CONTENTS

ABOUT THE AUTHORS

Liz Hill and Brian Whitehead are a husband and wife team who run a consultancy and publishing business, Arts Intelligence Limited.

Liz's primary role is as co-editor of the arts industry's leading fortnightly arts management magazine *ArtsProfessional*. She also manages research, consultancy and training projects for a wide range of clients. She has written and co-authored a number of books and articles for various publishers, including *Creative Arts Marketing*, *Foundation Marketing*, *Conducting a survey using SPSS* and *Commissioning Market Research*. Prior to the launch of *ArtsProfessional* magazine and its predecessor *ArtsBusiness*, she was a Senior Lecturer in marketing at Anglia Polytechnic University in Cambridge since 1991, where she designed and launched its MA in Arts Administration. She was also Senior Moderator for the Chartered Institute of Marketing.

Brian spent fifteen years in marketing roles within the arts and leisure sectors. His early career was in local authority leisure and arts management, for Three Rivers District Council and subsequently Northampton Borough Council. There he was Marketing Director for the Derngate Theatre which became a charitable trust in 1993. He left in December 1998 when his commitments to the consultancy and publishing activities of Arts Intelligence became full time. Brian has belonged to a number of voluntary, professional and non-profit organisations as a paid member, supporter and often as board member. His interest in friends and membership schemes has extended to both voluntary involvement and professional consultancy. He takes an active interest in all aspects of arts and cultural management, most notably through his co-editorship of *ArtsProfessional*.

ArtsProfessional and Arts Intelligence

ArtsProfessional is the UK's leading fortnightly arts management magazine, providing the arts and cultural industries with a vehicle for sharing good practice. Published by Arts Intelligence, it is written by industry practitioners and its readership ranges from board members and chief executives to academics, policy makers, funders, consultants, students and commercial suppliers to the arts and cultural sector. The publication is supported by a free fortnightly e-mail news digest, *APe-mail* and a fully searchable website at www.artsprofessional.co.uk. In addition to publishing *ArtsProfessional,* Arts Intelligence also supplies professional business and marketing services to the not-for-profit sector, as well as developing major projects with key clients and serving the research needs of other consultants, agencies and freelances. The company specialises in quantitative and qualitative market research and data management and analysis and offers consultancy services in relation to the setting up and management of membership schemes. For further information see the website at www.artsintelligence.co.uk.

About DSC

The Directory of Social Change (DSC) aims to help voluntary and community organisations become more effective. A charity ourselves, we are the leading provider of information and training for the voluntary sector.

We run more than 350 training courses each year as well as conferences, many of which run on an annual basis. We also publish an extensive range of guides, handbooks and CD-ROMs for the voluntary sector, covering subjects such as fundraising, management, communication, finance and law. Our trusts database is available on both a CD-ROM and a subscription website.

Charityfair, the annual three-day conference, events programme and exhibition, is organised by DSC and takes place each spring.

For details of all our activities, and to order publications and book courses, go to www.dsc.org.uk or call 08450 77 77 07.

PREFACE

Our decision to write *The Complete Membership Handbook* evolved over a number of years and has built upon a passion we share for the core values in our work relating to best practice in the arts and cultural sector. Our initial interest was triggered through our work relating to 'friends' of arts organisations and has developed into a deeper concern for understanding how groups of people organise themselves to promote a common interest – usually for the benefit of the common good. Some arts organisations worked closely with and gave considerable support to their friends groups and some were keen to establish a friends group for the first time. Others were struggling to work effectively with an existing group; or even, sadly, displayed only a grudging acceptance of their friends and either overtly or covertly sought to curtail or even terminate their activities.

When we looked beyond the cultural sector, we found many similarities in the way that membership schemes operated. Furthermore, we identified many successful organisational models, and lots of examples of good practice in management and marketing. It is our hope to share those models of good practice between sectors and promote the undeniable benefits that can be generated through a well-managed membership scheme.

Some elements of this book will be of interest to just about anyone tasked with setting up or managing almost any type of membership scheme; but the key themes are of particular interest to those who wish to bring together a group of people in support of a charitable or social cause or activity. The primary focus is on membership schemes that aim to support not-for-profit activity, for which the involvement of a core group of loyal supporters can bring major benefits.

The book will be of particular interest to:

- board members, trustees, directors and chairs of membership organisations, and organisations to which membership groups are affiliated – for solutions to strategic issues faced by their organisations, including long-term financial planning, objective setting and goal achievement, advocacy and public relations;
- chief executives and senior managers – for solutions to strategic issues, but also for advice on creating and implementing these solutions, monitoring and evaluating their achievements;
- managers of membership schemes – for advice on how best to run their day-to-day activities, and for guidance on operational matters such as

managing the finances, communicating with members, marketing and sales and general administration;

- managers of other functional areas such as finance or marketing – for an overview of how a membership scheme can fit alongside other marketing, sales and fundraising activities;
- volunteers involved with a membership scheme – for a better understanding of where their scheme fits into an affiliate organisation or other social cause (and for those involved in boards and committees, this book offers guidance on discharging those responsibilities);
- academics and students – those with an educational or research interest in the operation of membership schemes;
- government and policy-makers – to understand how this special area of the not-for-profit sector operates, and to recognise its potential in co-ordinating special interest groups and the delivery of revenue streams.

More than 100 examples illustrate the work of a diverse range of membership organisations, the problems they have faced and the solutions they have found to those problems. Hopefully, almost anyone involved with a membership organisation or scheme can find inspiration from their experiences, and by learning from these examples, can avoid the pitfalls that lie in wait for the unwary.

Liz Hill and Brian Whitehead

Spring 2004

ACKNOWLEDGEMENTS

We are indebted to so many people who have helped in ways too numerous to mention.

Our colleagues Emma Bonsall and Kim Horan who, having recently completed their Masters' research into friends and membership schemes, continued to work tirelessly in researching and writing case studies for this book.

For their efforts in checking the legal and financial passages: Sean Egan of Bates, Wells & Braithwaite solicitors; Mahmood Reza of Pro Active Accounting; and Jenny Sanders.

The rest of our own team at *ArtsProfessional* and Arts Intelligence including Sharon Collier, Serah Gautrey, Damian Hebron, Paul Minett and Rachel Priestman for keeping the ship afloat during our absences of body and mind.

The following have all assisted in one way or another with advice, case studies, experience or suggestions:

Julie Aldridge, Arts Marketing Association
Emma Boniwell, Society of Authors
Alex Burford, Gateway Arts Industry Network
Bob Bustance, Gordon Graig Theatre, Stevenage
Sarah Carthew, Flora Smith, Judy Ridley and Philippa Ouvry, Victoria & Albert Museum
Karen Dawe, Birmingham Contemporary Music Group
Alice Devitt
David Emerson, Association of Charitable Foundations
Monica Ferguson, The Stables at Wavendon
Kathleen Fetigan and Susan Fisher, Royal Opera House
Susan Foster, Watermill Theatre, Newbury
James Gambrill, Sadler's Wells Theatre
Nick Hallam, Royal and Derngate Theatres
Mark Hazell, Norwich Theatre Royal
Amy Hillcroft, Friends of Chelsea and Westminster Hospital
Jim Hutchinson, Imperial War Museum, Duxford
Andrew Ladds, Coeliac UK
Polly Larner, National Maritime Museum
Alice Lemon, Making Music
Bernard Martin, TEAM, Liverpool

Ed McKeon, London Sinfonietta

Sophie Moxon, Edinburgh International Book Festival

Rebekah Polding, City Screen

Carolyn Pugh, City of Birmingham Symphony Orchestra

Stefan Rosu, University of Music and Performing Arts Vienna

Adrian Salmon, The Phone Room

Alix Slater, University of Greenwich

Geoff Sweeney, Derby Playhouse

Sally Trower, British Association of Friends of Museums

Sally Anne Tye, Nottingham Playhouse

Pat Westwell, Ambassador Theatre Group

Paul Whitehouse, Ludlow & District Community Association

Dawn Yates, Manchester Art Gallery

... and staff from the Ramblers' Association, Royal Botanic Gardens and the East Manchester New Deal for Communities.

... and of course, thanks to Alison Baxter at DSC for commissioning this book, and to Donna Bridgwater for seeing the project through.

We would also like to take this opportunity to thank those individuals and organisations who have given us permission to use and adapt material for this book. Every effort has been made to trace the owners of copyright material, though in a few cases this has proved impossible and we apologise to any copyright holders whose rights may have been unwittingly infringed. We trust that in the event of any accidental infringement, the owners of the material will contact us directly. Please note also that where membership fees have been quoted in the book these figures were correct at the time of going to press.

If you have any suggestions, comments or corrections, please contact us through our website at www.completemembership.co.uk or by e-mail to info@completemembership.co.uk. Updates and other useful information on managing membership organisations will be posted on the website from time to time.

Dedication

To our children Christopher and Joanna, with love always.

1 WHAT DO WE MEAN BY A MEMBERSHIP SCHEME?

The concept of a 'membership scheme' may be one that is widely known, but it is also one that is seldom clearly defined. Such schemes are found to operate in a diverse range of organisations and contexts, with widely varying purposes. They exist under a range of different names and perform a diverse range of functions. This chapter aims to clarify the confusion that often surrounds the terminology relating to membership schemes, to explore the range of contexts in which they operate and to examine their most common structures.

A membership scheme is quite simply a mechanism for connecting like-minded individuals who are motivated to make links with others because they recognise that there are personal and/or societal benefits to be generated by their joining forces in a more formal way. It is a formal structure through which eligible individuals (usually, but not always, those who pay a membership fee) are permitted access to certain benefits which can only be obtained by joining the scheme.

The scope of membership schemes

Membership schemes can be found in just about all walks of life. For example, people who are interested in playing tennis will become members of a tennis club if they can see the benefits of gaining access to both courts and opponents; business people will join a Chamber of Commerce if they sense that there are good networking opportunities to be found, or that it will give them more influence over local government policies; and someone who cares for a disabled child may join a support group if they feel it will help them to cope better with the day-to-day realities of their situation and/or provide support for others.

Membership schemes are sometimes better known under other names. For example:

- **A friends scheme** (e.g., friends of a hospital or of a theatre): members tend to be individuals who are united in their affiliation to an organisation or project – usually referred to as the 'host', 'patron' or 'parent' organisation. Such schemes generally exist (and people join them) because they provide an opportunity for people to show their support for an organisation, whilst also benefiting themselves through giving that support.
- **A supporters group** (e.g., supporters of a particular football club or a fan club for a rock band): members of a supporters club join primarily to express their solidarity with others who support the same team. By forming a group, they can access special privileges from that organisation and meet with other fans.

Football Supporters' Federation

The Football Supporters' Federation (FSF) is an independent, democratic organisation with an elected national council that currently represents over 100,000 football fans throughout the UK. Members include both individual fans and local supporters organisations from every professional football club in England, as well as other leagues. The organisation campaigns by lobbying government and football authorities and supporting the views of fans on major issues. The FSF also supports England fans through the Fans' Embassy, which provides information, confidential advice and support to those travelling to away games, and through JFFA – Justice for Football Fans Abroad. The organisation is also involved with other European fans' groups through Football Supporters International. It has five regional divisions, each of which elects two members to the national council. The chairman, vice-chairman and other council members are elected at an annual conference.

Current campaigns include, Say No to Football Franchising, based on issues arising from the relocation of Wimbledon Football Club to Milton Keynes; The Campaign for Safe Standing; and support for the traditional 3pm Saturday start times for major games. The FSF produces a range of publications including a quarterly magazine and members also receive discounts on other football publications.

Source: www.fsf.org.uk (12 December 2003)

- **A sports or social club** (e.g., members of a film society or a hockey club): people are most likely to join these clubs to enable them to participate more fully in pastimes that they enjoy – and in particular those which require them to interact with others. For example, a hockey player won't have much fun on the pitch on his/her own; and film buffs tend to need a group of people to join them in order to share the cost of hiring films from their distributors.

- **A pressure group** (e.g., a lobbying charity or a politically motivated group): groups of people working together are far more likely to be able to effect change within social, political, economic, legal, medical and other walks of life. For example a group of residents, threatened with environmental damage if proposed gravel and sand extraction pits are developed, may unite to influence local planners and national government to withhold the necessary planning consent.
- **An alumni scheme** (e.g., groups of former school pupils and ex-students of colleges and universities): generally such groups are organised and managed by the school or college concerned and are used as a vehicle for keeping former students in touch, raising funds for the institution and creating networking opportunities. With large colleges, or those with a celebrated history, alumni groups can extend across the world and spawn national and regional sub-groups as well as special interest groups.
- **A loyalty scheme** (e.g., a supermarket rewards scheme or travel club): people who join these schemes tend to do so in order to be eligible for financial rewards. They become eligible for certain discounts and incentives, and in return, the organisation running the scheme can gather valuable data about their purchasing habits. Whilst a loyalty scheme offers benefits to customers, the nature and extent of those benefits are largely discretionary, and in the gift of the scheme's operator. This is a key difference from most other membership schemes.
- **A trades union** (e.g., an association which represents employees within a particular industry sector or across a number of industry sectors). Trades unions exist purely to represent the interests of workers. They are mutual associations set up and owned by the workers, primarily to negotiate employment terms with company bosses. These days the services offered extend to mortgages, insurance, legal advice and much more besides.

Society of Authors

The Society of Authors is a trades union, founded in 1884 to 'protect the rights and further the interests of authors'. An independent non-profit making organisation, it exists to assist professional writers, illustrators, translators and broadcasters in their dealings with publishers, with contracts and with financial matters. Member benefits include a quarterly journal, Quick Guides dealing with common concerns, opportunities to meet other members, and discounts at bookshops and on a variety of other products and services. An Associate category of membership is available, for one year only, to unpublished authors. There are currently 7,631 full members of the Society, which is managed by nine full-time and four part-time staff. Membership increased by 12.4% in 2003, and 91.3% of members renewed their subscriptions in 2002.

Source: Emma Boniwell, Membership Secretary, Society of Authors, (December 2003)

- **A professional body** (e.g., doctors may belong to the British Medical Association, or music teachers to the Incorporated Society of Musicians): members of professional bodies may comprise people who have similar levels of professional standing or career interests. They may join primarily to access specific services or facilities relating to their specialist professional field of interest, or possibly to demonstrate official recognition of their professional expertise.
- **A co-operative** (e.g., a worker's co-operative or a retailing organisation such as the Co-operative Group, founded in 1840): as its name suggests, in law a co-operative is owned by all its members, each with voting rights. A co-operative is defined as an autonomous association of persons united voluntarily to meet their common economic, social and cultural needs and aspirations through a jointly owned and democratically controlled enterprise.[1] Such entities are often created for the social good, for working with disadvantaged people and self-help groups, for example.
- **A friendly society** (e.g., a mutual healthcare trust operated on behalf of employees of a particular sector such as the Benenden Healthcare Society Limited which assists post office and civil service workers and their families): a friendly society is a mutual organisation which provides a wide range of assurance, insurance and healthcare products, often tax free. They offer investment and protection to people of all backgrounds, and are owned and governed by the members.
- **An owners club** (e.g., a classic car club): those who join an owners' club have a common interest because they own, and are enthusiasts about, a particular product. It is their desire to share their enthusiasm with other like-minded people that drives them to become members, though their existence may not be of much significance to the organisation that produces the product.[2]
- **A product user group** (e.g., comprising a group of businesses who use the same software systems): non-competing business customers of organisations producing high value products and services may like to get together from time to time to discuss issues and problems that arise through the use of those products. Jointly, they are able to lobby and exert more pressure on the producing organisation to develop their products to meet their needs than they would individually. Such groups may be formally constituted or simple informal gatherings, and they may be inspired and managed by the users, the producing organisation or a mixture of both.

Clearly, membership schemes are in essence very diverse. Some are open for anyone to join (such as a supporters group), while others have strict membership criteria (such as a professional body). Some are affiliated to specific organisations (such as a friends scheme) while others focus on a cause or activity (such as a pressure group, or a hockey club). Some function as legal charities, some as trading companies and others as mutual societies, with their agendas governed by their own constitutions. However, all membership schemes, whatever they are called and for whatever purposes they exist, share two core characteristics:

- they offer tangible and/or intangible benefits to their members and
- to become a member involves a conscious decision to join.

In the absence of the former, there would be no reason for anyone to join; and in the absence of the latter, there are no grounds for suggesting that a 'scheme' actually exists – simply a 'market', perhaps.

Whilst its general themes are relevant to all types of schemes listed above, the content of this book refers specifically to membership schemes that bring together groups of people in support of charitable or social causes or not-for-profit activity. Members of these schemes join in order to be affiliated with the work of a particular organisation, and it is the setting up and management of these schemes, and the relationship between them and their affiliated organisations, that are discussed in detail here.

The development of membership schemes

Membership schemes tend to come about through one of two routes. Traditionally they have emerged from the activities of a small group of enthusiasts who have given their time to support the work of an organisation or cause they believe to be of value to their community. As the activities of those individuals expand however, so does the requirement for more formal structures to ensure that those activities continue to be managed effectively and sustained for the benefit of the affiliate organisation or cause, as well as for the enthusiasts themselves. The formalisation of these activities within some sort of scheme becomes increasingly important as founder members begin to withdraw and continuity becomes a problem.

In recent years, however, more and more membership schemes in the not-for-profit sector have been initiated by organisations themselves as part of their marketing or development activity. Faced with the need to generate new streams of income to support their work, they have become gradually more marketing-oriented and started to recognise the benefits that a core of committed enthusiasts can generate for their organisations. Whereas traditional marketing thinking focuses on an organisation's ability to sell, the more recent concepts of 'relationship marketing' and 'relationship fundraising' recognise the value of building high levels of loyalty by treating customers or donors as individuals, not markets. They emphasise the importance of supporting long-term one-to-one relationships through which transactions will inevitably follow.[3] A membership scheme is found to be a valuable mechanism through which such relationships can be nurtured.

Although few figures have ever been published about the number of membership schemes that exist, it is clear that from the 1990s onwards, there has been an increasing awareness by organisations of the potential that such schemes can offer them. The number of schemes operating appears to have grown, and membership levels within many of those schemes have grown too. Despite their sometimes haphazard development, membership has become big business.

The value of members

People with whom not-for-profit organisations conduct one-off transactions are certainly valuable to them, as are people who support a cause as an occasional donor or volunteer. These people are important revenue (or resource) generators, without whom many such organisations would cease to exist. However, the intermittent nature of their transactions with the organisation means that the extent to which their long-term support can be assumed is generally unknown, and the level of support given may be limited. Customers and donors tend to come and go, and unless an organisation acts to draw these people closer to them, they may be missing an important opportunity to develop a valuable relationship.

Those who join a membership scheme show a commitment to an organisation beyond that of simply being a 'customer' (see Figure 1.1). These people reveal themselves to be willing to demonstrate their sympathies for an activity or cause and to build a relationship with an organisation that supports this activity or cause. Furthermore, a person joining a membership scheme supplies personal data about themselves which permits the organisation to target future database marketing and relationship management activities at an audience that is known to be sympathetic to its aims.

The value of such overt commitment to the organisation is inestimable, but it is by no means a one-way street. Members usually enjoy a balance of both tangible ('hard') and less tangible ('soft') benefits. In other words, they will benefit from a combination of financial advantages and preferential treatment, together with the satisfaction that they have made a positive contribution to the resources of a worthwhile organisation, project or cause, to enable it to further its activities. The benefits to both parties are discussed further in Chapter 2.

Figure 1.1 The pyramid of loyalty

Source: adapted from Christopher, M., Payne, A. and Ballantyne, D. (1993) *Relationship Marketing*, Butterworth Heinemann, p22, with permission from Elsevier

A well-designed and well-managed membership scheme, which places the interests of the organisation at its heart yet still delivers real benefits to its members, has the potential to generate the most beneficial relationships of all. People who belong to a membership scheme can deliver a valuable source of income to the organisation, act as a supportive resource and form a vocal and influential lobby when hostile external forces threaten the organisation (see case study below), or indeed when on-going visible support is required by the organisation, to justify and endorse and promote its activity. The pinnacle of the relationship is reached when a scheme member not only offers support to an organisation, but is also willing to act as an advocate for it.

Save Watersmeet Action Group

Rickmansworth's 500-seat local authority controlled arts centre, Watersmeet, was threatened with closure when councillors decided to withdraw its subsidy as part of a strategy to reduce overall council expenditure. The centre, which had been built and operated by the same local authority for the previous 30 years, had provided a popular mix of films, professional comedy, dance, drama, music events and amateur dramatics throughout this time. It was not particularly regarded by stakeholders or customers as a cutting edge arts organisation, or even a particularly important focus of local pride. However, the council's unexpected decision to remove its funding led to an immediate outpouring of contempt for the politicians and support for the survival of the venue.

During the first weekend following the funding announcement, nearly 9,000 signatures were collected in a petition to save the centre and near-violent demonstrations took place. An *ad hoc* support club subsequently named 'SWAG' – the Save Watersmeet Action Group – was immediately created by the most vociferous of the lobbyists. The politicians, coincidentally in the midst of an election campaign, appeared taken aback by the strength of the public reaction and attempted partially to retract their announcement. They offered to keep the venue open for a further period of months, whilst arrangements were made to transfer the future management of the organisation to SWAG. SWAG formalised its structure, registered as a charity, formally constituted itself as a lobbying and support group and set up a charitable trust company, with the intention of taking over the running of the venue from January 2004. It also prepared a fundraising plan to raise £300,000 towards the long-term survival of the organisation.

Sources:
Former staff of Watersmeet
Watford Observer, www.watfordobserver.co.uk (2 November 2003)
www.savewatersmeet.org.uk (2 November 2003)

Membership schemes in context

Although membership schemes generally have the potential to generate passionate advocates from among their midst, not all are designed to do so. Some organisations may, for example, be quite happy for their members to sit at the third level on the pyramid of loyalty (Figure 1.1), as good clients, conducting a series of transactions with them. In that case, they may offer a package of benefits that encourages the ongoing patronage of their members by offering them incentives to make further purchases or partici-pate in the organisation's work, but make no attempt to harness any deeper involvement. Others may want more active support from their members and create schemes which are primarily used to generate otherwise scarce resources such as time or money, in which case their scheme objectives might revolve around volunteering or fundraising. Consequently, even though a scheme is termed a 'membership' scheme, it may be very different from other schemes with the same name.

Who runs membership schemes?

A membership scheme tends to flourish when its affiliate organisation delivers a service or supports a cause deemed to be of high social value, yet which faces certain external pressures. These pressures are often financial and sometimes political, and could potentially undermine its work. Consequently, organisations with charitable status and those which offer obvious public benefits are the most likely to have membership schemes associated with them. However, such schemes also exist in the commercial sector. For example, Ambassadors Theatre Group owns or manages over 20 theatres on a commercial basis right across the UK, and runs highly successful friends schemes at many of its venues, generating significant income from them. There are also membership schemes that support the work of local and national government departments. The Friends of Dundee City Archives, for example, whose affiliate organisation is a department of Dundee City Council, support the work of that office and aim to raise public awareness of the archivists in their city. Similarly, there are many friends schemes thriving in hospitals alongside the National Health Service.

Membership schemes affiliated with not-for-profit organisations exist across a wide range of sectors. They are particularly common in organisations whose missions relate to culture, education, health or the environment. For example – though this is by no means an exhaustive list – they are affiliated to:

- museums and galleries
- performing arts organisations
- festivals
- zoological and botanical gardens
- heritage properties
- archives
- sports and recreation-based organisations
- hospitals and hospices
- animal welfare organisations
- schools and colleges
- libraries.

The nature of a membership scheme is likely to be determined, at least in part, by the type of organisation, cause or activity to which it is linked. For example, a theatre venue running ticketed events will be keen to fill its seats, especially on less popular nights of the week and for little-known productions which are unlikely to attract capacity audiences. It may provide ticket discounts, priority booking and other benefits through its membership scheme to encourage ticket bookings for events which may otherwise attract under-capacity audiences. A hospital, on the other hand, may wish to provide patient services, such as a shop or tea trolley, which would be un-economic should paid staff have to be employed to deliver them, or for which the capital costs could not be justified from the public purse. So a scheme affiliated to a hospital is likely to try to promote the value of 'doing good' in order to attract volunteers and fundraisers. In yet other contexts, such as galleries and museums, members may be attracted by an opportunity to attend private views or press launches, and to join a social circle with similar interests for special talks and events. In the case of lobbying groups, however, such financial or social benefits are less likely to be relevant, as the attraction may simply be the opportunity to 'make a difference' to a particular cause or community.

The structure of membership schemes

The context in which a membership scheme exists will affect the way that it is established and the structure within which it operates. Fundamentally, schemes fall into two categories: those existing independently of the organisation with which they claim an affiliation, and those which are an integral part of the organisation itself. Within these categories are a whole raft of different organisation types (see Figure 1.2), each with their own strengths and weaknesses, and each appropriate in different circumstances.

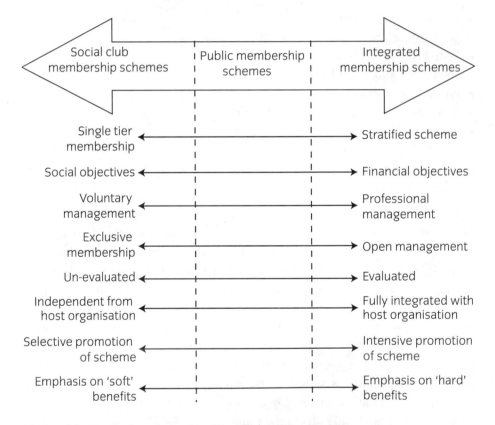

Figure 1.2 Typologies of membership schemes

Source: adapted from Hayes, D. and Slater, A. (2003)

In recent years, economically motivated pressures and political demands for accountability, access and democracy have led some schemes to move out of one category and either grow into another, or to be completely re-launched under a new structure. (Chapter 6 examines how that process can be managed).

Independent membership schemes

These types of scheme exist when a group of people creates a formal structure through which to express its support for and/or interest in the work of an organisation with whose aims it has sympathies. Such schemes may, however, have few, if any formal ties with the organisations they support and their members are usually free to govern their own activities, and all the incomes and expenditures associated with their schemes, without reference to those organisations. Research into major London-based museums and galleries[4] found that two distinct types of independent schemes exist, both of which also occur in a wide range of other membership contexts.

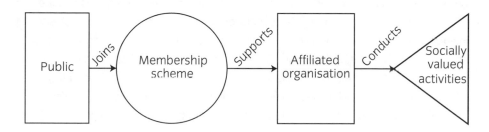

Figure 1.3 Independent membership scheme

The social club group

This type of membership scheme is one which evolves from a social group of enthusiasts whose active involvement with an organisation has grown over time. Manchester City Galleries (see case study below) provides an example of such a scheme. A more formal organisation emerges to embrace other enthusiasts, though membership of such schemes is likely to remain small and selective, and is expanded, if at all, primarily through word of mouth – through both social networking and personal invitation. The formalisation of the group into a membership scheme generally occurs as much to further the social interests of the founders as to benefit the affiliate organisation. Although members usually have altruistic motivations towards their affiliate, the activities of the members are likely to be driven by a core group following their own social agendas. Recruiting new members is not a priority, (even if it were, the skills may not exist within the group to support this function) and it may even be seen as a threat to the exclusive feel of the social club experience that constitutes the main reason for people to join.

Manchester City Galleries

Manchester City Galleries manages four venues in and around the city: Manchester Art Gallery, Gallery of Costume, Heaton Hall and Wythenshawe Hall. The Friends of Manchester City Galleries is a registered charity, established to support the work of Manchester City Galleries. It provides assistance with funding, interpretation and educational activities, as well as the purchase of artworks for the collection. Over £200,000 has been raised since the charity's launch in 1979.

The Friends are an autonomous group run by an independent, self-appointed committee, which has ex-officio staff members of its affiliate organisation present at committee meetings. The Galleries' Marketing Manager acts as a coordinator between the committee and the affiliate organisation. The Friends raise money through subscriptions and regular events organised by the committee. Events include lectures, visits to country houses, art galleries and museums, trips abroad and other social activities. There are currently around 700 members. The membership scheme is managed on a voluntary basis by the Friends themselves, many of whom also volunteer to join a small team of Gallery Guides, giving tours for visitors and helping to interpret the collections for organised groups and individuals.

Membership benefits include:

- Contributing to the success of one of the North West's foremost cultural organisations
- Free admission to all exhibitions where a charge is made
- Invitations to private views and other Friends' events
- Opportunities to work in our venues as a volunteer guide
- Free subscription to the Friends' bi-annual newsletter including details of forthcoming events and activities
- Free mailings of information on all exhibitions and public events.

The Friends control their own funds and have a separate bank account. Manchester City Galleries makes requests to the Friends committee for funds to purchase new acquisitions. The Friends are the primary source of support for acquisitions as there are few other sources from which to meet those costs. The majority of requests are usually fulfilled but particular purchases are sometimes refused, and funds are retained pending further requests.

Manchester Art Gallery has recently been re-opened and re-branded following a four-year closure for refurbishment. The Friends scheme continued to exist during this period, but membership dwindled. When the Gallery re-opened the organisation wanted the Friends to have a higher profile to help attract new members, re-establish their audience and encourage attendance, so Manchester City Galleries' own branding was incorporated into the Friends scheme. For example, the two logos were made more similar; professionally printed tickets were introduced for

Friends events; and the Friends newsletter was designed and produced by the Galleries themselves. The latter created an opportunity for the organisation to have more control over its content, and to include news of the artistic programme and events, articles and photographs of acquisitions. There was resistance from some members of the Friends committee over the increased costs of the new branding, particularly when comparing the printing costs of the new newsletter to the previous newsletter (a photocopied letter from the Chairman). For these few members the increased costs were perceived to be counterproductive to their giving to Manchester City Galleries. However, the members have in general received the newsletter very favourably, and the relationship building and communication aspects have been to the mutual advantage of both parties.

Sources:
www.manchestergalleries.co.uk (13 January 2004)
Dawn Yates, Marketing Manager (13 January 2004)

In terms of management, members of social club schemes usually adopt formal mechanisms for self-governance including constitutions, memoranda and articles of association, and appoint themselves to posts such as chair, treasurer, secretary and trustee. Thus they are completely autonomous from the organisation to which they claim to be affiliated, and may even apply for their own charitable status. Members tend to be affluent and well connected, often possessing professional expertise and being highly regarded within their community. Some may view a properly constituted scheme as an opportunity to exert influence over the affiliated organisation, particularly as some individuals will make large donations and expect to receive recognition in return. Other fundraising activity can be somewhat *ad hoc*, and may well focus on issues deemed by the members themselves to be important. For example, friends of galleries and museums might be very interested in raising money for new acquisitions, but much less so in supporting education projects or the core running costs of the organisation. The fundraising activity itself tends to be relatively unsophisticated, and is more likely to involve events with a social dimension. It is unlikely that any objective evaluation of the scheme will ever take place, though even in the absence of any evidence, a high degree of self-congratulation takes place, and these members have a tendency to overestimate their value to any affiliate organisation.

From the perspective of that affiliate organisation, the social club membership scheme is not usually the most beneficial structure. The complete autonomy of the members means that the organisation itself has no formal control over or say in the activities of the group, which in itself can be a major cause of conflict. There is a danger that groups will raise funds for projects that the organisations do not support or which are not regarded as priorities, or use the funds raised in the name of the organisation to benefit their members rather than the organisation itself. Such independent fundraising is likely to provide far from optimal returns – either to the members or the organisation – and indeed the net financial effect on the organisation may even be to undermine its own fundraising programmes since conflicting approaches to donors will inevitably be detrimental to both parties. Some such groups have an elitist, ageing, stagnant or even declining membership base, but the organisation has no legitimate power to change this. The reason the affiliated organisation continues to support the membership scheme usually has as much to do with a fear of alienating its members as with the benefits gained from their existence. These members, who may be advocates and donors as well as high profile members of their local communities, can be sufficiently influential as to make them a force to be reckoned with, whether for good or ill.

The public members scheme

This type of scheme is run as a semi-professional organisation, usually an independent registered charity, with its own autonomous management and sometimes even its own paid employees. The Royal Botanic Gardens (see case study below) provides an example of such a scheme. In a public members scheme, democratic processes are in place to ensure that a transparent system is in operation, and there are usually strong links between the members and the affiliate organisation, sometimes including representation by the members on the organisation's board.

Royal Botanic Gardens

The Foundation and Friends of The Royal Botanic Gardens, Kew, is a registered charity which was established in September 1990 to support the work of the Royal Botanic Gardens and to raise awareness of the organisation's scientific and conservation work world wide.

Friends join a scheme that offers a range of benefits including unlimited free entry to Kew Gardens, free guest passes, free entry to other gardens, a quarterly magazine, events and activities, and discounts in the shops and on adult education courses. The Friends are also eligible to apply for volunteering opportunities relating to scientific, horticultural and education projects, and the visitor and events programme. However, they are not entitled to voting rights on matters relating to the activities of the charity. The highly tiered membership scheme is priced for individuals, joint members, and concessionary members, and it is possible to make a gift of membership to a third party. The membership categories include Friends, Premier Friends, Associate Friends (available outside the UK), Season Tickets, Life Membership and Founder Membership.

There are now over 50,000 Friends of Kew, and a staff of 22. Despite the fact that the affiliate organisation is itself a charity that receives the majority of its funding from government and has many statutory obligations, the Friends still play a crucial role within the organisation. They support the Royal Botanic Gardens by raising funds from a whole range of sources including charitable trusts, major donors and the corporate sector, and generated an income in excess of £3.5 million in the financial year ending March 2003. Many conservation and research projects would not have been successful without their help. For example, the Friends have raised funding for the Millennium Seed Bank, research into the conservation of island flora, and education programmes for plant scientists from the developing world.

Sources:
www.rbgkew.org.uk/friends (2 November 2003)
www.kew.org (2 November 2003)
www.charitiesdirect.com (2 November 2003)
www.charity-commission.gov.uk (2 November 2003)
Interview with the Foundation and Friends of the Royal Botanic Gardens, Kew

The mission of a public members scheme is likely to be formalised and reflected in a written constitution. It will usually be focused on generating revenues and other resources for the organisation, especially through fundraising, but also volunteering. However, these functions may be separate from and in addition to the organisation's own activities. Other functions of the scheme, including the social dimension and advocacy activity, tend to become the domain of key stakeholders and small sub-groups within the membership.

A public members scheme will have a much broader membership base than a social club group. Its members may be geographically widespread and will have a wide range of motivations for joining, so a 'stratified' or 'tiered' set of membership categories is often made available to offer a set of benefits – of which social networking will be only one – to those who join the scheme (see Chapter 3 for more about benefits and tiered schemes). Considerable importance is placed on expanding the membership base, so open invitations to prospective members are publicised by the affiliated organisation, as well as in any literature or website produced by the members themselves.

Despite their relative sophistication, these schemes are unlikely to be subject to any real evaluation. If they are, then the research is unlikely to be comparable with or integrated with any research undertaken by the affiliate organisation, though it may be shared with them.

Conflict is less likely to emerge between an affiliate organisation and a public members scheme than a social club group, as the scheme may be well managed, effective at raising significant resources, and attract a strong membership base. However, it is still possible that a small sub-group of enthusiastic, vocal and active members will form an inner clique within the membership and that this will deter others from participating. Furthermore, the lack of evaluation makes it impossible for the organisation to tell whether the costs of running the scheme are appropriate relative to the financial benefits gained from it, or whether there is scope for improvement.

Integrated membership schemes

These schemes exist when an organisation is supported by a group of people whose membership is integral to the organisation itself. This occurs in two circumstances: firstly when an organisation sets up its own membership scheme for marketing, development or advocacy purposes, and secondly when a group of people formalise themselves into a membership organisation with a view to collectively pursuing a set of its own (normally) charitable aims.

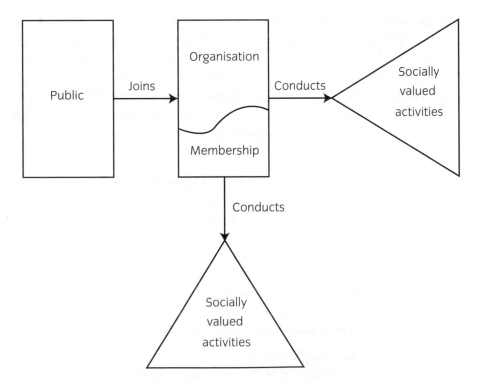

Figure 1.4 Integrated membership scheme

Organisation 'owns' the membership

The most significant characteristic of this type of scheme is that it is created by an existing organisation and integrated into that organisation's own strategic plans. It is managed by the organisation's own staff, normally within its marketing or development department, and the emphasis tends to be firmly on revenue generation rather than volunteering. English National Opera (see case study below) is a good example of such a scheme.

With these schemes, aggressive marketing is likely to take place in order to continually attract new members, and this is often underpinned by professional database management to track and evaluate the activity of members. Promotional literature relating to the scheme will carry the organisation's own brand identity, and details of the scheme will be integral to the organisation's website. In larger schemes, the membership categories on offer are likely to be highly stratified, to the extent that different levels of membership may even have their own brand names and brand values, and those attracted to a particular tier within a scheme may not even be aware of the benefits being offered to other tiers. The scheme may also be designed to embrace corporate members as well as individuals.

English National Opera

The Friends of English National Opera (FNO) was set up to support the ENO company, which is dedicated to providing high-quality, low-cost opera in the language of its audience. ENO is a registered charity and the Friends department sits within the development section of the company, responsible for corporate, capital and major donor fundraising as well as the Friends scheme.

There has been a supporters scheme attached to ENO (originally known as the Opera Club) since the 1970s. Until the mid-1980s this was run by volunteers, who looked after ticket applications and catered at events. Gradually, paid staff were brought in to complement the volunteer team and the committee who ran the Friends. Eventually, as the scheme developed still further, its management was brought in-house and run by a small team of dedicated professionals comprising a Friends manager, an assistant and an events officer.

In recent years, the emphasis has been on building a successful, consistent membership base. As well as delivering a revenue stream for the company, the scheme aims both to attract and retain members who, through the Friends, develop a closer relationship with ENO. A 'ladder of giving' is in place to encourage members to move up through the different tiers of membership – from ordinary 'Friends', who receive a basic package of information and booking benefits, through to 'Fellows' (donating £3,000 or more) who are also offered other exclusive entertainment opportunities. They are offered significantly more involvement with the top management of the organisation, including an invitation to the exclusive annual Fellows' Dinner, hosted by the General Director and Chairman of the Board of ENO.

The source of all new membership applications is tracked, so that the effectiveness of each initiative and campaign can be monitored. Through this, ENO has learned that a direct mail campaign to the audience is more effective in recruiting new members than a seat drop of membership leaflets. This type of monitoring enables the organisation to determine how and where to publicise the scheme and how much should be spent on the campaigns.

The membership level has risen to a steady 7,000 members. The full-time paid staff are in a position to provide regular and efficient feedback to members and respond promptly to queries and letters. There is competition in London between arts organisations for a relatively small pool of prospective Friends with a specific interest in the arts, and the high level of service provided is one of the reasons why Friends are believed to stay loyal to ENO.

Following ENO tours to the United States in recent years, a separately branded 'American Friends of ENO' was created in 2000, to exploit the relationship with its many American attenders. Although the benefits offered to these members closely emulate those of the UK scheme, the new organisation has been set up under US law as a Section 501 (c) 3 charitable organisation, enabling members to enjoy tax relief available to US taxpayers.

The main scheme has been re-launched twice in recent years and there are plans to examine it yet again before the re-opening of the Coliseum in 2004. Each time, much care is taken to ensure that members are well informed of changes to the scheme, and that the financial demands made are not beyond their means. The most popular reasons for becoming a Friend of ENO are to receive priority booking for performances, to have access to tickets to dress rehearsals and Friends events, and to support the company. Whenever the scheme is reviewed, every effort is made to sustain these core areas. Any amendments are approved by the Friends council, an advisory board which meets three times a year to discuss the scheme, initiatives and upcoming projects.

Sources:
Cantrell, S. (2001) 'A Professional Scheme', *ArtsProfessional*, issue 15, 3 December, p6
www.eno.org (22 November 2003)

The membership of this type of scheme will have a similar profile to a public members scheme, and is likely to comprise a mixed group of people who come from a cross-section of geographic areas and social backgrounds, having been recruited through a range of channels. Members are motivated by both hard and soft benefits, and those who make greater financial commitments will be recognised and offered a superior package of benefits, designed to deepen the relationship with them. Members are not formally represented in the organisation's governing body (see Chapter 3), but meetings are usually held to maintain good levels of communication between the two parties.

Evaluation is key to this type of scheme (see Chapter 5). Much of the management activity associated with it will be database-driven, enabling scheme managers to analyse members' behaviour, calculate their lifetime value, membership 'churn' (the rate of turnover of members within a scheme), and determine the most effective approaches to marketing and fundraising. As the entire operation of the scheme is within the affiliate organisation's own control, the types of conflict that arise in independent membership schemes are less likely, but other problems do occur. For example, the emphasis of this type of scheme on recruiting and retaining members can mean that high levels of 'hard' benefits have to be provided, often in the form of financial inducements such as price reductions. The organisation must watch out that the costs of running the scheme do not outweigh the benefits realised through it; and be aware that the proportion of its members who are genuine enthusiasts for its work, as opposed to bargain hunters, may be quite small.

Membership 'owns' the organisation

In some circumstances, though, the membership scheme is inseparable from the organisation. In this case, it is the members rather than the organisation's executives who determine and control the strategic direction of the organisation itself. In joining the scheme, a member is in effect joining the organisation and acquires influence over the whole organisation, not just the activities pursued by members. The National Autistic Society (see case study below) provides a useful illustration of this.

Members may exert their influence through an electoral process. As well as receiving benefits, those who join such a scheme become eligible to stand for election to the governing body of the organisation and to vote in elections for its officers. The governing body will then determine the policy and strategy of the organisation, and direct the employed staff in how to implement these. Members, whether or not involved in the governing body, can have their voices heard formally, by raising issues for the agenda at the organisation's formal general meetings (see Chapter 5).

National Autistic Society

The National Autistic Society (NAS), formerly The Society for Autistic Children, was founded in 1962 by a group of parents who were frustrated with the lack of provision for children with autism and their carers. Initially working out of Helen Green Allison's back room with a handful of members and minimal funding, the organisation has grown into the UK's foremost organisation for people with autism and those who care for them. The NAS is registered both with the Charity Commissioners and the Registrar of Companies. Its trusts and powers are laid down in its articles of association which state that its objects are 'to provide education, treatment, welfare and care to people with autism and related conditions'. The society now has over 12,000 members, all of whom are all entitled to vote at the general meeting of members which controls the Society's direction.

The NAS is structured into six operational regions. This allows the development and support of services reflecting local needs and the identification of gaps in local provision. Regional coordinators, as well as contributing to an integrated regional plan, seek to involve other bodies such as local authorities and other groups representing the needs of people with autistic spectrum disorders, in order to make the most of scarce resources.

The NAS also has over 60 branches around the country, varying in size and levels of activity. These are run by parents and are able to provide mutual support at a local level. In addition it accommodates independently registered charities, which have the same basic aims but who restrict their work to smaller geographical areas, as affiliated societies. There are over 20 service-providing affiliates of the NAS and over 30 non-service providing ones.

In November 2003 the NAS won the BT Telephone Helplines Association award for 'Developing Effective Networks'. This was in recognition of the work of its Advocacy for Education Service, which has developed a Special Educational Needs Network, consisting of over 50 national, regional and local voluntary sector organisations providing advice on special educational needs.

Source: www.nas.org.uk (5 December 2003)

Under these circumstances, the members of a scheme are potentially very powerful – quite the reverse of the situation when the organisation 'owns' the membership (see above). This brings both advantages and disadvantages. On the plus side, the organisation should, in theory, be very responsive to the needs of its members – even to the extent that if the membership declines significantly, members may vote for the organisation to disband itself completely. However, in large membership schemes members are likely to be apathetic about exercising their voting rights, and this may permit small factions to dominate the democratic process. Provided that these dominant individuals make sensible decisions that are to the benefit of the whole membership, this will cause few problems, but should their views be unrepresentative of those of the membership as a whole, they can undermine the fundamental purpose for which the organisation exists.

RSPCA

In 2001 the RSPCA (Royal Society for the Prevention of Cruelty to Animals) won the right to exclude or remove pro-hunting members who were believed to be part of an infiltration campaign. The judgment clarifying the membership rules of the Society followed the charity's decision to seek guidance from the High Court when it put on hold around 600 applications for membership believed to be from pro-hunting supporters, applying to join the charity in an attempt to change its long-standing policy against hunting with dogs. Judge Mr Justice Lightman concluded that, under the rules of the Society, applicants could not be arbitrarily rejected. Rather each case would have to be considered by the full 25-strong RSPCA council, at which time those challenged must be given the chance to explain their primary motives for joining. Malcolm Phipps, chairman of the RSPCA's ruling council, welcoming the ruling and said 'The RSPCA is a democratic organisation, but clearly concerted efforts to join the society for an overriding reason other than animal welfare makes a mockery of this democracy. Today's ruling has given the Society a mechanism to protect itself against infiltration'.

Source: Wilson, J. 'RSPCA wins right to bar pro-hunting activists', the *Guardian*, 27 January 2001

In order to avoid such problems, some organisations take steps to limit the extent to which members can influence the activities of the organisation by creating a trust. Members join the trust, rather than the organisation itself, and the revenues generated through their membership are transferred back to the organisation. Members are given the opportunity to vote on matters relating to the trust, but not specifically on the policy and strategies of the whole organisation. Thus, although they are indeed integral to the organisation, members who belong to a trust may share much common ground with those who belong to public members' schemes (see above).

Summary

Although membership schemes exist in all walks of life, this book focuses on schemes which bring together a group of people in support of a charitable or socially valuable cause or activity. These schemes generally exist (and people join them) because they provide an opportunity for people to show their support for an organisation or cause, whilst benefiting themselves through giving that support. Some schemes discussed in this book are set up and managed independently of the organisation with which they are affiliated, whilst others are integrally involved with them, or indeed are one and the same organisation. In both situations, organisations can benefit from these schemes, as their members can provide a valuable source of income, act as a supportive resource and form an influential lobby group. Members can benefit from a combination of financial advantages and preferential treatment, and/or the satisfaction that they have made a positive contribution to a worthwhile cause or organisation.

---

1   National Co-operative Business Association, USA

2   Butscher, S. A. (2002) *Customer Loyalty Programmes and Clubs*, 2nd edition, Gower

3   Berry, L. (1983) 'Relationship Marketing' in Leonard L. Berry, G. Lynn Shostack and Gregory D. Upah (eds) 'Emerging Perspectives in Services Marketing', Proceedings of the American Marketing Association, Chicago, pp25–28

4   Hayes, D. and Slater, A. (2003) 'From "Social Club" to "Integrated Membership Scheme": Developing Membership Schemes Strategically', *International Journal of Nonprofit and Voluntary Sector Marketing*, Vol. 8, No. 1, pp59–75

2 WHO BENEFITS FROM MEMBERSHIP SCHEMES?

The key to success for a membership scheme lies in identifying the benefits that each party needs in order to make it worth their while being involved with the other. This chapter explores the reasons why organisations may establish membership schemes. It also reviews the benefits that might be sought by members from these schemes, as it is only when an organisation understands the motivations of its potential members that it is in a position to create an effective scheme.

For an organisation, the prospect of always having a loyal group of supporters on hand is an attractive one, as a close relationship with its members can reap a number of benefits that are more difficult to replicate in other ways. Having said this, some of these benefits will be more important to some organisations than to others, and those involved in setting up or running schemes need to be crystal clear as to what the priorities are for their own scheme.

Why run a membership scheme?

There are five generic types of benefit that organisations can gain from their friends and membership schemes:

1 **Revenues from membership fees:** probably the most obvious benefit of all, this often proves to be the most elusive too. There is an ever-present danger that the costs of running a scheme that is attractive to members will outweigh the revenues generated by the membership fees themselves.

2 **A source of trading income:** the loyalty of members to their affiliate organisations or causes pre-disposes them to trade with those organisations, rather than others who make similar commercial offers. For example, members of charities will be an important target group for trading activity

through Christmas cards and gift catalogues, and friends of theatres will be a key target market for ticket sales.

3 **A source of fundraising income:** friends and members are invariably good prospects for anything from telephone campaigns to prize-draws. Their support for the aims of the affiliate organisation, demonstrated through the very fact that they have joined the membership scheme, suggests that they may be amenable to giving more support.

4 **An enlarged pool of affordable staff:** a corps of volunteers can be drawn from a membership base. The joining of a membership group reveals a person's genuine interest in the affiliate organisation, which will invariably be one of the selection criteria for volunteers. It should be said however that not all volunteers will wish to join a friends or members scheme (see below), and it should not be assumed that all members will wish to volunteer!

5 **A formalised group of advocates:** a membership group can give critical mass to what might otherwise be rather dispersed support for an organisation or a cause. It can harness the combined power of a wide range of voices and exert more influence than any individual would be able to achieve.

Revenues from membership fees

On the surface, setting up a membership scheme is a very attractive proposition for not-for-profit organisations, as it can appear that some people are willing to join them simply because they want to support that organisation. The reality is somewhat different. People only ever part with money because they expect to get something in return (see motivation, below) – either tangible or intangible. But whether it be a regular newsletter, discount vouchers, social gatherings or any of the hundreds of other benefits that could be offered through membership schemes, the organisation has to prepare itself in order to deliver to members what they want. This invariably costs money, so it is important that the both income and cost projections are assessed before a scheme is established. Failing to take the likely costs into account can lead to inappropriate decisions about, for example, how much to charge for membership and the level of benefits to offer (see Chapter 3).

Trading income

Perhaps understandably, the concept of 'marketing' has historically been viewed with some suspicion by the not-for-profit sector, dismissed as a commercial vehicle for aggressive sales and preventing existing ones being lured away by the competition. The more recent concept of 'relationship marketing', however, looks at the whole issue of retaining loyal customers in a slightly different way and is highly relevant in considering how a charitable or other not-for-profit organisation could generate a long-term stream of trading revenue through its close ties with a membership group.

Whereas traditional marketing thinking emphasises an organisation's ability to continually make a series of single sales to a group of potential customers, relationship marketing focuses on the quality of interaction between the two parties. It holds that a more effective way of going about things is to offer exceptional service levels over a long time-scale,[1] which in turn will build customer commitment and lead to ongoing relationships, rather than a series of one-off transactions.

Membership schemes are valuable means through which quality interactions and exceptional service can be delivered. It is no coincidence that supermarket chains have, over the past ten years, developed their own 'membership clubs' (known as loyalty schemes) through which they provide their customers with information about their products, publications, special offers and discount vouchers. Being large commercial operations, they are unlikely to attract loyalty or support on philosophical or philanthropic grounds, but through their membership schemes they can enhance their marketing to existing customers, which translates into increased sales at the check-outs.[2] This could be described as 'benefit-driven' trading.

Benefit-driven trading

Not-for-profit organisations sometimes go down the same route as the supermarkets, and use their membership schemes primarily to stimulate demand for the services they offer. In order to achieve this, they draw members into their schemes by creating a highly attractive package of benefits that leads potential members to believe that their personal interests will be best served by joining the scheme. For example, a theatre might create a package of benefits that includes ticket discounts for certain nights of the week, priority booking and a ticket-exchange facility. From the theatre's perspective, this might stimulate sales by encouraging people to book more regularly, and to book their seats for less popular performances. From a potential member's perspective, joining the scheme is an attractive proposition, enabling them to take advantage of discounts, to gain access to scarce tickets and to minimise the impact of unforeseen circumstances. Similarly, the Scottish Council for Voluntary Organisations (SCVO) offers a range of benefits to its member organisations, many of which are likely to be motivated to join by virtue of the range of benefits offered, especially those services which are offered to members on a financially preferable basis compared to non-members (see case study below).

Scottish Council for Voluntary Organisations

The Scottish Council for Voluntary Organisations (SCVO) is an industry membership body for other voluntary membership organisations. However, whilst its members may make considerable use of the facility to network with their colleagues from similar voluntary membership organisations, SCVO also provides and actively promotes a range of services for its members that are in many cases cheaper and more targeted than those available through the open marketplace to non-members. Services such as payroll management, advertising, a credit union for members, cheap office supplies, tax advice and appropriate pension schemes are but a few of those offered, and lead to significant cost-saving and time-saving benefits. With the strapline 'Let us do your chores, while you deliver your promises', SCVO reminds potential members of its ability 'to maximise your efficiency and effectiveness – and of course to safeguard your resources'.

Source: www.scvo.org.uk/membership (7 October 2003)

Loyalty-led trading

Organisations in the not-for-profit sector, however, tend to enjoy a natural advantage over their supermarket equivalents. For many, the motivations people will have for joining their membership schemes will be based as much upon a recognition of the intrinsic value of their work to wider society as upon the benefits that might accrue to them personally. The potential for stimulating profitable trading activity amongst members such as these is consequently all the higher. Those who are not just customers, but also advocates of the work of an organisation, have been proved to buy more, stay around longer and be willing to pay more than their more commercially minded counterparts.[3] This has important implications for those managing membership schemes. They are in a good position to engage in 'loyalty-led' trading. In other words, they do not necessarily have to offer costly financial incentives to stimulate trading. Instead, because they are a 'preferred supplier' in their members' minds, they can seek opportunities to sell products and services that will be acceptable, even at higher prices, than those available from other suppliers. Even the many charitable organisations for whom trading is not an integral part of their core operation can take advantage of their members' willingness to buy from them. The ever-growing number of charities that sell Christmas cards and create gift catalogues is an obvious example of this; and others, such as the Royal Horticultural Society (see case study below), have a vast array of products available for sale through subsidiary trading companies.

Royal Horticultural Society

Founded in 1804 and awarded Royal Charter status in 1987, the Royal Horticultural Society states its charitable purpose as 'the encouragement and improvement of the science, art and practice of horticulture in all its branches'. Membership in January 2003 stood at 323,350, and its turnover during the previous year amounted to around £19 million. There are currently around 3,000 gardening and horticultural clubs up and down the country which are affiliated to the RHS and with such a substantial operation to fund, one of the many revenue streams exploited by the organisation is the sale of RHS-branded products through its subsidiary trading company, RHS Enterprises Limited. Products are commissioned and sold exclusively through shops at RHS Garden Wisley, Rosemoor, Hyde Hall and Harlow Carr.

Other items are sourced and sold as part of its 'Licensing Programme'. This enables products and services to be developed under the RHS brand name and sold across the world, with RHS earning royalties from their sale. The RHS is, understandably, very protective of its brand name and is therefore extremely careful about who may use it. Business plans are evaluated by its licensing team and put into practice using a contract which is scrutinised by its intellectual property lawyers and trade mark agents. Since its reputation rests on, amongst other things, the perception of its brand by purchasers of its products, the RHS insists on being deeply involved throughout the process of concept, design, quality and production of licensed products and services. In the year to January 2003, RHS Enterprises Limited generated record a turnover of £12.6 million, representing a 20% increase on the previous year. Of this, profits of £2.3 million were covenanted back to the charity.

Sources:
www.rhs.org.uk (23 November 2003)
RHS Trustees' Report and Annual Statement, Year Ended 31 January 2003

Fundraising

Just as the concept of 'relationship marketing' supports the rationale for using membership schemes to stimulate trading income, the concept of 'relationship fundraising' highlights the role that membership schemes can play in fundraising activity. This concept holds that the whole process of raising money should be donor-based.[4] Treating fundraising just like any other kind of commercial transaction is an approach that is doomed to fail, because donors hate to be sold to. More appropriate is to view both fundraisers and donors as being on the same side of the table – the donors being colleagues in the process of supporting a cause, rather than customers.

A membership scheme can act as the table at which the two parties sit. Activities aimed at building trust can be built into a scheme and used to share the needs of the organisation with members, thereby stimulating them to contribute more than they might otherwise have done. Regular communication between members and an affiliated organisation and structured opportunities to volunteer, for example, can both draw members closer to the organisation and help it to build a relationship with them that predisposes them towards giving.

A membership scheme should not be thought of as a fundraising tool in itself, as the motivations for people for joining a scheme are likely to be quite diverse. For example, some schemes will have been designed primarily to attract members who are more interested in accumulating financial benefits (see benefit-driven trading, above) than anything more altruistic. Their joining illustrates an interest in the affiliate organisation or its work, but not necessarily a commitment to it. However, the existence of a scheme can offer a number of valuable opportunities in the process of fundraising:

RSPB

The Royal Society for the Protection of Birds (RSPB) operates a membership scheme with individual, joint and family categories. In addition the charity offers a variety of opportunities to support its work further, through donations, gift aid, legacies and a 'sponsor a species' scheme. Through associations with external organisations, the RSPB offers preferential terms to members and supporters such as the RSPB Wine Club, in association with Adnams Wines; a Visa card through the Co-operative Bank; and renewable electricity and natural gas at a small premium, through Scottish and Southern Energy PLC. The RSPB has also worked with solarcentury, a solar energy solutions provider, to develop a renewable energy package for RSPB supporters. A solar loan from the Co-operative Bank allows members to spread the cost over three years. RSPB Leisure offers deals on cottage holidays, boating holidays and hotel breaks; a breakdown service is arranged through the Environmental Transport Association; and there are also opportunities to purchase gifts, bird feed and accessories, bird call mobile phone ringtones and wildlife-friendly food. 'Our corporate partners have become an increasingly important source of funding. We value them all but, to mention just two, the Co-operative Bank Visa Card contributed £500,000 (and £2.5 million in the last five years) and income from our partnership with CJ WildBird Foods was certainly not peanuts at almost £250,000.'*

Sources:
www.rspb.org.uk (2 December 2003)
*RSPB Finances for 2002–03; Humphrey Norrington, Honorary Treasurer; Alan Sharpe, Director, Finance

---

Identifying potential donors

One of the criticisms frequently levied at fundraisers is that they try to build relationships with the wrong people – people who are not really open to having relationships with them.[5] A second criticism is that they start to build their relationships too late – after an initial gift has been made. A more consistent pattern of giving can be achieved if a relationship is formed before a first donation is made, informed by a more detailed understanding of individual members' needs. The commitment made by a person to joining a membership scheme identifies them *by definition* as a person with something to gain out of a relationship with the affiliate organisation, and thus creates an invaluable pool of potential donors.

National Kidney Federation

On the 'Donations' page of its website, the National Kidney Federation (NKF) says to donors 'If you are donating a sum of £12 (the minimum membership subscription fee) or more, then you may prefer to become a 'Friend' of the NKF. This will entitle you to a Welcome Pack and four issues of 'Kidney Life' magazine'. It then directs the donor straight to its 'Membership application form' using a link to its membership page.

Source: www.kidney.org.uk (18 January 2004)

Cultivating entry-level donors

Another problem that frequently faces fundraisers is 'churn and burn' – attracting a one-off donation which never goes further. It is, of course, much easier to elicit a one-off donation from someone than a ongoing stream of financial support; yet the cost of attracting that first donation can be high, and for that support to simply 'burn' off is a wasted opportunity. A membership scheme can provide a mechanism through which relationships with first-time donors can be developed over a period of time. Less threatening than the prospect of being the target of further fundraising efforts, a scheme can nurture ongoing goodwill amongst donors and make them more receptive to future approaches.

Shared Earth Trust

The Shared Earth Trust is a unique conservation body which pioneers the restoration of biodiversity to Britain's farmed countryside and runs a visitor centre and community group resource, 'Denmark Farm Conservation Centre', in West Wales.

It promotes the importance of supporting its endeavours as a way of 'adding your voice to those who care about the countryside'. It welcomes donations, but actively encourages membership as the preferred way of supporting the organisation for two broad reasons. Firstly, it is keen to benefit from the financial implications of longer-term commitments to the organisation, and states that 'Membership allows us to plan ahead and make us less dependent on other funding. It can also release "match funding", making your contribution worth twice as much'. But equally important, many supporters of the Shared Earth Trust are landowners or land use advisers, responsible for huge areas of the countryside. The aim of the Trust is to help these people to make a direct difference themselves, either on their own land or by influencing the way other areas are managed. A membership scheme is an effective vehicle for meeting this aim and encouraging ongoing partnerships.

Source: www.shared-earth-trust.org.uk (3 December 2003)

Special project support

Sometimes an affiliate organisation needs to attract non-routine funding. This might be for a capital project to establish a new building, for example, or in response to a natural disaster or financial crisis. Under circumstances such as these, a membership scheme can be a useful place to start looking for support. Even benefit-driven members might be willing to give towards a capital project, where they can see how their own experience of the organisation's work might be enhanced as a result. Those who are more committed to the intrinsic value of the work of the affiliate organisation are likely to be better prospects for disaster fundraising.

Greenpeace

Greenpeace successfully raised $400,000 from its supporters to pay anticipated court costs for a case involving British Nuclear Fuels. Despite Greenpeace losing the case the judge did not award costs to its adversary and the charity wrote to its supporters offering to give their money back. Only six took it. The rest told Greenpeace to keep it, and some sent even more money.

Source: Burnett, K. (1996) 'The Future of Relationship Fundraising: What's Next', *The Grantmanship Center Magazine*, Spring

Community fundraising

Some members are enthusiastic about giving their time and energy to support an organisation (see Volunteering, below). Others are willing to be its active advocates (see Advocates, page 36). This combination suggests that, within an organisation's membership scheme, there are likely to be people who will be both able and willing to perform a community fundraising function on behalf of the organisation. The commitment that these people have to its aims – demonstrated through their membership – can mean that their approach to potential donors is a particularly enthusiastic, engaging and ultimately profitable one. However such approaches to fundraising should be undertaken with care, ensuring that volunteer fundraisers are adequately trained, fully understand the values and beliefs of the organisation, and are able to communicate these to potential donors.

Friends of Victoria Hospital

The Friends of Victoria Hospital is a voluntary organisation that exists to provide additional comforts, amenities, services and equipment not available through official funding channels. The first phase of the hospital's re-development was undertaken by the Friends, who not only raised 95% of the £2 million cost of the new extension, but also took responsibility for overseeing the building project. The new building opened in December 2001 and provides a new Outpatients Department and a Clinical Investigations Unit, as well as an extended X-Ray Department and new administration offices. It was named in memory of Leslie Adams, the Chairman of the Friends from 1987 until his death in May 2000, whose vision it was to raise £1 million for the expansion of the hospital.

Source: www.southandeastdorsetpct.nhs.uk/data/Community%20Hospitals/Wimborne%20 Community%20Hospital/friends.htm (18 January 2004)

Volunteering

Whether or not a membership scheme confers on its members any actual voting rights over the activities of the organisation, the very act of joining a scheme tends to create in people a sense of ownership and participation in its work and a commitment to its goals. It is this commitment that can predispose some members to volunteer their services to the organisation. This potential pool of voluntary labour can be a very useful resource for not-for-profit organisations operating on limited funds; but there are key issues to consider:[6]

- **Not all members want to be volunteers:** people join membership schemes for a range of reasons and it is dangerous to assume that all people will be willing to give their time to an organisation. Schemes that emphasise the importance of volunteering above other benefits may alienate those who are unwilling or unable to do so.

- **Not all members are suitable to be volunteers:** organisations recruiting volunteers will require them to have specific skills and qualities to undertake the work they need to be done. As well as a commitment to the organisation and a willingness to give time, volunteers must have an aptitude for the work involved. Any training needs must also be considered.

- **A membership scheme is not a pre-requisite for recruiting volunteers:** not all volunteers want to belong to membership schemes. For example, students willing to give their time in exchange for work experience may have relatively little commitment to the goals of the organisation, but their skills may still be extremely valuable. The cost of joining a membership scheme would deter many for whom the primary reason for volunteering has more to do with their own career progression than the activities of the organisation itself.

- **The affiliate organisation may already operate a separate corps of volunteers:** the potential for muddle and confusion through attempting to manage two separate volunteer resources may be detrimental to meeting the organisation's needs.

- **Legal constraints apply to volunteers too:** legislation relating to, for example, health and safety, disability discrimination and public liability insurance need to be considered in exactly the same way as they would be for salaried staff.

- **Defining the barrier between paid staff and volunteers:** any organisation which operates with both paid staff and a volunteer corps must clearly define the roles expected to be performed by each type of worker. This is for a combination of reasons (see below), but also to protect the morale of paid staff who might have cause to believe their paid roles might be subverted by replacement volunteers.

Sutton Park

The Friends of Sutton Park Association (FOSPA) was formed in 1950 in response to suggestions at the time that parts of the Park could be made available for building. Now that the Park has been designated as a National Nature Reserve and its future is secure, the organisation concentrates on funding voluntary conservation projects in Sutton Park. Affiliated to the British Trust for Conservation Volunteers and working in partnership with the Sutton Park Ranger Service, all work carried out by the FOSPA Conservation Team is based on management plans drawn up by English Nature and other expert bodies. All members of the management committee and conservation team are volunteers, and the revenue from membership fees is used to pay for tools, safety equipment, sapling trees and other items to support current conservation projects. FOSPA also has two representatives on the Park advisory committee, which considers all matters related to the running of the Park. Membership is open to all. Members receive a regular newsletter by post, which contains details of current work and of a variety of social events and conducted walks which take place throughout the year. 'By becoming a member you will join a loyal and supportive group of people who are keen to save and protect the Park for future generations…If you have any concerns about the Park, FOSPA wants to know about them. If there are any issues that need further investigation, FOSPA will take them up. And if there are any developments that you need to know about, FOSPA will keep you informed.'

Source: www.fospa.btinternet.co.uk (2 December 2003)

Benefits of using volunteers

It is beyond the scope of this book to cover in detail the role of volunteers in not-for-profit organisations, but is worth considering here the benefits that they can bring to an organisation. By encouraging the use of volunteers, the organisation can:

- **Make otherwise uneconomic activity economically viable:** the value of volunteer activity to the not-for-profit sector in the UK in Volunteer's Week during May 2002 was estimated by the National Centre for Volunteering to be a staggering £10 billion annually. Volunteer work involved 22 million adults in the UK, who contributed over 90 million hours each week to charities and other agencies across the country.[7] Indeed, in many not-for-profit organisations the value of labour contributed by volunteers makes the difference between the organisation's viability and insolvency.
- **Provide support to paid staff:** invariably, in a non-commercial environment where every attempt is made to keep costs to a minimum, paid staff manage considerable workloads, often under continuous pressure. Volunteer support for them can dramatically increase their effectiveness, by enabling them to delegate.
- **Provide a substitute for paid staff:** certain roles in organisations can sometimes be fully covered by volunteer staff, keeping the payroll to a minimum.
- **Provide an opportunity to give:** people who are time-rich yet cash-poor still like to give to those causes which they support. The opportunity to give time, rather than money, may, for example, particularly suit people who are on low incomes, retired, studying, or between jobs.
- **Provide a flexible workforce:** some roles for which there is only an intermittent need in an organisation can be difficult to fill, as casual staff may have insufficient knowledge of the organisation to undertake the required

tasks. A trained pool of volunteers can be an effective solution in these circumstances.

- **Provide access to professional advice:** professional knowledge and skills, for example relating to financial or legal issues, can be so expensive that not-for-profit organisations may choose to 'get by' rather than seek expert help. Yet volunteers can come from all walks of life and qualified professionals are often happy to share their expertise with organisations to which they are committed.

Volunteering roles for members

It is quite possible for membership schemes to deliver suitable volunteers to various roles across an organisation; but certain roles tend to be particularly well suited to those who join membership schemes.

Running the membership scheme

Depending on the structure of a membership scheme (see Chapter 1), there may well be a vital volunteering role connected with the management of the scheme itself. The self-centred nature of social club groups, for example, will invariably mean that the scheme members have only themselves to rely upon for tasks such as membership renewals, communication with members and event management. Public members schemes and integrated membership schemes may be better resourced with core staff, but nonetheless, certain of the tasks – from stuffing envelopes to hosting social events – can be cost-effectively undertaken by volunteers. A lot of skills required for running a scheme tend to be related to business activities. Accounting, database management and marketing are all central to the health of a membership scheme, so the criteria for the appointment of volunteers to membership management roles should be quite specific. If those skills are not present among those willing to volunteer, then other solutions may have to be investigated, including an investment in training.

Network marketing

People who are passionate supporters of an organisation, cause or activity are generally the best people to enthuse about it to others, and word of mouth can be a very powerful communication tool. If managed carefully, such enthusiasm can be channelled into the development of a network of marketing activity. 'Ambassadors' schemes, for example, help people encourage friends, colleagues and local societies and clubs to share their enthusiasm. Those who join membership schemes are good prospects for becoming volunteer ambassadors for an organisation, as the enthusiasm that led them to become members can be channelled into encouraging others to do the same (see also Chapter 4).

City of Birmingham Symphony Orchestra

In 1999–2000 the City of Birmingham Symphony Orchestra (CBSO) recruited 20 volunteers to work as 'ambassadors' in the first year of a pilot scheme intended to bring 500 new attenders to its concerts. The Cultural Ambassadors scheme was funded by the Arts Council of England's New Audiences Programme and aimed to increase the number and range of people attending concerts. CBSO Society members and patrons, as well as frequent attenders and subscribers, were targeted by direct mail, asked to register their interest and invited to an introductory evening, which explained the benefits of the scheme for both the ambassadors and their guests. These included a 25% discount on parties of 10 or more new attenders; a free ticket for the group organiser; free programme; interval reception with members of the orchestra and the personal attention of a member of staff throughout the evening.

The ambassadors, who were already passionate supporters of classical music, encouraged friends, colleagues and local clubs and societies to share their enjoyment of the music and to take advantage of the benefits of the scheme, which included discounted tickets, the opportunity to meet members of the orchestra. Twenty-eight groups of personal friends, neighbours, work colleagues, church groups and societies/clubs came to 10 CBSO concerts over the season and the project reached its target of 500 guests, 440 totally new attenders and 60 lapsed and current attenders.

At least half the ambassadors said they had joined the scheme not because they had decided to 'convert' friends, but because they were already involved in other groups or societies and wanted to provide these organisations with a benefit or service. As one said: 'I belong to the association of retired persons…and this was an ideal starting point for getting people to listen to music'. As a result of feedback from the ambassadors, a young person's price has been introduced to encourage young attenders. Further recommendations include sending information on future concerts to ambassadors at least four months in advance so they have time to advertise the events and provide a better service in-house for attending groups.

Sources:
www.newaudiences.org.uk (18 January 2004)
www.cbso.co.uk (18 January 2004)

Asking for money

When it comes to generating income, those who are most committed to the core objects of an organisation are also those most likely to volunteer to raise money on its behalf (see Fundraising, above). Anything from the sale of raffle tickets to door-to-door collections and coffee mornings can be set in motion through those who belong to membership schemes. Particularly for the type of fundraising activity which relies more heavily on enthusiasm than on technical skills, the membership body can provide an invaluable bank of willing volunteers.

Advocates

The commitment shown by members to an organisation suggests that they may be broadly supportive of its aims. Under some circumstances it is possible to convert these latent sympathies into more pro-active support. Organisations which themselves exist to promote a specific cause or ideology are best placed to rally their members to action. However, even those which exist for other primary purposes can find that a membership base is an important place to look when they need to fight a particular issue or make representation to the authorities, communities and electorates.

Members can provide advocacy in a variety of ways.

A rapid response to a crisis

Two types of crises can benefit from a swift response from a membership body. A crisis may affect the members of the organisation itself, perhaps threatening the very existence of the organisation. Proposed changes in the law, for example, may unintentionally create problems for an organisation's members, and the support of the entire membership base can help the organisation put forward its case. Other crises requiring an urgent response can arise through the causes that an organisation supports.

Amnesty International

Amnesty International is a human rights campaigning organisation with over a million members in more than 140 countries. It was founded in Britain in 1961 by lawyer Peter Berenson and has more than 100,000 volunteers and 80 paid staff worldwide. Three hundred and thirty local groups, 600 youth groups and 100 student groups have been established in the UK.

The organisation seeks the 'release of all prisoners of conscience as long as they have not used or encouraged violence'. With the help of its members, thousands of prisoners have been released and helped since it was established. There are several ways in which members can help. The core method of campaigning is to flood the authorities concerned with letters and messages of protest. Members are also encouraged to support the following initiatives:

- **Urgent actions:** In 1974 the Urgent Action Network was set up as a means of campaigning rapidly in an effort to save a particular prisoner from torture, death or medical neglect; from unfair trial, the judicial death penalty or extrajudicial execution; or from repatriation where the return to a person's country of origin may lead to further abuse of human rights. If an immediate international response is judged to be the most effective method of dealing with specific human rights violations, the Urgent Action Network is set in motion. Amnesty compiles an Urgent Action case-sheet with details of the individual(s) concerned, some background information, advice on the wording of appeals and the government officials to whom such appeals should be addressed. The case-sheet is then sent to Amnesty's national offices for immediate distribution to the members of their networks.

- **Crisis response actions:** Crisis response actions are issued by Amnesty on occasions when massive human rights violations are taking place, or when an event in the UK necessitates an immediate coordinated mass response from UK Amnesty supporters. Members who agree to assist Amnesty in the event of a crisis are sent a simple request, usually for a letter to be written urgently to an MP or foreign government official. Pre-printed postcards and online e-mail actions are also sometimes produced or invitations are made to participate in a demonstration.

- **Individual actions:** The AIUK Urgent Action Donor Pledge scheme was set up in 1987 to ensure that telegrams and faxes are sent from the AIUK office in response to each urgent action. Members of the scheme donate a sum of money annually for faxes and telegrams to be sent out in their names. This provides people with busy lives with an easy way to contribute effectively.

Sources:
www.amnesty.org.uk (12 December 2003)
FitzHerbert L. and Becher, K. (2002) *The Major Charities, An Independent Guide*, Directory of Social Change

A lobbying force

An organisation that wishes to address fundamental issues relating to its core activities is in a good position to mobilise a membership group. For example, an organisation competing for public funding against a variety of other good causes may call on its members for support. Other organisations may wish to draw attention to and campaign for a change in practice relating to something they consider to be an injustice or malpractice (and this may even be a primary reason for their existence). Members may join to support them because they consider that the 'public good' will suffer if they do not.[8]

Baby Milk Action

Baby Milk Action is a non-profit organisation which aims to save lives and to end the suffering caused by inappropriate infant feeding. The organisation works with an international network with the aim of influencing the marketing activities of the baby feeding industry. The organisation campaigns itself against what it sees as the irresponsible marketing of baby foods, and also encourages members of the public to protest against company tactics, and coordinates an international boycott of Nestlé, the world's largest baby milk manufacturer. Members who wish to become active in the campaign are supported with advice and materials, including blank anti-Nestlé petition forms and 'Boycott Nestlé' stickers, and teachers are offered a pack containing 14 activities to help students to 'See through the Spin'.

Source: www.babymilkaction.org (15 January 2004)

High-level political influence

It is possible for an organisation to tap into certain key networks by identifying members who not only have sympathy for the aims of an organisation, but also have themselves a high public profile, or high-level political connections. These members are sometimes trustees or board members, but there may be others who do not wish to involve themselves in the running of the organisation, yet would be willing to speak out about a specific issue.

Trade Justice Movement

Formed at the end of 2000, the Trade Justice Movement is a fast-growing group of organisations that include aid agencies, environment and human rights campaigns, fair trade organisations, faith and consumer groups. The movement is supported by more than 50 member organisations that have in total over 9 million members. Together they are campaigning for trade justice – not free trade – with the rules weighted to benefit poor people and the environment. The movement calls upon world leaders to:

- stop forcing poor countries to open their markets; and champion their right to manage their own economies
- regulate big business and their investments to ensure that people and the environment come before profits
- stop rich countries promoting the interests of big business through trade interventions that harm the poor and the environment
- ensure trade policy is made in a fair, transparent and democratic way.

The Trade Justice Movement aims to show the world that by acting together, organisations can have a much bigger impact than they could ever have if they worked in isolation, and consequently can bring about change. All the coalition members support the policy positions outlined the organisation's founding statement.

Source: www.tjm.org.uk (18 January 2004)

A supportive voice in the community

A membership base is a valuable tool for disseminating the ideology or beliefs of an organisation further afield. The enthusiasm and commitment of members can be harnessed to 'spread the word' throughout the communities in which they live. For example, a membership body can be a catalyst for anything from talks at Women's Institute meetings to education work in schools, though to achieve this type of advocacy, the organisation itself may have to provide some resources and support. At a less formal level, the membership disseminates the values, beliefs and objects of the organisation through social networks, whether through impromptu dinner party conversations, or whilst waiting to be called for an appointment at the doctor's surgery.

La Leche League

The La Leche League (LLL) is an international voluntary organisation, founded in 1956 in the USA, which is recognised by UNICEF and the World Health Organisation as a world expert in the field of breastfeeding. It provides information and support to women interested in breastfeeding and undertakes national breastfeeding campaigns world wide.

Members believe in the value of 'mother-to-mother support' which they can find in their own vicinity or 'a warm voice to reach by telephone'. La Leche League leaders are mothers who would like to give something back to the organisation that has helped them to breastfeed their own babies. They are all fully trained by LLL to help other mothers to breastfeed. LLL leaders are always available to listen to a mother who would like to breastfeed, is experiencing problems breastfeeding, or just wants to share her concerns with another mother. In the UK LLL groups meet monthly for informal discussion meetings led by LLL leaders. Pregnant mothers, as well as mothers with their babies, discuss all aspects of pregnancy, breastfeeding, weaning and parenting, and have access to a lending library of books and leaflets. Members receive a bi-monthly magazine for mothers with stories, latest research and information, publication lists and details of conferences. They also have access to professional advisers and use of the group library. Health professional members receive in addition, specialist publications, a sample set of tear-off information sheets, leaflets, details of seminars and study days and reduced rates for medical research enquiries.

Sources: La Leche League Membership Form
www.lalecheleague.org (18 January 2004)

Why join a scheme?

If, as suggested above, membership schemes attract people who have some sympathies with a particular cause or with the aims of a particular organisation, then it might also be assumed that their motives for joining such a scheme would be predominantly philanthropic. However, just as pure altruism may not fall at the heart of most individuals' decisions to give money to charitable causes,[9] neither is it the most common motive for people to join a membership scheme. More likely, a wide range of underlying reasons explain why they are willing to give their support, and a membership scheme may be the most appropriate vehicle for capturing that support.

Transaction versus transfer

Even when people say they want nothing in return for their support of a worthwhile cause or activity, the chances are that they do have expectations. They expect the organisation to put the resources they contribute – money, time, influence and so on – to effective use in the pursuit of some reasonably well-defined aims, and chances are they expect the organisation to show them some gratitude as well.[10] Rather than view a charitable donation – or indeed, the joining of a membership scheme – as a no-strings-attached transfer of funds from a supporter to a cause, it is more helpful to view the process as a two-way transaction between an individual and the organisation soliciting their support.

Those who join membership schemes can be broadly separated into two main categories[11] – 'givers' and 'takers' – within which a wide range of sub-categories can be found, depending on the nature of the affiliated organisation or cause.

Givers

These people use their membership primarily to demonstrate their approval of and appreciation for the work of an organisation. This demonstration tends to take the form of giving either time or money, or both. Some givers could, perhaps, more usefully be described as donors. In other words, they view the joining of a membership scheme as one way (possibly one of a range of ways) of giving financial support to an organisation or cause. Other givers may, instead of – or as well as – giving money, be willing to volunteer their time. For them, a membership scheme may provide the framework they need to encourage them to participate in the work of an organisation whose aims they support.

An interesting range of motivations may lie behind an individual's desire to give money[3] or time[12] to an organisation through a membership scheme.

Self-esteem

Giving can make people feel good and build their self-image. Thinking of themselves as 'contributors' can be a source of personal pride, and their self-perception is enhanced by feeling needed. A membership scheme can provide a relatively safe environment in which people can test themselves, and prove their self-worth. There may be a 'safety in numbers' aspect in developing self-esteem. Some people will join in order to gain knowledge about the organisation and its particular brand of work – whatever it is – through the safe environment, in which other like-minded people are also keen to share in the mutual informal learning process.

Public recognition

These people use giving as a way of building their social status or enhancing their prestige in the eyes of others. Wealthy individuals with millions to spare may choose to have buildings named after them. Those with less to give may enjoy the status afforded to members of a scheme, which provides a public vehicle through which they can demonstrate their support, perhaps including a listing in the organisation's programme, newsletter or brochure.

Birmingham Contemporary Music Group

A key group of Birmingham Contemporary Music Group's supporters each pay £1,000 a year to ally themselves with BCMG's mission to bring the most exciting new classical music to diverse audiences and change young people's lives through a dynamic education programme. Individual and corporate givers are invited to join the BCMG Foundation, and in return receive invitations to see Foundation projects in action, including an annual BCMG concert supported by the Foundation. There are regular, exclusive opportunities to meet composers, conductors and players and members are invited to an annual dinner with BCMG artists. Members' support is acknowledged in BCMG's print and publicity.

The launch of the Foundation followed the success of the 'Sound Investment Scheme', which has helped to commission many new works since it was set up over a decade ago. Each new work is divided into £100 Sound Units, and members of the scheme can buy Sound Units in the work of their choice. Sound Investors receive further information about the chosen work, news of its progress during composition and invitations to rehearsals and a special première reception. At this reception, the composer offers members either a signed copy of the score's title page or the exclusive opportunity to buy the full signed score. Members of the scheme are also named in the score and concert programme, are guaranteed tickets for the première performance and afterwards receive any press reviews and news of future performances.

Sources: BCMG press release (October 2003)
www.bcmg.org.uk (18 January 2004)

Ideology and altruism

Concern for a cause is a great motivator for giving, stemming from a sense of moral obligation that it is the 'right' thing to do. A membership scheme can provide a sense of belonging and an opportunity for people to interact with others who share similar convictions.

Fear of losing a service or facility

Self-interest is firmly at the root of some giving. Services provided through the not-for-profit sector are often at risk of disappearing unless people are willing to finance them. Some view membership schemes as, not only a mechanism for supporting, but also as a formal means of registering their own stake in services or activities of which they themselves wish to take advantage.

Re-paying a debt

Doing good is used as an expression of gratitude by people who feel that they have benefited from a service or from the work of a particular organisation. A membership scheme can create an opportunity to give that might otherwise not be available. For example, whilst few people would volunteer to donate money straight into the government's coffers, or to work for the government without pay, a significant number are willing to join the friends of a hospital, hospice, through which they will give both time and money. They are often motivated by gratitude for the quality of care that they or a relative have themselves received, and are happy to provide services which are highly valued by patients yet do not fall within the remit of National Health Service funding.

Chelsea and Westminster Hospital

The Friends of Chelsea and Westminster Hospital raise funds throughout the year and use their money to provide equipment, services and facilities for patients. The Friends are constituted as a charitable trust and are entirely separate from the Hospital. All funds raised are controlled by the 25-strong Friends committee, which is also responsible for spending decisions.

Almost a thousand members pay an annual membership fee to join the scheme, and grateful or indebted patients are encouraged join. The only direct benefit offered for membership is a copy of the AGM report. However, the Hospital is not bereft of wealthy neighbours, so fundraising events are directed towards activities that may encourage Friends to participate, such as golf tournaments or cricket matches.

The nature of the fundraising events is seen as a reflection of the profile of the committee, and also of the sort of people who would be willing and able to give money. The committee recently organised a charity clay pigeon shoot, which raised £33,000; £10,000 of this went on event costs, and £23,000 went towards purchasing new equipment for the Hospital's Burns Unit. One hundred and ten people participated, and it was felt that a number of these were more interested in the shooting itself than in the cause for which funds were being raised. Having said this, the Friends are aware that some people may not be happy to support certain fundraising campaigns, as they may feel that the National Health Service should provide certain equipment. Consequently, the anal ultrasound equipment that is desperately needed in another department of the Hospital, and which could help change thousands of lives, is seen by the Friends as a very worthy cause, but a difficult one for which to run a fundraising campaign.

Sources: www.nhs.uk/root/localnhsservices/Orgs/voluntaryServices1.asp?id=RQM&t=vol (18 January 2004)
Interview with Amy Hillcroft, Friends committee (December 2003)
Friends of Chelsea and Westminster Hospital Constitution and publicity literature

Social interaction

Social networks of like-minded people develop through membership schemes, and people value the opportunity to mix with others for a specific and 'worthy' purpose. Membership schemes that enable people to work together towards common goals can, as a by-product, create very enjoyable opportunities for them to meet others and to form deep and lasting relationships with them. This can be particularly valuable, for example, for people who are now to a community and want to make new friends.

Fantasy fulfilment

Belonging to a membership scheme can create opportunities to have a depth of engagement with an organisation or activity that would be unattainable in other ways. This form of self-development can be very attractive to some people. For example, someone who has always wanted to work with animals but instead has ended up with a career in accountancy might seek a deeper involvement with an animal charity or a zoological society than they achieve simply being a donor. Membership can provide a form of escapism from the rigours of daily life and an opportunity for engagement at a more satisfying level.

Career development

The opportunity to enhance career prospects is an important motivator for some people's involvement in a membership scheme, which can create a range of attractive career development scenarios. At its most basic level, membership of the scheme may create useful networking opportunities with potential employers. Schemes that encourage volunteer participation can satisfy a range of motivations beyond this. For example, a scheme may present risk-free opportunities for people to explore the realities of other jobs; it can give them a chance to take a leadership role; it can help them keep alive skills that they no longer need to practise at work; it can provide an opportunity for them to learn new skills; the work experience can look good on a resumé or CV; and it can also provide a stepping stone into paid work from other employment, unemployment or for college-leavers.

Exercise influence

An opportunity to have a say in the development of an organisation or cause will motivate some people to give active support. If they have a passion for the core activity of the organisation and a view as to how that activity should be performed, they may choose to become members of a scheme in order to gain influence over the inputs to and outputs of the organisation. That said, not all schemes permit such involvement from their members, and from the organisation's point of view, the involvement of members, however well-meaning, may present some serious drawbacks.

Business and Professional Women UK

Business and Professional Women UK (BPW) is an organisation for working women that has operated for 65 years. It aims to help increase members' self-confidence and levels of skills, leading to more successful careers. It is a non-party political lobbying organisation. Membership is open to all working women, in any type of career and at all levels of responsibility. Women who are on career breaks, or in unpaid work that would normally have market value, are also welcomed.

Benefits of membership include:

- the opportunity to influence local, national and international decision-making and the formation of policies
- events and social activities which give members the opportunity to meet and enjoy the friendship and support of other like-minded women
- regular newsletters and information on local and national issues
- training and development programmes to help women increase their self confidence and so to achieve their career goals.

There are also clubs around the UK, which hold meetings once or twice a month, giving members the opportunity to meet other working women, and a Young BPW branch of the organisation for members under the age of 35 years.

All BPW UK members are automatically members of both BPW Europe and BPW International, which campaign for equal opportunities and status for women in economic, civil and political life, and for more women to be employed in decision-making positions. BPW Europe is the largest network of business professional

---

women in the world with over 20,000 members. It has representatives at several United Nations and European Institutions, including the United Nations Educational, Scientific and Cultural Organisation, the World Health Organisation, and the United Nations Industrial Development Organisation.

Source: www.bpwuk.org.uk (18 January 2004)

Takers

These people join membership schemes primarily as a means of obtaining rewards that are not available by other routes. From their perspective, if membership fails to deliver these rewards, then membership is pointless. The potential recruit will usually fail to join in the first place, but if they do join, they will permit membership to lapse. The types of rewards that people seek include the following.

Status

Although public recognition may be a motivation underlying the actions of 'givers' (see above), it can also be an important motivator for 'takers'. Schemes offering exclusive 'members only' benefits can provide a route through which those seeking social status and recognition can set themselves apart from others. For example, membership of a museum or gallery friends scheme may permit access to private views which are denied to others. The scheme may be viewed as a means for buying a passport into an otherwise impenetrable social circle. In practical terms, there is often the feeling of being on 'the inside track' of an organisation, through maintaining membership. Whether through a perception of 'having the ear' of the organisation or simply accessing privileged information and opportunities not made available to non-members, 'takers' will seek the benefits of enhanced personal status afforded through joining.

Financial gain

For some, tangible economic benefits will be paramount in their decision to join a scheme. For example, membership may offer access to goods and services that would be far more expensive if obtained in other ways. Alternatively, membership may offer discounts to those who become heavy users of a service. Schemes such as those operating within theatres, wildlife parks and zoos, museums and heritage establishments are often founded on this premise, which without further benefits on offer are little more than a crude form of loyalty scheme, more commonly associated with high street retailers. Ticket discounts enable more regular visitors to make considerable savings through such schemes, provided members are willing to adapt their behaviour to meet the conditions of the discounts (for example, attending on a weekday, booking well in advance or by buying at least three tickets).

Perhaps unsurprisingly therefore, households with children are more likely to be financially motivated than those without.[13]

Preferential treatment

Certain types of preferential treatment offered through schemes can confer perceived status on members (see above), but this preferential treatment may also take many other forms and some people will be motivated to join a scheme simply to gain access to it. Here again, some theatre schemes provide good examples. They may give their members the opportunity to book tickets for popular shows before the box office opens to the general public; and some offer ticket exchange schemes for people who have pre-booked tickets but wish to change their arrangements as the date of the event approaches.

Social interaction

The motivation for social interaction through a membership scheme is not necessarily rooted in a desire to 'give' to an organisation (see above). Some people like to be involved in membership schemes because of the social events that they run for members. These can create valued opportunities to meet and mix with other people who have similar interests.

Serving multiple motivations

What is clear from the motivations of 'givers' and 'takers' (above) is that certain benefits of membership can be sought for quite different reasons by different people. Social interaction, for example, can be a motivation for joining a membership scheme whether or not a person is inclined to support the affiliated organisation. Fundraising events can take advantage of this. One group of members may enjoy being involved with the process of setting up and managing events, and others will enjoy actually attending them. A desire for social status is another motivation that may drive both 'giving' and 'taking' behaviour. Some arts organisations will be only too familiar with the distinction between members who are motivated by the opportunity to socialise with the stars and partake in its aura of glamour,[14] as opposed to those who wish to be acknowledged as ambassadors for a well-respected institution.

On the other hand, some motivations appear to be mutually exclusive and in the process of satisfying some people's needs, others are alienated. In some instances, one segment of the membership will be solely interested in the economic benefits they can derive from membership, while another views the opportunity to contribute to a cause or organisation in which they believe to be fundamental to their membership. True altruists sometimes disparage those who view philanthropy as an exchange for benefits (even though they still expect some form of recognition for their own donations).[15]

The needs of these people may be best served outside a membership scheme unless the scheme is used primarily as a vehicle for fundraising.

The design of a successful membership scheme is dependent on recognising the range of motivating factors that may lead a person to belong, and on presenting tangible benefits that permit these needs to be met. The issue of catering for a diversity of motivations and needs consolidates the theories of 'relationship marketing' and 'relationship fundraising' and implies that a tiered or multiple-category membership scheme will be most effective at attracting all the different segments of a potential membership base. The development of such a scheme is explored in detail in Chapter 3.

Umbrella bodies

In addition to membership schemes designed for individuals and corporate bodies, there are also those set up for the benefit of other membership groups. Umbrella bodies are membership organisations to which other membership organisations belong. They tend to provide services, networking opportunities, high level advocacy and other forms of support that enable their members to deliver their own services more effectively. For example:

- **The National Association of Hospital and Community Friends** (representing over 700 hospital friends schemes) provides member organisations with automatic insurance cover for public liability, products liability, employer's liability, trustees' liability and personal accident.

  Source: www.hc-friends.org.uk (19 January 2004)

- **Making Music** (the National Federation of Music Societies) runs a Music Exchange scheme to enable its member groups to borrow musical scores at a fraction of the publishers' costs, and provides a 'Programme Note Bank' to help them compile their concert programmes.

  Source: www.makingmusic.org.uk (19 January 2004)

- **The National Association of Toy and Leisure Libraries** offers a one-day course entitled 'Introduction to Toy Libraries', which focuses on the processes involved in setting up and running a toy library.

  Source: www.natll.org.uk (19 January 2004)

- **The British Association of Friends of Museums** provides member organisations with a sample Heritage Volunteer Charter, the 'Handbook for Heritage Volunteer Managers and Administrators' and a wide range of information sheets on issues such as gift aid, running an appeal, and relationships between museum friends and the governing bodies of museums.

  Source: www.bafm.org.uk (19 January 2004)

- **The Long-term Medical Conditions Alliance**, the umbrella body of national voluntary organisations working to meet the needs of people with long-term health conditions, is active in influencing health policy. The organisation responds to key documents and consultations, selects representatives from across its member organisations to sit on committees and boards, campaigns on specific issues and influences policy through its research and consultation with members.

Source: www.lmca.demon.co.uk (19 January 2004)

- Membership of the **National Council for Voluntary Organisations** is open to all voluntary organisations, whether large national bodies or small community groups and development agencies working at a local level. It runs many network groups, covering specialist areas of work, providing an opportunity for professionals to keep up to date with latest developments, share experiences and to learn from others. For example, the Computer Support Worker's Forum is aimed at any individual in the voluntary sector with a responsibility for ICT, whether in a formal or informal capacity.

Source: www.ncvo-vol.org.uk (19 January 2004)

Summary

Organisations potentially have a lot to gain from running membership schemes. They can generate revenues from membership fees, create a market for trading income, benefit from increased donations, identify a willing pool of volunteers and establish an enthusiastic group of advocates. There are also important benefits for members – not just the tangible benefits delivered through the scheme, but also the psychological benefits that can be gained by belonging to a body for which one has an affection, empathy or interest. The design of a successful membership scheme is dependent on clearly identifying and matching the objectives of a scheme to the needs the organisation and in doing so, developing membership benefits that will motivate a person to join.

---

1 Gummesson, E. (1987) 'The New Marketing – Developing Long-term Interactive Relationships', *Long Range Planning*, Vol. 20, No. 4, pp10–20

2 Wright, C. and Sparks, L. (1999) 'Loyalty Saturation in Retailing: Exploring the End of Retail Loyalty Cards?', *International Journal of Retail and Distribution Management*, Vol. 27, No. 10, pp429–440

3 Smith, S. and Wheeler, J. (October 2002) *Managing the Customer Experience*, FT Prentice Hall, p45

4 Burnett, K. (1996) 'The Future of Relationship Fundraising: What's Next', *The Grantmanship Center Magazine*, Spring

5 Fox, R. (1996) 'The Future of Relationship Fundraising: What Goes Wrong', *The Grantmanship Center Magazine*, Spring

6 Further information on all aspects of volunteers and volunteering is at www.volunteering.org.uk

7 Press release: *Volunteer's Week* (7–13 June) sees celebrations of the UK's 22 million volunteers, www.volunteersweek.org.uk, 7 October 2003

8 Jordan, G., Maloney, W. A. and McLaughlin, A. (1994) 'Collective Action and the Public Interest Problem: drawing a line under Olson?' Conference Proceedings: 1994, Political Studies Association, referring to Olson, M. (1971) *The Logic of Collective Action*, 2nd edition, Harvard University Press

9 Price, R.A and File, K.M. (1994) *The Seven Faces of Philanthropy: A New Approach to Cultivating Major Donors*, Jossey-Bass

10 Kotler, P. and Andreasen, A. (1995) *Strategic Marketing for NonProfit Organisations*, 5th Edition, Prentice Hall, p252

11 Arts Intelligence Ltd (2002) 'Northampton Theatres: Delivering an Effective Membership Scheme', research report (unpublished)

12 Ellis, S.J. (undated) 'Why Volunteer?' Energize, Inc. at http://charityguide.org/charity/motivation/whyvolunteer.htm, 9 October 2003

13 Slater, A. (2003) 'Users or Supporters? Understanding Motivations and Behaviors of Museum Members', *Curator: The Museum Journal*, Vol. 46, No.2, April, pp182–207

14 Burns Sadek Research Ltd. (1992) Qualitative research conducted to examine the motivations for membership of friends' schemes, Arts Council of Great Britain

15 Price, R.A. and File, K.M. (1994) *The Seven Faces of Philanthropy: A New Approach to Cultivating Major Donors*, Jossey-Bass

3 DEVISING A MEMBERSHIP SCHEME

The design of a membership scheme has a fundamental impact on what it can achieve and how effectively it can achieve this. A number of vital foundation stones must be put in place when a scheme is first set up in order for it to thrive in the longer term. The overall objectives for the scheme must be identified; a structure through which the scheme is managed must be set up; and a range of benefits and an associated fee structure (in most cases) or other qualifying joining criteria must be devised to attract members. This chapter explores these foundation stones in more detail.

The initial design of a membership scheme is critical to its long-term impact and fundamental issues such as the basic structure of the scheme, its relationship with the organisation and its objectives should be established at the outset. A useful preliminary exercise in this process would be to work through the checklist for starting up a scheme given in Appendix A.

Selecting an organisational framework

As explained in Chapter 1, membership schemes can take a number of forms, and the most appropriate structure for a scheme will depend upon the context in which it is being set up and the purposes for which it will exist. For example, if an existing organisation wishes to set up a membership scheme in order to create a mechanism through which fundraising activity can be channelled, and through which a regular corps of volunteers can be recruited, it might conclude that an integrated membership scheme would work to its best advantage. In this case there would normally be no need for a separate legal entity to be established for the scheme, which would simply slot into the organisation's overall management structures. In general, the creation of an integrated membership scheme as opposed to an independent one is preferable for an organisation, since this structure offers it maximum control. With such control assured, the organisation is able to review and update the scheme's objectives, benefits and pricing strategy, for example, as its own aims and objectives develop over time.

There are a few circumstances under which an organisation may decide that an integrated membership scheme is not the optimum solution. In the case of organisations constituted as private companies or local authorities, neither are charitable bodies so some form of arms-length membership structure may be desirable. Potential members might not wish to support such organisations directly, but might consider contributing to a ring-fenced or restricted initiative.

On the other hand, if the concept of a membership scheme is being driven by a group of individuals who wish to support an already-established organisation, an integrated scheme may be inappropriate unless the individuals involved are particularly keen to engage the direct support of the organisation. Instead, the group will have to consider whether to set itself up as a public members scheme, complete with semi-formal, semi-professional associated structures, or to remain as a less formal group of voluntary individuals.

Setting objectives

At the very root of the scheme must be a shared understanding by everyone involved as to precisely why the scheme exists at all, and what it aims to achieve.

Given the wide range of benefits that can accrue both to organisations that set up membership schemes and those who join them, it is vital that the primary and any secondary purposes of a scheme are pinned down at the very outset.

Basic aims

The benefits sought from a scheme, described in Chapter 2, will be the main determinant of its overall aims, and these aims tend to fall into two categories.

To generate revenues

A not-for-profit organisation may wish to set up a membership scheme with a view to establishing a source of income that is unrelated to its core income generation activity. For example, a charity that depends on fundraising activity to achieve its objectives may find that the fees payable for membership of a scheme can deliver a valuable new income stream, and some organisations use a membership scheme as the primary mechanism by which supporters can make donations to the organisation. In these cases, the high cost of membership (especially for the top tiers of membership) is usually disproportionate to the financial value of the benefits on offer, as such schemes aim to harness philanthropic behaviour. They are, in essence, quite different from schemes that appeal on the basis of the financial incentives they offer, where the majority of the fee covers the cost of discounts and privileges provided (though these types of schemes may still deliver a charity with a donor prospect list that is of value in other fundraising activity). They may also be inappropriate in organisations where fundraising through a membership scheme is secondary to other quite separate individual fundraising initiatives.

The Institute of Contemporary Art, Boston

The Institute of Contemporary Art in Boston (USA) operates a membership scheme which distinguishes between 'Supporting Membership' and 'Active Membership' in its promotional leaflet. The lower levels of Active Membership, comprising both 'Individual' ($40) and 'Dual/Family'($60) categories, confer benefits such as free admission, newsletters both in print and by e-mail, a membership card, and invitations to openings. Supporting Membership covers friend, patron, donor and director's circle levels at prices ranging from $125 to $5,000. Membership of the Ars Longa Society is also available at $10,000. These categories enjoy all the benefits of Active Membership, together with added elements such as guest passes, previews, reciprocal benefits at other art museums, and at the top levels, private exhibition tours on request, and an annual special event.

Sources:
Membership leaflet: 'Let the ICA bring you the art, ideas, people and energy of our time'
www.icaboston.org (13 January 2004)

Trading organisations such as theatres, can also benefit financially from the ticket sales revenues that may accrue as members take advantage of special deals aimed at encouraging them to attend performances for which they would otherwise have not booked tickets. The economics of any scheme designed primarily to generate revenues must be carefully assessed, however, as there can be significant management and administration costs associated with it, as well as the prospect of significant incomes (see Budgeting, below). Consequently, most schemes are driven by more than the prospect of simple commercial gain, and strive to generate loyalty and goodwill among members, as well as money.

Theatre Royal, Newcastle

A fundraising campaign on behalf of the Theatre Royal, Newcastle also tested responses to a 'revenue ask' from the theatre's attenders. Five target groups were selected comprising, Friends of the Theatre (who pay £40 a year), Stage 2 members (who pay £5 a year), and three groups of attenders, subdivided by frequency of attendance over the previous two years. Between two hundred and five hundred people in each group were contacted with the following results:

Segment	Number contacted	Pledge rate (%)	Total pledged over 4 years	Average pledge per contact	Average value per definite pledge	Return on investment
Friends	442	33.9	£27,625	£62.50	£184.17	10:1
Stage 2	470	25.3	£14,943	£31.79	£125.57	5:1
T5+	304	22.7	£11,040	£36.00	£160.00	6:1
T3–4	237	17.3	£5,793	£24.44	£141.28	4:1
T2	250	16.4	£3,978	£15.91	£97.03	2.5:1
Total	**1,703**	**24.7**	**£63,379**	**£37.22**	**£150.90**	**6:1**

Of the T2 group (those attending only twice in two years) 16.4% pledged a donation. The more frequent attenders (those attending three or four times in two years) produced both a higher success rate and pledged more on average, and these results increased again in the group of attenders who visited the theatre five or more times in the two-year period. For every £1 spent on the campaign this group realised £6 for the Theatre.

The Stage 2 group provided a lower success rate and levels of donation than the T5 group suggesting that although these 'members' were willing to pay for information their involvement and indeed attendance rates may be less. However much higher returns were achieved from the Friends group, both in levels of donation and pledge rate and it was felt that the 'ask' to this group could have been increased.

This test suggests that infrequent Theatre attenders can be a profitable source of income from donations, but that on average, Friends are far more likely than non-Friends to respond to such an 'ask' and to pledge more. However, Friends who make only a minor commitment (Stage 2) show no more propensity to give than regular attenders.

Sources:
Adrian Salmon, The Phone Room
Arts Marketing Association 2002 Day Event, 'Stairway to Heaven' (www.a-m-a.co.uk)

To generate loyalty

Many schemes are set up with a view to involving supporters, attenders and/or participants more closely with the work of an organisation. The scheme can provide a framework that encourages the loyalty of its members. This is a common objective in the arts sector, where in theory a membership scheme can help establish and maintain a group of regular attenders by stimulating their interest and making them feel rather more involved than merely being on a free mailing list or being a subscriber.[1] There is always, of course, the danger that the enthusiasm exhibited by members stems more from the financial benefits accruing to them through a scheme than any emotional commitment to an organisation or activity, and that any perceived loyalty is in reality little more than the inevitable response to the stimulus of a highly desirable set of tangible benefits.[2]

In other parts of the not-for-profit sector, the desire to establish a loyal core of supporters may stem from a need for a more powerful voice in the community, a stronger base for fundraising activity or a more active corps of volunteers. It is important to recognise the range of motivations that lead to loyalty among the members of a scheme, and to permit these to be expressed. For example, some potential donors may wish to use a membership scheme as an opportunity give financial support to an organisation, and may feel that a scheme offering extensive tangible benefits fails to accommodate their philanthropic motivations. In other circumstances a member's loyalty may not be to the organisation itself but rather to a social peer group or business community that is associated with the organisation. Even these motivations can be developed to the benefit of the organisation indirectly, provided they are understood and rewarded appropriately.

Friends of the Earth

The environmental pressure group Friends of the Earth (FoE) concentrates its efforts in three main areas: campaigning, activating citizen action and research; and providing information and ideas about environmental problems and solutions. The FoE Trust Ltd, which is a registered charity, carries out mainly education activities which qualify for charitable status, and campaigning activity is carried out by the non-charitable, but not-for-profit FoE Ltd. The two organisations, which share offices and staff, and are almost wholly funded by donations from individuals, are also supported by over 200 local FoE groups. Although authorised by the main body, these groups are legally independent and do not have charitable status.

In return for a regular donation of £5 per month, the organisation provides a welcome pack with information on its work, regular updates on urgent campaigns and the magazine *Earthmatters*, which contains news, contributions from experts

---

in the field and information and advice on ways of supporting campaigns. The organisation offers to refund all donations if, after a year, the supporter does not feel that the organisation has lived up to its promises.

Sources:
FitzHerbert, L. and Becher, K. (2002) *The Major Charities: An Independent Guide*, Directory of Social Change, pp136–138
Leaflet: 'Join Friends of the Earth'

Needless to say, there is an important relationship between bringing in revenue and fostering loyalty. Income generation from membership schemes is found to be largely dependent upon loyalty, which itself is a precursor to increased purchase, individual giving and advocacy.[3] It is an understanding of this inter-relationship that tends to underpin successful membership schemes. As a result, many schemes are devised to comprise a series of tiers, enabling multiple objectives to be served through a single scheme.

Objectives

The setting of specific objectives for a membership scheme is a critical part of its development, as these objectives will form the baseline against which the scheme's success or failure can be measured (see Chapter 5). The discipline of attempting to set concrete goals is valuable, as it focuses attention on the likely impact of a scheme and sets appropriate levels of expectation in relation to it.

Although not always an easy process, it helps if these objectives are written in a SMART way. In other words, they should, if at all possible, be:

Specific (make it quite clear as to what the precise target is)
Measurable (be capable of evaluation of progress)
Agreed (supported by all who are involved in achieving them)
Realistic (not unattainable dreams)
Time-constrained (to be achieved by a specific deadline).

Thus, such objectives may include targets for:

- revenues from fee income
- numbers of members
- revenues from trading income arising through the membership scheme
- levels of participation in advocacy work
- estimated value of volunteer activity through the scheme
- number of volunteers per work category
- average life-time value of members
- average life-time period of membership
- fundraising revenues from members

- advocacy targets (possibly qualitative rather than quantitative targets)
- renewal rates, joining rates and 'churn' (loss rates).

The above objectives should not only be measurable in total at any point in time, but also by membership category (e.g. family, student, individual rate), by tier (e.g. bronze, gold, diamond levels), and across specific periods of time such as financial years and seasons. (See Chapter 4 for a more detailed explanation of tiers and membership categories.)

These objectives will also have a major knock-on effect on a number of other key decisions that have to be made in the setting up of a membership scheme, such as its management structure and the package of benefits that should be offered to members. Consequently, before finalising any objectives, it is important to undertake an assessment of the needs of potential members.

Assessing the potential market

As explained in Chapter 2, the range of motivations that might prompt a person to join a membership scheme is both wide and varied. In the absence of any tangible evidence, making assumptions about the factors that might trigger a response to the opportunity to become a member is a risky approach. For example, it would be dangerous to assume that a person who covenants money to a charity regularly would enjoy any greater involvement with that organisation. The very act of giving may provide a sufficient level of engagement for them. Similarly, just because a person holds a season ticket for entry to a botanical garden, this doesn't mean that they have any interest in becoming a volunteer, joining a social group associated with the organisation or giving further support in a crisis.

Individuals present a complex range of interests, needs and desires which extend in several dimensions, and it is important to understand which benefits should be clustered together and offered to which segments of the potential membership population. This, however, is an inexact science, so before setting up a membership scheme (and at regular intervals thereafter) it is extremely valuable to undertake some research to determine what sort of people are attracted by the idea of becoming a member and what will be the factors that influence their behaviour in this respect. Such research should be used to understand the size and range of potential member market segments, and the optimum package of benefits to deliver to each segment.

Conducting research

The key to an effective research exercise usually has very little to do to with the amount of money spent on it, and everything to do with the clarity of thinking behind the exercise. Research into the needs of members and potential members should involve a number of very clear steps.

Identify the purpose of the research

Membership research will normally aim to understand the reasons why potential members might join a scheme, and/or why current members continue to belong. When researching an existing scheme, it also helps to gain an insight into the perceived value of current benefits on offer. Listing a set of information needs – the specific facts you would like to know when the research is complete – is a useful starting point.

Identify the 'population of interest'

Not everyone in the world is a good prospect for membership of a scheme, and in order to assess the market as efficiently as possible, it is helpful to identify at the start the sort of people who may be minded to join, and to target the research at them. This may include a range of different groups involved with your organisation, including those who:

- have previously given money
- subscribe to the organisation's services
- attend regularly or undertake frequent transactions with the organisation
- volunteer their services
- are on the mailing list
- are known to support similar organisations or to have an empathy with the cause
- have a demographic profile similar to existing members.

The population of interest for research into the views of current members is, self-evidently, somewhat easier to pin down, being the members themselves!

Decide on a research budget

Small organisations with very limited resources may decide that they do not wish to spend any money on research. Whilst the scope of their research will inevitably be limited, it is still possible for them to make relatively informal inquiries of their membership or potential membership. The more structured the process for making these inquiries and analysing the responses to them, the more valuable the process will be. For larger organisations, that have more to gain and more to lose in the running of their membership schemes, it is best to set a realistic research budget that will enable the research objectives to be met and a suitable approach to be used for the research. External expertise may be required to conduct the research professionally, and this too should be factored into the budget.

Identify the most cost-effective approach

The most appropriate process for conducting the research – the methodology – will depend upon a wide range of factors, especially the scale of the organisation. Effective research seeks out the views of a broadly representative group of people, whose answers to a range of questions are assumed to be representative of the whole constituency. Two forms of research can be used.

'Qualitative research' is used to explore in some detail the thoughts of a relatively small number of people, in order to try and understand their views as well as possible. This approach might be taken, for example, if an organisation was thinking of setting up a scheme for the first time, and wanted to understand the types of benefits that it should offer in order to trigger membership. One-to-one interviews and focus groups are commonly used to collect this type of information.

'Quantitative research', on the other hand, is conducted amongst a much larger group of people and uses questionnaires to find out quite simple information. The findings can be used to predict the proportion of people as a whole who have similar views to each other. This is a very valuable approach, for example, for examining what existing members like and dislike about a scheme to which they belong, and to investigate the sort of support there would be for new benefits of a scheme. (For example, any of the series of questions at Appendix B could be useful on such a questionnaire for a cultural organisation.) A rough estimate of the potential financial value of a membership scheme and the optimum fee-benefit calculation can also be established.

Implement the research programme

The logistics of conducting research are seldom straightforward. Responsibility for the administration of the research, the practicalities of distributing questionnaires and ensuring they are completed, making arrangements for focus groups and analysing incoming questionnaire data are the sorts of issues that should all be considered before the project kicks off – not half way through.

Use the findings to inform decisions

There's no point going to the trouble of conducting a research exercise unless the findings are used to inform decisions. So the final step is to use the findings of the research to make better decisions about how a scheme should be structured, managed or implemented.

Much of the research process described here can be handled in-house for small membership schemes. But for larger schemes with more to gain from effective management practices, it is usually advisable to commission professional external agencies[4] both to devise the research programme and subsequently to undertake and report on the programme. Poorly conducted or wrongly interpreted research findings are likely to be more damaging in the long run than relying purely on gut feeling and instinct.

Building an organisational structure

Fundamental to the smooth running of a membership scheme are the mechanisms put in place for its governance and management. Three key areas have to be considered at the outset: the legal status of the organisation, its management and staffing structure, and the administrative systems that will support it.

Legal status[5]

Different forms of legal entity will be appropriate for a membership scheme, depending on whether the scheme is to be integrated within an existing organisation or to remain completely independent. Professional legal advice is almost always valuable at this stage, as any decisions made will have far-reaching implications for matters such as taxation, responsibility for the liabilities of the organisation, the eligibility of the organisation for grants, the nature and composition of its governing body (see below) and the voting rights of its members.

In the UK the legal frameworks within which membership schemes can be managed categorised into two groups:

- **unincorporated organisations:** such as membership associations, partnerships and occasionally trusts
- **incorporated organisations:** such as a company limited by guarantee, company limited by shares, an industrial and provident society.

Charitable status[6]

Both incorporated and unincorporated organisations can register for charitable status if they qualify under the regulations governing the designation of charities. This means that some membership schemes can take advantage of a range of tax benefits granted to charities, but it if they do, they must also comply with the accounting requirements of the Charities Act 1993. Generally, organisations whose aims are charitable and who wish to be eligible for the tax concessions available must register with the Charity Commission if they are based in England and Wales. Exempt charities in England and Wales and all charities based in Scotland and Northern Ireland must register with the Inland Revenue for recognition of their charitable status. There are a few exceptions.[7] Those that:

- do not have an annual income over £1,000
- do not have use of land or buildings
- do not have any permanent endowment (i.e. capital which cannot be spent like income)
- are exempt or excepted charities.

To be charitable, an organisation's objects must be wholly charitable under one of four headings:

- the relief of financial hardship
- the advancement of education
- the advancement of religion
- certain other purposes for the benefit of the community.

A decision to apply for charitable status should not be taken lightly, and should involve serious consideration of all the formal reporting, taxation and legal issues related to it. Professional advice is usually required in these areas, as well as reference to the Charity Commission[8] for specific guidance concerning any application for charitable status.

The governing document

Whatever the legal entity chosen as a framework for the activities of a membership scheme, a 'governing document' will have to be devised to formalise its status. This is a legally binding set of rules according to which the organisation is permitted to function. It may take the following forms:

- **constitution or rules:** used by unincorporated associations such as amateur sports clubs and social club groups
- **trust deed:** used by grant-making bodies
- **memorandum and articles of association:** for incorporated organisations such as companies limited by guarantee (including many not-for-profit organisations and cultural organisations such as theatres, museums and galleries).

Management structures

From the point of its inception onwards, any membership organisation is dependent upon people to develop its initiatives and take responsibility for its decision-making and administration. Fundamentally there are four types of people who may be involved in the direction, management and/or administration of a membership body.

The governing body

If a membership organisation has independent status its governing document (see above) will dictate the structure of its governing body. This governing body will comprise a set of individuals who will, usually in a voluntary capacity, take overall legal responsibility for the decision-making relating to the organisation. In circumstances where a membership organisation has no committee, the governing body will comprise all the members. However, this is an unusual scenario. Usually, the governing body will be variously defined as a 'board of trustees', a 'board of governors', 'board members', 'committee members', or an 'executive committee', depending upon the legal status of the organisation.

For the avoidance of possible confusion, the term 'management committee' should not normally be used to describe a governing body as it more commonly describes a team of individuals who are paid or volunteer to carry out the wishes of the elected governing body, and therefore are not empowered to take final decisions affecting the organisation. Were a management committee to act in the capacity of a governing body, those managers might be regarded as shadow directors, and be held legally and financially accountable for any disasters that may befall the organisation. For incorporated organisations, the governing body will generally have limited liability for any debts of the organisation, unless it has been shown to have operated irresponsibly or illegally. However, for non-incorporated organisations, the individuals who comprise the governing body together carry personal liability for any legal or financial troubles.

Irrespective of legal structure, the governing body's key responsibilities comprise, in brief:

- **Constitutional objects and powers:** ensuring that the organisation's objects (i.e. its aims and purposes) are made clear, and that policies and strategies are put into place to achieve these.
- **Procedures and accountability:** ensuring that the organisation operates within the rules of its governing document and adopts procedures that adhere to current laws and reflect good practice. For example, this will involve setting up effective democratic processes for the election of the governing body and promoting adequate communication between the governing body and any management committees, sub-committees or the general membership. The governing body must also adhere to the requirements imposed upon it by its members at general meetings, as well as externally imposed conditions, for instance those demanded by grant funders, sponsors and donors.

- **Legal requirements and obligations:** ensuring that the organisation meets all its legal obligations, for example with respect to:
  - contracts of employment
  - equal opportunities legislation
  - leases, licences or tenancy agreements for premises
  - contracts for services
  - insurance requirements
  - health and safety legislation
  - income tax, National Insurance and VAT
  - data protection legislation
  - charities and/or companies legislation.
- **Financial and accounting responsibility:** ensuring that the organisation has sufficient funds to enable it to operate, including the ability to meet future financial obligations when they become due. This will involve taking steps to prevent the organisation from getting into financial trouble and these will include ensuring proper records are kept of all financial transactions and implementing appropriate security procedures to protect the organisation from theft and other financial abuse (see Chapter 5). Essentially, it must have an adequate system of internal control and must maintain transparency and accountability.

Management committees

Whilst all membership organisations will have one form of governing body or another, some larger organisations may also set up management committees, working parties and sub-committees to undertake specific aspects of the day-to-day administration of their affairs. In some cases, a management committee is one and the same as a governing body, but more often it will be a separate group which may include a mixture of governing body members and other co-optees. A combination of factors is key to sustaining successful management committees: the delegation of specific tasks, the clear definition of requirements ('terms of reference') and responsibilities ('delegated powers'), and involvement of people with the motivation, skills, vision and drive to achieve the task. To prevent confusion between the roles of the governing body and a sub-committee, it is especially important to ensure that there is clarity about the roles and responsibilities of each. Such clarity should be apparent not only in the governing document, but also in the day-to-day tasks involved in the management and running of the organisation.[9]

Paid staff

Some independent membership schemes and all integrated membership schemes will be led by paid staff who work in a professional capacity. To them will fall the workload directly associated with the scheme, such as recruiting members and delivering membership benefits, and they will operate through reporting lines that lead to more senior management levels within their respective employing organisations. They may seek the assistance of volunteers in undertaking these tasks, but the ultimate responsibility lies with the paid staff.

Paid staff can be appointed to undertake work in two ways. If appointed as employees, whether full- or part-time, they become subject to employment law and as such are usually appointed on a permanent basis, or under a fixed-term contract. If appointed on a freelance basis, a contract for services will usually be drawn up. Legal advice is valuable to ensure that the organisation understands the implications of any given route, particularly as the Inland Revenue applies strict rules in assessing whether such freelancers are bona fide self-employed under a contract for services or whether they should be regarded as staff under a contract of service. Irrespective of employed status, there are a number of laws which relate to 'workers'[10] in general.

Volunteer staff

Certain membership schemes, in particular social club groups, are very reliant on the voluntary activities of its members. In an ideal world, it is desirable to select volunteers using the same criteria as would be used in an employment situation or when appointing freelance staff. In practice, however, it may be difficult to attract people with the most appropriate skills to fill any vacancies if those posts are not paid; and the extent to which managerial control can be exercised over volunteers is therefore limited.

The decision as to whether to appoint paid staff or rely on volunteers can be a tricky one. The benefits of running a scheme through paid staff include:

- the ability to select professionals with a pre-determined skills base
- availability of time and expertise
- accountability to senior managers and ultimately the governing body
- ability to manage large and complex organisations.

On the other hand, relying on volunteers can be more appropriate if:

- available funds are limited;
- there are a number of relatively simple manual tasks required where using volunteers can save considerable money for the organisation;
- the organisation and membership is small in size and limited in scope;
- membership management issues are relatively simple and straightforward;
- schemes are based in geographic areas where paid staff are expensive and difficult to recruit.

Administrative systems

As well as the governing body, management committees, staff and volunteers, a range of systems has to be put in place to enable a membership scheme to function effectively. The systems relating to the money generated by and spent through the scheme are particularly important.

Budgeting

A budget is a plan that reflects, in financial terms, an organisation's proposed activities over a period of time.[11] A budget is an important tool for any membership scheme. It focuses attention on the projected costs of managing a scheme, and sets these against the projected revenues. This gives those responsible a sense of the extent to which the scheme is financially viable. In the absence of a budget, it is all too easy to fail to notice when the costs of keeping a scheme running begin to outweigh its financial benefits, and few independent membership organisations enjoy the luxury of being able to exist without a reasonable certainty that their income will at least equal their expenditure. An integrated scheme may, however, be in a better position: if its objectives are being met and an affiliate organisation is willing to subsidise its costs, for example, then a scheme that fails either to break even or generate a surplus may be quite acceptable. However, it is important that the financial model is recognised at the outset, so that an affiliate organisation itself can budget its support for the membership scheme. The process of budgeting will be made easier by using tools such as spreadsheets.

A list of potential revenues and costs that may need to be factored into a budget appears at Appendix C, and there is further discussion of budgeting in Chapter 5.

Income/revenue and expenditure

Mechanisms for managing and accounting for incoming cash and outgoing expenditure are needed. For an integrated membership scheme, this will be a relatively straightforward process. Any revenues generated through the scheme will be payable directly to the affiliate organisation (albeit in some cases a separate account may exist in order visibly to demonstrate that such transactions are kept separate from the other trading activities of the affiliate organisation), and expenditure will be authorised and processed by it. That organisation will therefore have full control over the ways in which any surpluses generated through the membership scheme are spent.

Independent schemes will need to account for all income and expenditure. They must ensure that both the rules of the scheme and the requirements of the tax authorities are complied with, and that the full liabilities of the scheme are known. In order to accomplish this, they have to set up their own banking arrangements, and create systems through which money is deposited and paid out. (For further details of the financial management issues, see Chapter 5). In many cases, a treasurer or financial manager will take responsibility for this, but he or she may not be authorised to sign cheques above a certain value. Routine decisions about expenditure can be pursued effectively by giving delegated powers to a sub-set of the governing body – such as a financial sub-committee – to make payments which fall within its previously agreed limits. For decisions on large items of expenditure – for example, how any funds generated through the membership scheme should be used in support of the affiliate organisation or cause – other mechanisms may be needed. For example, the approval of a meeting of the full governing body may be required, or if decisions relate to fundamental issues such as the objects and powers of the organisation, there may also have to be a majority vote by members at a general meeting.

Taxation

Different tax regimes mean that the tax implications for membership schemes will differ widely across the world. In the UK, independent membership bodies may in some circumstances be liable for corporation tax on any profits, and may need to register for value added tax (VAT), depending on the value of goods and services that they sell which would normally attract VAT (known as 'taxable supplies'). However, where income is classified as a donation, this is outside the scope of VAT, and thus the value of donations received should not be included within the calculation of VAT-able revenues. An affiliate organisation that operates an integrated membership scheme in-house may already be registered for VAT though, and should be aware of any corporation tax liabilities.

The law relating to VAT[12] is both complex and subject to a fair amount of case law and interpretation by accountants and HM Customs and Excise (HMCE) officials (who implement the VAT rules on behalf of the government). It is essential that, whether running an independent membership organisation or an integrated membership scheme, detailed professional advice is sought and adhered to. There are complex rules relating to which goods and services are charged at the standard rate of VAT and those which are zero-rated or reduced tariff. Charitable donations are exempt and not subject to VAT at all (see above). In some cases only a proportion of the revenue generated from a membership scheme is viewed by HMCE as being a payment for goods and services, with the balance treated as a charitable donation. Therefore, it is vital that HMCE[13] is consulted. In some circumstances, a written ruling about the tax due on membership fees is advisable, rather than relying on assumptions which may turn out to be wrong, and therefore both costly and illegal. Adding to the complexity, membership subscriptions paid to a cultural organisation may be exempt from VAT, depending on the nature of benefits offered to members and the status of the organisation (e.g. if it supplies cultural services). New advice from HMCE was made available[14] in 2003.

A final health warning on VAT: the amount and level of VAT that can be claimed back by a membership organisation may be restricted. However, if VAT rules are not followed, an organisation will be liable to pay back any VAT due, plus interest plus potential penalties. Ignorance is no excuse.

Systems and procedures relating to tax should be agreed by the governing body before being implemented. However, tax rules change from time to time, so such systems should be held under regular review.

Gift aid[15]

Gift aid is a tax concession through which charities in receipt of donations can increase the value of these donations by 28p for every £1 received, by reclaiming the basic rate of income tax already paid by the donor. In general the Inland Revenue does not treat membership schemes as eligible for gift aid, since membership fees are payments made to acquire benefits in the form of goods or services, hence not regarded as donations or gifts. However, it is possible to set up a scheme that can benefit from gift aid rules, and to claim gift aid on eligible elements of a membership scheme.

The Inland Revenue[16] is prepared to treat membership fees as if they are gifts, provided that they meet certain conditions. Firstly payments must do no more than secure membership of the charity, and secondly they must not secure a right to the personal use of any facilities or services provided by the charity. For example, the provision of newsletters explaining the work of the charity or admission to its sites to visit and view the work of the charity would not breach these conditions as they are not regarded as services or facilities for personal use. However, memberships that include, say, individual tuition or coaching, or free or discounted use of sports facilities that are not available on similar terms to non-members, are regarded as personal use of services or facilities and would therefore not be recognised as gifts or donations. If the charity is able to separate the element of a membership fee that provides the basic rights of membership from any part that relates to the provision of services or facilities, then the membership element can be treated as a gift.

Organisations should contact the Inland Revenue in order to establish formally the proportion of the membership fee (if any) that is eligible for gift aid,[17] and a written decision can be requested. As is the case for VAT, if gift aid rules are not followed, an organisation will be liable to pay back to the Inland Revenue any gift aid claimed.

Payments made for membership must also satisfy donor benefit rules. These rules place limits on the value of the benefits that a donor may receive. If the value exceeds these limits, the donation will not qualify as a gift aid donation. There are also rules for particular situations including educational school trips, church collections and donations allowing free admission to view heritage property or wildlife. Special rules also apply to family membership, and when an individual pays another's subscription, as occurs with gift membership.

It is usually helpful if a membership scheme that is eligible for gift aid is identified as such to potential members, so that they are aware of the extra funding that their fees are generating, courtesy of the tax man. With this in mind, an organisation called 'The Giving Campaign' has created branding that organisations may use to help promote the charitable nature of their work and its eligibility for gift aid, and offers downloadable toolkits including advice, logos and suggested wording for promotional materials.[18]

Different approaches to gift aid

Because the tax rules governing gift aid vary depending upon the nature of the benefits offered through a membership scheme, organisations vary in the way that they communicate the benefits of gift aid to potential members. For example:

- **The Friends of the Imperial War Museum** state that they are able to reclaim income tax from any subscription or donation received in accordance with a gift aid declaration. Members are then asked to sign the standard gift aid declaration, which tells donors that they must pay enough tax overall to cover tax reclaimed; that non-taxpayers should not sign a declaration; and that the organisation can only reclaim tax at the basic rate, even for higher rate taxpayers. It is also made clear, however, that higher rate taxpayers can obtain further tax relief through their tax returns.

  Source: www.iwm.org.uk/IWMFriends/index.htm (19 January 2004)

- The membership subscription form for **The Jewish Genealogical Society of Great Britain** offers a lower level of annual fees for those who have signed the gift aid declaration. The standard annual subscription fees are £25 for individuals and £30 for families; but for those who have not signed the gift aid declaration the annual fees are £32 and £38.46 respectively.

  Source: www.jgsgb.org.uk (19 January 2004)

- The membership body of **The British Cartographic Society** (The BCS) includes a wide range of corporate, academic and other bodies, plus individuals, with an interest in maps. The organisation's membership and renewal forms ask members quite simply to sign a declaration saying 'I am a UK taxpayer. I would like the Society to treat all membership subscriptions I have made from 6 April 2000 as gift aid donations until I notify you otherwise'.

  Source: www.cartography.org.uk (19 January 2004)

- **The V&A Patrons scheme** has three levels of supporters (see case study in Chapter 6, page 179). The value of the membership benefits which have been approved by HMCE and the Inland Revenue are stated on the joining form for each level. It is made clear that the remainder of each membership fee level is treated as a voluntary donation, for which gift aid can be claimed.

  Source: www.vam.ac.uk (19 January 2004)

- **The Watermill Theatre** in Newbury operates a friends scheme which requests a membership donation rather than a joining fee. Although a minimum donation of £20 for single membership and £30 for joint membership is suggested, it remains nevertheless a discretionary amount. The application form asks members to sign the following declaration for gift aid purposes 'I am a UK taxpayer, and I would like this donation to the Watermill Theatre (and all subsequent donations until I notify the theatre otherwise) to be tax effective under the gift aid scheme'. Benefits offered by the scheme include regular newsletters, priority booking, dress rehearsal tickets when available, ticket exchange facilities and invitations to special events.

  Sources:
  Information from Susan Foster, Watermill Theatre (December 2003)
  Membership leaflet: 'Everyone needs Friends and the Watermill Theatre is no exception'
  www.watermill.org.uk (19 January 2004)

Subscriptions and renewals

The process of collecting subscription applications and money from members, and the subsequent renewals system associated with this, can be complex, particularly for tiered schemes (see below) and especially for schemes which operate 'rolling' as opposed to 'fixed point' renewals (see below and Chapter 5). For any but the smallest of independent membership schemes, a computer-based relational database system will be needed, and a web-based system is becoming increasingly desirable. Specialist membership management software is available, and may be essential for more complex schemes. On the other hand, simple database software will be adequate for more basic schemes.

This raises a series of questions, firstly as to whether the membership and renewals process should be handled in-house or contracted out to a subscription agency. The resources available through an affiliate organisation may mean that it is both feasible and desirable to keep the operation in-house. For example, an arts centre may use an integrated box office and web-based ticketing system which records transaction details as its customers book tickets. To these records may be attached each person's membership details, including renewal dates. For much smaller schemes it may be possible to keep adequate membership records on a simple spreadsheet or relational database. For those in between – larger schemes which do not have access to the resources of an affiliate organisation, and particularly those with a very limited staff base – contracting out to an agency which runs specialist membership management services may be the most cost-effective route to follow.

The technology being used is inextricably linked with another membership management decision – that of whether to renew all members at a specific date in the year (a fixed point renewal), or whether to sell full 12-month memberships at any point in the year (a rolling renewal). For some organisations, such as sports clubs which run matches during a specific season only, it is normally most appropriate to renew all memberships at the same time, and to offer a sliding scale of discounts depending on how much time is left before the renewal point. For other organisations which experience no specific 'peak season', selling 12-month memberships all year will be preferable, though this makes the administrative system for renewals considerably more complex (see Chapter 5 for a more comprehensive guide to renewals and membership retention).

City Screen

Established in 1989, independent exhibitor City Screen, which operates the Picturehouse chain of city centre arthouse cinemas, offers a membership scheme in 17 of its sites as part of a focus on customer loyalty. Individual site managers take responsibility for the day-to-day operation of each scheme in association with City Screen marketing staff. The benefits offered by the scheme vary from site to site as part of a commitment to individuality and independence but reciprocal membership benefits are available at other participating sites.

In City Screen's early stages, the majority of box office systems used in the venues did not include database capability. Therefore membership records were maintained separately involving considerable amounts of management staff time. Paper lists of current members were supplied to box office staff, which proved increasingly cumbersome as the membership base increased, for example in allocating tickets for special events or validating discounts for customers who had lost or forgotten their cards. In addition this system could not provide information on the purchasing patterns of members which would facilitate direct marketing initiatives or allow comprehensive evaluation.

In 2002 City Screen developed a specialised box office system, Boxman, which is gradually being rolled out across its cinemas. This system integrates membership data and purchase histories with ticketing functionality. As a result, membership applications and renewals can be processed by box office staff at the point of sale, releasing management time and simplifying validation. The facility to export data into other software applications not only allows detailed reporting but also creates opportunities for targeted marketing which were not previously available.

Overall the scheme enjoyed a 21.9% increase in levels of membership during the financial year 2002–03. In November 2003 the scheme showed an average of 1,792 members per site, with over 5,000 members in one of the longer established schemes.

Source:
www.picturehouses.co.uk (18 January 2004)
Interview with Rebekah Polding, Events Manager, City Screen (22 December 2003)

Designing a scheme

Effective membership schemes recognise the needs of potential members and set about fulfilling these needs in a way that will also meet the objectives of the scheme.

Segmenting the market

As explained in Chapter 2, the needs of members and potential members, and their motivations for joining a membership scheme, can vary widely. In catering for the needs of the widest possible group of potential members, it is seldom that a single-price, one-size-fits-all scheme is the most effective one. Instead, it is often appropriate for the principles of 'market segmentation' to be applied in order to offer different packages of benefits to different people (normally at different prices), but all within the boundaries of the same overall scheme. For example, people who are highly committed to an organisation or cause may view joining a membership scheme as a valuable opportunity to meet and socialise with other like-minded individuals, and may be willing to pay more for this opportunity. Others may have no interest in participating socially, and simply be interested in deriving financial benefits themselves from a scheme. For these people the benefits must, in cash terms, outweigh the joining fee (albeit the benefit to the organisation should be the continued loyalty and income which might otherwise not be forthcoming). Different membership categories can be set up to enable these segments of the market to obtain what they want from a scheme, without having to sign up for benefits that are of no value to them, or that are, in their view, too expensive.

Royal College of Nursing

The Royal College of Nursing (RCN) is the leading professional union for nursing, campaigning on behalf of the profession and working to develop practice. The RCN maintains a network of local advocates in the form of fully trained RCN stewards, safety representatives and practice nurse representatives and offers a 24-hour information and advice service through RCN Direct.

The scheme is segmented into 12 categories to suit individual circumstances:

Category	Criteria for membership	Subscription (per year)
Full member	Qualified for over a year and registered with the National Medical Council (NMC).	£146
Full newly qualified	Transferring from RCN student membership after gaining a nursing or midwifery qualification enabling staff to register with the NMC for the first time. For one year only.	£73
Full member – concessionary	1 For new members joining the RCN within one year of registering with the NMC for the first time. 2 Existing RCN full newly qualified members at the end of a year in that category of membership. 3 Internationally recruited nurse members upon notification that they have successfully registered with the NMC. For one year only.	£73 rising to 75% of full membership cost from Jan 2004
Student	Currently in nurse training for first nursing or midwifery qualification.	£10
Internationally Recruited Nurse (IRN)	IRN accepted onto an adaptation placement, currently undertaking an adaptation placement or awaiting registration with the NMC.	£10
Nurse cadet	Currently undertaking a Nurse Cadet training course recognised by the RCN.	£10

Assoc. member – non-practising	Been in another RCN category for at least one year but now non-practising.	£36.50
Assoc. member – retired	Been in another RCN category for at least one year but now retired.	£10
Assoc. member – career break	If taking a career break for up to two years (max.) or working less than 37.5 hours a month. Return to this category is only available after at least one year's full membership.	£73
RCN/RCM associate	RCN subscription if full member of the Royal College of Midwives (RCM).	£73
Joint (NATFHE/ EIS/AUT)	RCN subscription if in joint membership with these teaching trades unions.	£109.50
Healthcare assistant – full	If staff member has S/NVQ Level 3 in an area of care recognised by the RCN.	£96

Sources:
www.rcn.org.uk (12 December 2003)
Information from membership office (22 December 2003)

Some common bases for membership categories are described below.

Age

To encourage people on low incomes to join a scheme, it is common to offer discounted rates to young people and retired people. Sometimes it is appropriate for a scheme to offer the same benefits to these groups as to full paying members, but in other circumstances it may be appropriate to limit the benefits made available. For example, junior membership of a tennis club will often permit young people access to courts at specific times of day, when full members are less likely to require the facilities. Before introducing age-related concessions, it's important to understand the profile of a potential membership base. If it turns out that the majority of potential members are retired, for example, then to offer reduced-price membership on this basis could defeat the purpose of the scheme altogether.

Metropolitan Museum of Art

The Apollo Circle at the Metropolitan Museum of Art is a special membership group for individuals aged 21–39. Named after the Greek god of youth, the arts, culture, and music, The Apollo Circle provides for its members a variety of educational and social activities and offers unique insights into the Museum's collection and special exhibitions. Annual dues are $1,000 for individuals or couples, and individual members may bring a guest to all events. Proceeds from the scheme support The Apollo Circle Fund for Art Conservation.

Source: www.metmuseum.org (16 January 2004)

Family grouping

A membership structure that includes a family category may encourage a wider membership base, but the implementation of this needs some thought. For example, how families are defined can be a difficult issue. Using the concept of a 'household' may no longer be appropriate: not all families will be based in a single household, and not all households comprise single families. Furthermore, a computer database must accommodate the records of single parents, same sex couples and the marital status of co-habitees. It's also important to remember that a family membership category will only be attractive if the scheme offers benefits to all members of the family.

Family membership categories

Different membership schemes handle family membership in a range of ways. For example:

- At the **Royal Society for the Protection of Birds**, 'Family Membership' covers 'up to two adults and all children aged under 19 at one address' and the scheme also offers a 'Wildlife Explorers Family Membership' which covers 'all children under 19 at one address, but no adults'.

  Source: www.rspb.org.uk (19 January 2004)

- **Belfast's Linen Hall Library** offers family membership 'open to family members resident at the same address' which covers 'parents/partners and their children aged under 18'. Although all eligible family members receive individual membership cards, only one copy of mailed material is sent.

  Source: www.linenhall.com (19 January 2004)

- **Chicago Botanic Garden** offers a family membership which provides the option to buy four tickets for members-only events and free parking for two cars in addition to the benefits available to individual members. A 'Family Plus' membership increases the permitted number of tickets to six and includes six free tram tours of the garden.

  Source: www.chicagobotanic.org (19 January 2004)

- The family membership category offered by **Norwich Theatre Royal** allows priority booking and discounts on the purchase of eight tickets, without specifying numbers of adults and children or any relationship between them.

  Source: Forthcoming events brochure: Norwich Theatre Royal

- Family membership of the **Friends of the National Railway Museum** applies to 'a maximum of four persons, two or three of whom are under 18 years of age, residing at the same address'.

  Source: www.nrm.org.uk (19 January 2004)

- **San Diego Natural History Museum** offers a level of membership specifically for grandparents, defined as 'two seniors in the same household plus four grandchildren per visit'. This includes access to special activities and classes and allows grandparents to register their grandchildren for classes and programmes at special discount rates.

  Source: www.sdnhm.org (19 January 2004)

Access and disability

Those who suffer from mental and physical disabilities may live on low incomes, require carers, medical assistance and other support such as wheelchairs, guide dogs and so on. A special membership category with price discounts may help those who need to be accompanied to an event, and who may make use of any limited facilities that are available for people with certain types of physical disability, such as parking spaces or areas for wheelchairs.

Sadler's Wells

Sadler's Wells offers a variety of membership opportunities, including a friends scheme which provides discounts on tickets and programmes, a brochure mailing list and a free monthly e-mail bulletin which confers occasional special offers and discounts. In addition Sadler's Wells operates a free scheme for patrons with disabilities, the over 60s, students, and the unwaged, to demonstrate its 'commitment to access for all'. The scheme offers targeted benefits for each group, as well as information about the organisation's programmes. Potential members may join the scheme at the time of booking and enjoy the benefits immediately.

Source: www.sadlerswells.com (2 December 2003)

Corporate status

A membership category that provides benefits specifically aimed at businesses, rather than individuals, can generate a lot of interest in the business community and act as a mechanism for containing and directing any latent support for future advocacy. Such a scheme can be viewed by businesses as means of involving their staff in a particular cause or charity, and as a route to exercising corporate social responsibility. Under these circumstances, the 'price' of joining is often a commitment to a given fundraising target over a period of time. In other cases there may be a simple commercial case for a business to join a corporate membership scheme that provides financial and other benefits to employees. For example, leisure- and culture-based affiliate organisations may be able to offer a set of tangible benefits to staff and opportunities for corporate entertaining through their schemes. Given the potential value of such a package, corporate categories can normally be priced much higher than those offering only individual benefits.

Sight Savers corporate membership scheme

Sight Savers International (SSI) runs a corporate membership scheme that requires companies to make a two-year fundraising commitment. The scheme requires companies to raise £1 per staff member for two years, with a minimum target set at £30,000 per year and corporate members are also encouraged to help promote the aims of SSI. With support from Sight Savers' fundraising and PR team, funds are raised through a combination of activities such as staff fundraising or payroll giving, events, cause-related marketing, donations, gifts in kind and sponsorship.

In return Sight Savers offer an 'Eye Witness' invitation for board members or employees to visit a SSI project overseas, to see the outcome of their fundraising efforts. Programme officers will make presentations to company staff and guests; there is an annual reception and a high-profile fundraising ball; features are published in Sight Savers magazine (reaching 200,000 supporters); and there is coverage of corporate involvement on the SSI website and recognition in its annual report.

Source: www.sightsavers.org.uk (10 December 2003)

Location

A membership scheme that supports geographically-specific activity may provide a category for members located too far away to keep in regular contact. For example, a museum, a zoological garden or a sports ground might all run membership schemes for their supporters. However, the only people in a position to take advantage of the full package of benefits on offer will be those who live within a certain distance of the activity. Consequently, a more limited package could be made available at a reduced rate for people who live overseas or even beyond the reasonable catchment of the venues.

Institute of Directors

The Institute of Directors is a non-party-political membership organisation representing the interests of business leaders in the UK. It offers members a range of business benefits and services such as publications, an advisory service and various events. Meeting rooms and facilities for corporate hospitality are also available throughout the UK, and it has a library in central London. Membership and associate membership is offered according to professional status and membership fees relate to these categories. However, reduced fees are available to members resident outside the European Union who, it may reasonably be assumed, will find many of the UK-based services less advantageous.

Source: www.iod.com (16 January 2003)

Some membership schemes attract considerable overseas interest, even if they appear to offer few benefits that will be of specific interest to overseas members. Under such circumstances it can be helpful if overseas branches of the scheme are established, to provide overseas members with a sense of community and an opportunity to create a set of benefits that are more relevant to their particular needs.

The National Trust

The National Trust encourages overseas visitors to join as members and maintains reciprocal visiting arrangements with a range of heritage organisations in Australia, the Bahamas, Barbados, Bermuda, Canada, the Cayman Islands, Malta, New Zealand, Zimbabwe, Fiji, Guernsey, the Isle of Man and Jersey. Members of these organisations are generally entitled to free admission on production of a current membership card. Local clubs run by the members themselves, offering lectures, tours and holidays exist in both Belgium and Germany.

In the US, The Royal Oak Foundation, formed in 1973, exists as a membership affiliate of the National Trust, offering a chance for Americans 'to participate in the work of the National Trust and stay up to date with Trust activities. Royal Oak members enjoy free admission to all National Trust properties and sites open to the public, as well as a reciprocal agreement with The National Trust for Scotland'. However, Royal Oak Foundation members do not have voting rights within the National Trust. The Foundation offers Spring and Fall lecture programmes and special events in various US cities, some of which are only open to members. It also sponsors a biennial architectural competition and supports the International Council of Monuments and Sites and the Attingham Summer School. Membership dues and donations are tax deductible for US residents and revenue is used for conservation and preservation projects, primarily in Britain.

Sources:
www.royal-oak.org (13 January 2004)
www.nationaltrust.org.uk (13 January 2004)

Occupation or special interest

In some circumstances a membership category specifically for people who work in the same profession or share a particular specific interest may be appropriate. For example, many membership schemes are affiliated to organisations that have a broad educational remit, and a category that supplies particular benefits for teachers, such as group discounts, teaching materials and specialist lectures, may be popular.

Soil Association

The Soil Association, launched a new category of membership in 2002, in order to provide up-to-date and accessible information about developments in the organic sector to agricultural advisers and consultants. A joint initiative between Soil Association Certification Limited and the Soil Association producer services department, the specialist Organic consultant membership package offers technical advice, through Soil Association telephone helplines, and information in the form of Soil Association publications, research reports and news updates. It also permits access to the 'members only' area of the Association's website and priority booking and discounts on training events and conferences.

Sources:
Press release: New Soil Association membership scheme for agricultural consultants (27 September 2002)
www.soilassociation.org (13 January 2004)

Time of use

Some members may be in a position to use the benefits of a membership scheme at times of the day, week or year when others are either unwilling or unable to do so. A membership category that specifically limits benefits to those times, in return for a reduced membership fee, can be attractive to some. This is an important issue for organisations that provide popular leisure opportunities with limited capacity, such as theatres, cinemas, squash clubs and so on.

Whipsnade

Whipsnade Wild Animal Park ran a Winter Membership Scheme for four years, during which all full-paying visitors to the park between the end of October and the middle of February received a Winter Membership card which, when validated on the day of the visit, entitled the holder to unlimited free entry during the membership period. This scheme aimed to promote out-of-season visits, but also gave an opportunity to sample the benefits of membership and encourage visitors to join the main annual scheme when their Winter Membership expired. However, it soon became evident that these essentially free memberships were being passed around various families, and as a result, a passport format was introduced. These members could then claim a discount of 20% on full membership. Even the new scheme enjoyed limited success in increasing membership levels though, and when management structures changed, the scheme was discontinued in favour of other promotions.

Sources:
www.whipsnade.co.uk (18 January 2004)
Information from Whipsnade Membership Office (22 December 2003)

Level of involvement

Membership categories can be set up to reflect the different levels of involvement that potential members would like through the scheme. For example, some want nothing more than to be treated as preferential customers; some want to participate in the running of the organisation; some want to have access to an established social circle; and some will want any two or even all three of these. Membership categories which allow people to choose their level of involvement, and pay a membership fee which reflects this, can be very valuable to organisations and members alike.

British Museum

In 1901 a number of 'anonymous gentlemen' established a supporters club for The British Museum, in order to buy objects for the Museum's collections. However, in 1904 the 'Friends of the British Museum' merged with the National Art Collections Fund which also made (and continues to make) contributions to collections. The Friends were re-established in 1968 as 'The British Museum Society' (later re-instating its old name, 'Friends of the British Museum') with the principal objective being 'to gather support for a vigorous expansion of the Museum's services to scholars and to the general public'.

Other groups are linked with the Friends. These include the Townley Group, which was set up in 1997 and for which Friends pay £500 a year for the opportunity to develop a privileged relationship with the Museum's curators. They can choose to support specific projects in the areas they are interested in, whether excavations, conservation or research. Members are invited to go behind the scenes with the project curator and find out how their research is progressing, and are often among the first to hear of new developments and breakthroughs.

The British Museum Friends Volunteers were re-established in 1989 and around 150 members contribute further to the Museum by holding object handling sessions for the public, helping with shelving books in the Reading Room, acting as stewards for Museum functions and indexing Museum archives, as well as working behind the scenes in the antiquities departments. Members of the 'Young Friends' benefit from free entry to all exhibitions, a kids' magazine, and special events including sleepovers, behind-the-scenes visits, Sunday clubs and competitions.

The annual report of the British Museum Friends in 2002–2003 showed a total membership of over 15,000 for the first time, with over 1,000 Young Friends and over £600,000 in grants and donations to the British Museum.

Source: www.thebritishmuseum.ac.uk (12 December 2003)

Period of membership

Many membership schemes offer simple annual membership rates, but under some circumstances it may be desirable to offer membership over different periods. For example, an organisation which provides very seasonal benefits, such as an outdoor tennis club, may offer a special package for winter membership only. Another option is to offer life membership. There are two main benefits to this approach. Firstly, it can encourage relatively large cash injections into the scheme; and secondly, it can encourage members to sign up over a period of time beyond which they might otherwise have been interested in taking advantage of the benefits from the scheme. In some circumstances though, the disadvantages outweigh the benefits. In particular, a potential regular stream of income over a much longer period of a time is lost when a person buys a life membership, so the price charged for life membership must be set sufficiently high to offset that risk.

Tiered schemes

As the segmentation of a membership scheme offers potential benefits to all parties, tiered schemes tend to be the most effective. In effect, these are schemes which offer a basic set of 'entry level' benefits for a relatively modest sum, an enhanced series of benefits for more cash, and a very comprehensive package for more money still. Within each tier there may also be different prices set relating to, for example, demographics. Students or seniors wanting to join a scheme at any of the levels may be charged a lower membership fee than other adults, and a separate rate again may be charged for family groups.

The main disadvantage of tiered schemes relates to their complexity. Offering potential members such a wide range of options can confuse, and the administration associated with such a scheme is also more onerous. Clear and concise literature explaining the different tiers is essential, as is a computer-based membership management system (see above). In some membership schemes, the different tiers are branded and then marketed entirely separately to different target markets, thus the opportunity to confuse is reduced. In some particularly large schemes – especially those for major national and international organisations – members progress through the tiers, and only by personal invitation at the levels of higher commitment.

Norwich Theatre Royal

Norwich Theatre Royal is a 1,300-seat Art Deco theatre that re-opened in 1992 following three years of closure and extensive refurbishment. This re-opening provided the opportunity to re-launch the Friends scheme. The primary aim of establishing a new integrated scheme was to earn income, with the secondary intention of encouraging loyalty and frequent attendance. The scheme now has over 10,500 members. The scheme is kept firmly under the control of the theatre management and the Friends have no committee or representation on the Board. Detailed evaluation of the costs and benefits derived from the scheme is undertaken.

The scheme offers six levels of membership which include senior, family, student and group categories, plus a corporate scheme. Benefits of membership include priority booking, ticket discounts (including half-price first nights for drama productions), advance mailings, a regular newsletter and occasional special events (see below). No separate mailing list is offered, which ensures that customers who wish to receive programme information by post are encouraged to join the Friends scheme. The scheme demonstrates high levels of retention, at around 82%, and overall numbers are gradually increasing. Discounted fees are offered when paid by direct debit. In the financial year 2001–2002, the largest category of Friends were Senior Friends (5,533), followed closely by Personal Friends (4,267). Other categories showed much lower levels of membership in the same year with 79 Gold Friends, 16 Group Friends, 129 Student Friends and 280 Family Friends. It seems likely that the generous benefits available to Personal Friends may cost-effectively fulfil the requirements of those members who might otherwise be a target market for other higher level categories.

Personal Friend (£31/£29.50 by direct debit)

- £1.50 off each of up to six tickets for each production on any date at any price
- Half price tickets on first nights of all drama productions (excluding cheapest rate and special prices)
- One month's priority booking excluding cheapest rate on up to six tickets per production
- Free mailing of up to three programmes plus newsletters
- 10% discount on all food and drink at Norwich Theatre Royal
- £5 off cost of termly Adult Theatre Arts Courses for card holder only
- A numbered membership card together with a key ring and car sticker.

Senior Friend (£14.50/£13.50 by direct debit)

- Priority booking and discounts apply to four tickets
- All other benefits as for Personal Friend
- Members must be over 60.

Family Friend (£41/£39.50 by direct debit)

- Priority booking and discounts apply to eight tickets
- All other benefits as for Personal Friend.

Student Friend (£11.50)

- Priority booking and discounts apply to two tickets
- All other benefits as for Personal Friend
- Members must be in full-time education. Proof of status required.

Gold Friend (£135/£120 by direct debit)

- Benefits as for Family Friend
- Use of private bar facilities with other Gold Friend members unless previously reserved for a private corporate function
- Ability to make telephone bookings for each new season before other Friends.

Group Friend (£180/£170 by direct debit)

- 10% discount on group bookings of 20 and over (all prices except the cheapest) for every performance including Friday and Saturday evenings and all Sunday concerts
- One month's priority booking excluding cheapest range
- Free mailings
- Group membership card
- Special group rates on some performances.

Sources:
Norwich Theatre Royal Annual Survey 2001–02
Forthcoming events brochure: Norwich Theatre Royal November 2002–03
Bonsall, E. (2003) 'To what extent does membership influence ticket sales?', dissertation for the degree of Master of Arts Management, Anglia Polytechnic University
www.fuel4arts.com (August 2003)

Identifying benefits for members

Precisely what to offer members as part of their membership package should be informed by research findings – especially those benefits that are very specific to a particular cause or organisation. The following are common to many membership schemes across all sectors:

- newsletters and magazines
- opportunities for deeper involvement
- voluntary work running the scheme
- voluntary work for the affiliate organisation
- meet the management
- access to restricted opportunities
- superior service
- social occasions
- financial benefits
- opportunity to donate to a specific cause or initiative
- recognition for involvement.

The grid suggested at Appendix D shows how different benefits can be allocated to different tiers of a scheme.

Newsletters and magazines

At the most basic level, newsletters and magazines can provide an opportunity for members to be kept in touch with issues relating to the organisation (for further details of membership communications, see Chapter 5). For some schemes, this is more fundamental than for others. For example, a medical charity might wish to use its newsletter as a means of helping its members to manage their medical condition more effectively, and a sports club might use it to disseminate information about forthcoming fixtures and events.

However, printed communications cost money to create and distribute, and are extremely time-hungry and deadline-oriented, so whilst it is likely that newsletters and magazines can play a valuable role in a membership scheme, there should never be an automatic assumption that a regular publication has to be produced. In some cases, a year-book will be more appropriate, for example. Others may be better off relying on e-mail to communicate with members, as the associated costs are so much lower. The problem currently remains, of course, that not all households can receive e-mails, so a sector of the membership base may be excluded.

If printed material is used, there are further decisions to be made. Regular publications can range from highly sophisticated glossy magazines to single sheets of photocopied paper. The expectations of members as to the nature and content of newsletters will be determined by their perceptions of the financial status and brand image of the organisation and the extent to which they believe the publication is a fundamental part of their benefits package. For example, a person who joins the membership arm of a charity that works to support children in less developed countries may expect membership fees to be used primarily to support the work of the organisation, and may view a newsletter as a way of keeping in touch with that work. But to spend significant sums on high quality print may be viewed as inappropriate. On the other hand, someone joining a membership scheme relating to their hobby or leisure interest – an opera house, for example – may do so fundamentally in order to gain priority access to tickets. They may perceive a glossy magazine to be a valuable perk which helps them engage more deeply, not just with the organisation, but also with their leisure interest in general.

Given the sophistication of low-cost desktop publishing software these days, it is perfectly possible for presentable newsletters to be produced in-house by anyone with access to a computer. Consequently, most small membership schemes produce their own. By contrast, large schemes with sizeable member-ship bases may be better off sub-contracting their regular publication to a contract publisher who will not only manage the editorial and design work, but also sell advertising to third parties, the revenues from which can be offset against the costs of production. Occasionally such publications may even become net contributors to the membership scheme overall.

The contents of magazines and newsletters will, inevitably, depend on the role that they are intended to play, and this role should be determined at the outset. For example, a newsletter for the local branch of a national charity might include:

- information about forthcoming events
- reviews of recent events
- profiles of the work of local members/volunteers
- fundraising initiatives, such as competitions
- small ads
- recognition of the support of sponsors and donors
- relevant news from other regions
- relevant news from the national office
- activities for younger members
- details of national campaigns
- national and local press coverage of the charity's work.

By contrast, the magazine of a prestigious national museum may additionally contain:

- a foreword by the curator
- interviews with subject specialists and academics
- profiles of artists
- trading figures relating to the organisation's performance
- case studies about museum users
- an education column
- articles about the museum's preservation work
- display advertising.

RNIB

The Royal National Institute of the Blind (RNIB) introduced a mass membership scheme in 2002 in order to:

- Involve a greater proportion of blind and partially sighted people in the decision-making processes of the organisation through consultation and elections and thereby make the RNIB more accountable to its catchment area.
- Inform blind and partially sighted people about available services, both from within the RNIB and beyond; and through a membership magazine offer useful advice on benefits, daily living tips, accessibility issues and leisure opportunities.
- Build a large membership to strengthen the case of the RNIB when negotiating with government and other organisations on behalf of blind and partially sighted people.

The scheme, which is free to join, targets blind and partially sighted people and their families or carers as full members, and professionals in the field of sight loss and well-wishers who want to support the work of the organisation as associate members. Opportunities to donate, volunteer or contribute to campaigns are also available, but beyond the remit of the scheme.

The primary benefit offered to members is the exclusive quarterly magazine *Vision* which is available in a range of formats: print, Braille, analogue cassette, Daisy digital CD-ROM, disk or e-mail. *Vision* contains not only features on RNIB, services but also practical hints on daily living, interviews and information about national organisations and resources. Members receive three copies of *Vision* magazine as part of their joining package and then after five months may choose to pay to continue to receive it or remain as a free member without receiving the magazine. New members also receive a welcome call from a member of the RNIB team who can provide information about available services, local society or national organisations or refer particular needs to specialist colleagues within the RNIB. Members are invited to share their experiences and opinions with other members and to take part in RNIB's decision-making by voting for members of its consultative assembly or standing for election, and they are encouraged to support campaigns working for changes in policy or legislation.

Source: www.rnib.org.uk (10 December 2003)

Opportunities for deeper involvement

As explained in Chapter 2, a membership benefit that is commonly sought by some (but interestingly, one which may alienate others) is a deeper level of involvement with the organisation running the scheme. This involvement can be offered in a series of guises.

Voluntary work running the scheme

Integrated membership schemes generally have the support of a staff base to run the scheme, but this is not necessarily the case for other types of scheme, which may depend on volunteers for their very existence. The opportunity to get more deeply involved will positively attract some people, who may be keen organisers of social events, and/or enjoy the sense of community engendered by working with other like-minded people in pursuit of what they view to be a worthwhile goal.

Voluntary work for the affiliate organisation

When a membership scheme has close links with an affiliate organisation, it may be possible for members' services to be used more widely. For example, arts organisations may use members as volunteer front-of-house staff; museums may use them as guides; community groups may use them to run schools projects; and charities may use them to implement fundraising campaigns.

The advantage of recruiting volunteers from among the membership base, rather than the broader population, is that by their act of joining, these people have already identified themselves as having a commitment to a particular cause or organisation. The disadvantage, of course, is that the membership base may not possess the specific skills that are required. However, as discussed in Chapter 2, there is not always a direct correlation between those wishing to join a scheme and those wishing to volunteer. Offering opportunities to volunteer may deter some potential members if they perceive voluntary work to be an expectation of those joining a scheme. Instead an affiliate organisation may recruit volunteers directly, not through any membership scheme.

Friends of London's Transport Museum

The Friends of London's Transport Museum operates as a charitable trust, with a committee of elected members and others nominated by the trustees. Individual membership costs £18 for the first member at one address and additional family members at the same address can be added to the subscription at a rate of £7 each. Each individual receives a membership card and one copy of the newsletter is sent per household. In addition to free access to the Museum, discounts on other purchases, a quarterly newsletter, private views and meetings at the Museum, members are offered the chance to undertake voluntary work within the Museum and at its Acton depot.

The Friends supply a team of guides for the Museum. These guides are trained to engage Museum visitors by explaining and interpreting the Museum's collections, and they also act as stewards at open weekends at the Museum depot and at other special events. There are also many administrative jobs behind the scenes which are undertaken by the Friends. These include cataloguing books and other items, setting up the databases for the history of the different types of vehicles and for the complete history of London's bus, coach, tram and trolleybus routes. Other Friends volunteer to keep the fleet of buses and the Underground carriages in good condition. Those with the necessary licence and some experience with older vehicles can even help with driving buses to rallies and other outside events, and those without can act as conductors instead!

Sources:
Membership leaflet: 'Join The Friends of London's Transport Museum'
www.ltmuseum.co.uk/support/volunteers.html (19 January 2004)

Meet the management

An opportunity to meet the management of an organisation, to hear first hand about its activities and to air their own views on these activities, is valued by some members. This form of two-way exchange can be valuable for both parties, though the status of any meeting should be clearly established at the outset. Discussion is generally more appropriate than decision-making. Members' expectations can be raised if the management appears to agree to proposals at a meeting, but those proposals are not subsequently implemented. Conversely, the opinions expressed at a meeting may not be representative of the whole membership body, and well-meaning suggestions may not dovetail easily with the longer-term strategic direction of the organisation.

Access to restricted opportunities

Facilities and opportunities not available to non-members are highly-valued benefits in many schemes. For example, invitations to private views of exhibitions are commonly made to members only, as are 'meet the performers' events at theatres. Auditorium-based membership organisations where seat capacity is limited often send information about forthcoming productions to members first. They then restrict advance booking facilities for a period of time to give members a better chance of acquiring tickets for performances that will later sell out. They may also restrict their 'stand-by' seats to members too (though this may, of course, discourage advance booking).

Access to certain facilities is another important benefit of many schemes. This is self-evident for organisations such as sports clubs, which provide essential equipment without which participation in the sport would be impossible. But there are other circumstances under which access to restricted facilities can be very valuable. For example, room hire and much sought-after private dining facilities can be restricted to members only at visitor attractions such as historic houses; and in the performing arts, a private bar can sometimes be offered for interval drinks.

Finally, recognition by the affiliate organisation of members' generosity can be valued by some – particularly corporate members. It may be possible to acknowledge the support of members in an affiliate organisation's literature.

National Portrait Gallery

The National Portrait Gallery's Corporate Partnership Programme creates two levels of involvement which offer the benefits shown below. These benefits provide considerable incentives for holding corporate events at the gallery, including exclusive access to some areas, branding and promotional opportunities, and benefits for employees. In order to facilitate corporate entertaining the Gallery offers advice on catering and other services for events through an approved list of suppliers, as well as access to Gallery images for use on invitations, programmes and menu cards. Guided tours, special displays and talks by experts can also be arranged.

Corporate Members £6,500 plus VAT per annum

- 50% saving on all venue hire fees, without limit
- Free entry for employees to all paying exhibitions
- Priority booking for the upper Galleries including the new Tudor Galleries, Stuart, 18th Century Arts and Victorian Rooms
- One exclusive behind-the-scenes tour, Gallery talk and/or creative workshop for employees and/or clients (there may be small charge to cover the cost of materials)
- Five double invitations to each Private View (minimum five per year)
- One double invitation to the Director's Annual Dinner
- 10% discount in the Gallery's shops, Portrait Café and The Portrait Restaurant for all employees
- Two free catalogues for two major exhibitions per year
- Acknowledgement of your company's support on the Gallery's website, Partners' board within the Gallery, within one issue of the Gallery's quarterly information leaflet (80,000 print run) and the Annual Review.

Regency Partners £16,000 plus VAT per annum

- Entitlement to hire the Weldon Galleries for events
- One dinner with no hire charge in the Weldon Galleries or two evenings in other Galleries
- 50% discount on all further hire charges
- Free entry for all employees to all paying exhibitions (two per year)
- Priority booking for the upper Galleries including the new Tudor Galleries, Stuart, 18th Century Arts, Weldon Galleries and Victorian Rooms
- Opportunity for the Gallery's Director or senior curatorial staff to give a talk at the company's offices
- One exclusive behind-the-scenes tour, Gallery talk and/or creative workshop for employees and/or clients (there may be a small charge to cover the cost of materials)
- Ten double invitations to each Private View (minimum five per year)
- Two double invitations to the Director's Annual Dinner
- 10% discount in the Gallery's shops, Portrait Café and The Portrait Restaurant for all employees
- Five free catalogues for two major exhibitions per year
- Acknowledgement of your company's support on the Gallery's website, Partners board within the Gallery, within one issue of the Gallery's quarterly information leaflet (80,000 print run) and the Annual Review.

The corporate scheme operates in addition to a membership scheme for individuals, which offers free entry to paying exhibitions, invitations to first afternoon views of selected exhibitions, a quarterly leaflet, advance notice of special offers, and 10% discount in the shop, bookshop, café and restaurant.

Source: www.npg.org.uk (18 December 2003)

Superior service

In addition to offering special access to certain privileges, it is possible for some organisations to offer their members service levels that may not be economically viable if extended to their entire customer base. This is particularly true of service-based facilities. A theatre, for example, may offer its members:

- a ticket exchange facility, whereby members can exchange tickets they have purchased for one event for a different event;
- a telephone booking hotline which is only publicised to members, giving easier access to tickets for popular events;
- free mailings promoting all events;
- e-mail or text message notification of special discounts;
- options to reserve specific seats for extended periods without obligation;

- a membership manager to help members with, for example, group bookings or arranging social events.

Similarly, museums and galleries often allow members to jump the queue
for paid exhibitions.

Royal Opera House

The Royal Opera House operates a complex tiered Friends scheme divided into
three main sections, each of which is further divided to offer increasing levels of
involvement and benefits. It runs regular upgrade campaigns and recruitment
drives using direct mail, telephone, e-mails and its website and the scheme enjoys
a high rate of retention.

The first section is fundamentally an information service. £15 provides advance
information five times a year about performances and events; and an additional
£12 provides a subscription to *About the House* magazine.

Membership of The Friends of Covent Garden costs £69 per year and provides:

- advance information sent four times a year with *About the House* magazine
- personalised advance postal priority booking form for two tickets per production
- special Friends events, including celebrity interviews, masterclasses and the
possibility of attending open rehearsals
- membership card
- occasional discounts and offers.

Further opportunities are offered through the membership tiers known as 'Acts of
Support':

- Act 1: £205 – Friends benefits as above, plus an invitation to attend season
preview talks;
- Act 2: £360 – benefits as Act 1, plus invitation to a special annual event;
- Act 3: £770 – benefits as Act 2, plus enhanced priority postal booking for two
tickets per production ahead of Friends' advance postal booking; plus a guaranteed first choice of rehearsal ticket per booking period;
- Act 4: £1,445 – benefits as Act 3, plus priority postal booking for two tickets per
performance ahead of Friends and Act 3 members.

A higher level of involvement can be achieved through membership of the Trust.
Priority Trust membership is priced from £2,000 to £17,000, depending on the
number of seats that can be booked, but all tickets must still be paid for in addition
to the membership fee. This scheme provides the highest level of priority booking
for all productions; use of the Premium Box Office, including free ticket exchange;
priority access to the Royal Box and Directors' Box when available; and credit
accounts for tickets and dining. In addition Priority Trust members receive advance

information including the season guide, *About the House* magazine, and the Trust newsletter. They are also entitled to priority booking for catering and events, special events such as Season preview talks, masterclasses and visits behind the scenes, acknowledgement in programmes (if they want this) and rehearsal tickets.

Premium Trust membership provides benefits beyond those offered by the Priority Trust. Costing from £32,000–£40,000 per season, depending on the location of the seats, and charged on a pro rata basis if bought part way through the season, this level offers guaranteed tickets for all Royal Opera House productions in a chosen area of the House for a specific night every week throughout the season. Tickets for chosen performances are included in the fee and sent automatically. Two members of staff in the Trust office are responsible for selling and administering the higher levels of the scheme and the Premium Box Office, which is judged to be the most used and popular part of the membership, provides an exclusive phone line and employs two dedicated staff.

Sources:
www.roh.org.uk (12 December 2003)
Information from Kathleen Fetigan, Trust Office and Susan Fisher, Head of Friends, Royal Opera House (13 January 2004)

Social occasions

As discussed earlier, a membership scheme can provide opportunities for people to meet and socialise with others. This can be partially achieved through volunteering activity (see above) but more opportunities still can be created if social occasions are developed through the scheme. Where appropriate, social activity directly related to the affiliate organisation's own activity is ideal – such as theatre-going, specialist talks and lectures, or attending sports events. In these situations there is a delicate balance to be struck between events that benefit the affiliate as well as the members, and events which benefit only the members. For example, the friends of a particular historic building may choose to hold social events at that building itself, and the revenues generated, through say, the catering and room hire, will go to the organisation towards the upkeep of the building. Thus the event benefits both parties. However, the members may feel their social needs will be better met if the scheme also arranges trips to other historic buildings and stately homes, for which no revenues will be generated for the affiliate organisation. This may not please the affiliate, but given the importance of creating membership benefits that encourage people to join, it may have to tolerate it to an extent. If the membership structure takes the form of a social club scheme, then an affiliate organisation will have no option but to do so anyway.

The concept of relating social activities to the work of an affiliate organisation may be thoroughly impractical for charities whose core objectives relate to social problems rather than leisure interests. Under those circumstances, social occasions can be planned by and for members but are likely to be viewed as fundraising events rather than specific membership benefits.

Financial incentives

For certain types of membership scheme, cash-based incentives will be the primary reason why a person will join. In order for them feel that membership is worthwhile, they must believe that they will attract at least as much value in discounts and savings as the cost of membership.

This scenario is common amongst theatre-goers, whose primary motivation for membership can be very little to do with loyalty to an organisation, and a lot to do with getting hold of scarce and/or cheaper tickets. Consequently, discounts have to be managed very carefully, as they have the potential to undermine the affiliate organisation's core revenue-generating activities. There is always a danger that the value of the discounts given away outweighs the extra revenues generated through ticket sales, and that the tickets would have been sold anyway and at full price, had they not been sold to a member. Consequently, rather than give blanket discounts to members, most schemes are selective in the ways that financial incentives are applied, and attempt to provide benefits that will cost the affiliate relatively little, yet are of high value to members. For example, they will give discounts for less popular shows where there are likely to be spare seats available; reduce prices to members on weekdays and for matinées; offer free programmes; and provide interval drinks.

Discounts on merchandise are common too. These may take the form of savings on the affiliate organisations' own goods and services, but also third-party deals. It may be possible to negotiate discounts for members with commercial organisations who regard those involved with a particular scheme as being a good potential target market. For example, restaurant deals, cheap insurance and cut-price car hire might all be put into a membership package if commercial partners can be found.

Benefits for non-members

There are a few circumstances under which it may be advisable for some member benefits to be made available to non-members.

Reciprocal benefits

A reciprocal arrangement with other membership organisations can provide valuable additional benefits to each party's scheme, though these arrangements must be carefully thought through. For example, it is important that the benefits provided to those who belong to other organisations are not so valuable that they will encourage potential members to join those other organisations instead; yet they must be sufficiently valuable to encourage joining at all. Furthermore, all parties involved will need to provide their members with clear identification, usually in the form of a membership card (see above), if they are to police the system effectively.

Families and guests

Dilemmas can arise when schemes offer benefits to members that by definition spill over to benefit those around them, for example, a theatre that offers advance booking facilities to members, in order that they can acquire tickets that may otherwise sell out. But that member may wish to buy tickets on behalf of a group of people. Whilst on the one hand it is undoubtedly in the theatre's interest to sell lots of tickets, unless this benefit is limited in some way, the scheme could be abused. A single membership only need be purchased in order to gain access to the hottest seats in town. Each organisation must consider the extent to which potential abuse of its scheme could be a problem, and weigh this up against the potential benefits of greater goodwill which can arise when fewer restrictions are placed on members.

Chester Zoo

In addition to unlimited free access to Chester Zoo, annual members of its scheme also enjoy reciprocal free visiting rights at other leading zoological gardens which currently include Belfast, Bristol, Colchester, Dublin, Edinburgh, Marwell and Paignton Zoos, Woburn Safari Park and Fota Wildlife Park in Cork. These reciprocal rights are limited to free entry and require membership cards to be shown.

The Zoo offers a range of benefits to its members, including a quarterly colour magazine, 10% discount in its gift shops and a programme of meetings and talks. More unusually the scheme also offers free life membership after 25 years of continuous membership to those over 60 and a number of half-price vouchers to adult members of the society, which can be used to admit other family members to the Zoo at half the published admission price. All fully paid-up members of more than 28 days' standing can be involved in the running of the Zoo through the right to vote on any resolutions proposed at General Meetings of the Society, and automatically become members of The North of England Zoological Society.

Source: www.chesterzoo.org (10 December 2003)

Setting prices

The prices at which membership fees should be pitched will always be open to debate, but there are a few basic principles that can help guide the process of price-setting.

Understand the costs of running the scheme

The costs of running a scheme should be set out in a budget when the scheme is first devised (see above). A forecast of how many members the scheme will attract needs to be coupled with these costings to give an idea as to the cost per member of running the scheme. These figures, together with an estimate of the additional trading income that might be generated through the activity of the membership group, will help to create an understanding of the potential financial impact of the scheme on the organisation's finances. If the prices set are higher than this cost per head, then the scheme will be a net income generator; if lower, then unless predicted additional trading income is thought to be substantial, the scheme will incur a net cost to the organisation (see below).

Recognise the objectives of the scheme

Whether or not the organisation can tolerate the fact that the costs of running the scheme are higher than the anticipated revenues depends very much on the objectives of the scheme.

If revenue generation is at the heart of the scheme, then any suggestion that the scheme will cost more to run than will be returned in membership fees and other purchases means that the whole scheme needs to be reconsidered. Either membership fees will have to be raised or the benefits offered will have to be scaled down (though it is likely, of course, that both of these options will depress interest in joining, and they may be self-defeating). Ultimately, if the aim of the scheme is to make money, and it appears that this will prove impossible, then the whole concept of running a scheme should be abandoned.

If loyalty is at the heart of a scheme, then the fact that its costs may outweigh any revenues generated do not necessarily undermine its role. However, it is important that the organisation understands the extent to which it may have to subsidise the scheme in order to achieve its loyalty objectives.

Assess the value of the benefits

Although some potential members may be relatively philanthropic in their decision to join a scheme (see Chapter 2), others are likely to do some form of mental assessment as to whether the value of the benefits offered equates in any way to the costs of joining the scheme. The price set for membership fees should reflect perceived value to members, not just the costs, so it is important, when setting prices, to understand how much the benefits are worth. (This is also a calculation that must be done if gift aid is to be claimed on the membership fee, as explained above). This might be very different to the amount that these benefits cost the organisation to provide. For example, free entry to a paid exhibition is a valuable benefit to museum-goers, as it saves them the price of a ticket; but if they take advantage of this benefit, this adds nothing to the costs of running the organisation. Indeed, further revenues may be generated if the free visitor attends and then buys merchandise from the shop or refreshments at the restaurant. The only cost to the organisation is an 'opportunity cost' – the revenues lost if that member would have attended the exhibition anyway. By contrast, a glossy magazine can be very expensive to produce, unless its costs can be offset by advertising revenues. If that magazine is not highly valued by members, then it may prove difficult to justify its costs.

Be aware of price sensitivity

A potential member's willingness to pay a certain membership fee will be influenced by factors beyond their perception of its value, and research can help to pinpoint the boundaries of the market's price sensitivity.

Issues such as competition are relevant. Relatively few people are likely to join numerous schemes concurrently, as they simply wouldn't have the time to take full advantage of the benefits being offered. London's classical music-going audiences, for example, may choose between joining the membership schemes of a number of different orchestras resident in the city, and the cost of joining each may influence their choice. They may decide to join a scheme one year, but switch their allegiance the following year unless there is a financial incentive to remain.

The economic status of potential members is also relevant. Those who wish to join membership schemes run by medical charities, hospices and animal welfare organisations, for example, are likely to come from a wide cross section of socio-economic groups. On the other hand, those who are most likely to be attracted to membership schemes run by national cultural institutions often work in highly paid professional and managerial occupations. Clearly there is scope for setting high prices for membership relating to this type of activity. Indeed, it may be important to do so, as a scheme that seems too cheap may be viewed with suspicion.

Differentiate clearly between membership tiers

The concept of a tiered scheme is one that offers a range of different packages of benefits at different price levels. Pricing is an important tool for distinguishing between the different tiers. If the prices are too close together (and the packages of benefits too similar) then the process of choosing between them can be a confusing one for potential members. Conversely, if they are too far apart, then potential members may perceive the jump between levels as a costly one and scale down their commitment to a lower level than they would otherwise have done. Furthermore, the fees and benefits set for each tier should be considered in relation to any other schemes and benefits offered by the organisation, such as through subscription schemes, corporate sponsorship deals or concessionary pricing structures. (For an example of how these may be interrelated, see Appendix D).

Prickwillow Drainage Engine Museum

The Prickwillow Drainage Engine Museum operates a 'Friends of the Engine' scheme, the principal benefit of which is free admission. Membership fees are £10 for working members, who are actively involved in restoration and maintenance of the engines, as opposed to £15 for ordinary individual members and £30 for a family.

Source: http://web.ukonline.co.uk/jill.lawson/pwillow/engine.htm (16 January 2004)

Create opportunities for members to be generous

Finally, the scale of membership fees in a tiered scheme should normally include a bracket that permits people to exercise their philanthropy. A top price tier offering top level benefits can demand a significant fee, and even if no one takes up the offer, then it serves to make other tiers seem far more reasonably priced.

Another opportunity for generosity can be created if donations are sought in addition to membership fees. By including the option to give more, it is possible to permit those for whom price is not an issue to demonstrate further their appreciation of the benefits being offered.

Summary

Decisions have to be made when membership schemes are established that will impact on every aspect of their effectiveness. Fundamental issues, especially the objectives of such schemes, have to be addressed before any attempts should be made to set up structures for their management, or to devise packages of benefits for their members.

To ensure that any decisions relating to a scheme are sound from the beginning, they should be made on the back of a solid base of evidence which can be gathered through a process of research. A number of elements of a scheme's design can be helpfully informed by research, but it is especially valuable for assessing the benefits that will be most attractive to potential members, and the amount of money that is considered to be acceptable to acquire these benefits.

In order for the scheme to function, an appropriate management structure and associated legal framework needs to be put in place. These structures may initially seem onerous, especially for small social club membership schemes. However, their importance will become immediately evident if disputes arise between members or between those who run schemes and their affiliate organisations. Establishing solid frameworks at the start will mean that a scheme will have strong foundations and its prospects for long-term viability are improved.

---

1 Raymond, C. (1992) *Members Matter: Making the Most of Membership Schemes in the Arts*, Arts Council of Great Britain

2 Bonsall, E. (2003) 'To what extent does membership influence ticket sales?', dissertation for the degree of Master of Arts Management, Anglia Polytechnic University

3 Horan, K. (2003) 'To what extent is income generation from "Friends" dependent upon loyalty?', dissertation for the degree of Master of Arts Management, Anglia Polytechnic University

4 Hill, E. (2000) *Commissioning Market Research – A Guide for Arts Marketers*, Arts Marketing Association, p1

5 This book merely scratches the surface of the legal issues relating to membership schemes. For more comprehensive information see Adirondack, S. and Sinclair Taylor, J. (2001) *The Voluntary Sector Legal Handbook*, 2nd edition, Directory of Social Change, or take professional legal advice

6 Comprehensive information about charitable status and the process of registration (for charities based in England and Wales) can be found at www.charity-commission.gov.uk – 12 January 2004

7 Further information on becoming a charity, choosing and preparing a governing document and all other aspects of charity law is available at www.charity-commission.gov.uk – 12 January 2004

8 Charity Commission helpline – 0870 333 0123

9 Adirondack, S. (1998) *Just about Managing?*, London Voluntary Service Council, p11

10 Adirondack, S. and Sinclair Taylor, J. (2001) *The Voluntary Sector Legal Handbook*, 2nd edition, Directory of Social Change, p300

11 Reza, M. (2003) 'Budgeting Basics', *ArtsProfessional*, issue 59, October 6, p7

12 For full details about the UK rules on VAT see www.hmce.gov.uk/business/vat/vat.htm – 12 January 2004

13 HMCE National Advice Service – 0845 010 9000

14 www.hmce.gov.uk/forms/notices/701-47.htm – 23 December 2003

15 For full details of gift aid see
www.inlandrevenue.gov.uk/charities/claim_tax_back.htm – 12 January 2004

16 www.inlandrevenue.gov.uk/charities – 12 January 2004

17 An assessment of the value of benefits can be obtained through a helpline –
0845 302 0203

18 The Giving Campaign is at e: admin@givingcampaign.org.uk t: 020 7930
3154 and w: www.givingcampaign.org.uk – 12 January 2004

4 MARKETING A MEMBERSHIP SCHEME

Before a membership scheme is launched, and for as long as it is in existence, a marketing strategy should be in place to attract potential members and to encourage existing members to renew their memberships as they fall due. Marketing activities and techniques ranging from direct mail to web-based subscriptions and personal selling are covered here, as well as issues related to the identity of the scheme. In addition to this, 'internal' marketing should be ongoing, to gain the commitment and support of an affiliate organisation for the scheme.

The marketing of a membership scheme hinges on communication between those who are running the scheme with those who support it, namely current members, potential members and those who work for the affiliate organisation. For each of these groups, different forms of communication will be appropriate.

Targeting the message

Marketing communications with each of these groups should reflect their different communication needs.

Targeting current members

The process of targeting current members is very simple. An organisation should be able to identify them all by name, and will normally hold their full contact details, making it easy to get in touch with them. The most common reason for wanting to do this is to encourage them to renew their memberships. In theory, this should be a relatively straightforward task. Provided that valuable benefits have been delivered through a scheme, then members will have been building a subconscious commitment to an organisation during the period of their membership. When the time comes, they should be predisposed to respond positively to any invitation to renew (see Chapter 5 for more about the management of renewals). Nonetheless, a breakdown in communications at this stage can seriously undermine long-term efforts to sustain a viable scheme.

Other forms of marketing communications with current members may include efforts to encourage them to trade up in a tiered scheme to a more comprehensive package of benefits, or to offer them incentives to encourage them to recruit their friends, colleagues or neighbours to join the scheme.

Moseley Rugby Football Club

Moseley Rugby Football Club offers a membership scheme which allows free admission to the majority of games, privileges at away games, opportunities to apply for international tickets and free parking. In order to boost membership, the club offers a £25 shop or bar voucher to any member who introduces a new member and provides incentives for parents who are 'associate' members through their children, to join as full members.

Source: www.moseleyrugby.co.uk/moseley/members_price.asp (19 January 2004)

Targeting potential members

People who are not members, but may like to join, are much trickier to identify. They will exist both amongst an affiliate organisation's immediate supporters, as well as people amongst the wider population who have no recorded contact with the organisation.

The sort of people who may be most likely to join a scheme include:

- lapsed members of the scheme
- an affiliate organisation's most loyal customers
- friends, neighbours and colleagues of existing members
- previous donors to the organisation
- people with personal sympathies for the aims of the affiliate organisation
- people with a similar demographic profile to existing members
- staff of corporate sponsors
- current and lapsed members of similar schemes
- attenders at open days, seminars or other events run by the affiliate.

Coeliac UK

Coeliac UK was founded in 1968 in order to support people living with coeliac disease, a common long-term non life-threatening medical condition in which the body fails to digest gluten (a component part of wheat and many other cereal crops). The disease is believed to exist in between one in 100 and one in 300 people, but the vast majority of these people are never diagnosed.

The Society became incorporated as a company limited by guarantee in June 1995, and became registered as a charity shortly afterwards. Membership has grown significantly in recent years, as indeed has the entire scale of the Society's operation, due in part to the significant advances in testing techniques and subsequent diagnoses. There were over 50,000 members in June 2002, and by the end of that year the total had risen to more than 55,000 voting members with a further 2,000 professional members and 150 corporate members.

A major aspect of the organisation's activities in recent years has been its work informing the medical community of its existence, and the services it provides. Much of this educational and advocacy work is carried out by the Society's 750 volunteers and local groups, together with the support of several newly-created regional manager posts. Their work not only raises the profile of the Society within the health sector, but also generates new memberships and donations from newly-diagnosed suffers, who are given information by medical staff and dieticians on the services and support available from the Society.

Sources:
Crossed Grain, the magazine of Coeliac UK
Annual Review 2002
'A force for change: a summary of our plan 2000/2004'
'2004–2006 Strategy Plan'
www.coeliac.co.uk (14 January 2004)

Because these groups are so wide-ranging, marketing communications to attract them to a membership scheme usually benefit from taking a range of different forms (see below). Some of these communications can be targeted directly at individuals, as the contact details of some good prospects may be held by the affiliate organisation; but other people will only find out about the scheme if wider forms of mass communication, targeted print distribution and direct marketing are used.

The content of communications targeted at potential members invariably needs to be more persuasive than those targeted at current members, as it has to encourage them to join, as well as provide them with a mechanism for signing up and parting with their money.

Targeting internal audiences

It may seem somewhat excessive for those who run membership schemes to develop 'internal' marketing strategies. However, many schemes depend upon an affiliate organisation for financial support, for the provision of resources and benefits, and/or for access to potential members. Consequently, good communications between the scheme's managers and those who take top level decisions at the affiliate organisation (whether or not the two parties are employed by one and the same organisation) can make the difference between a scheme's success or failure – even its survival or extinction.

Most internal marketing communication is personalised. The marketing role usually involves providing an organisation's decision-makers with evidence that endorses the role of the scheme in supporting and achieving the organisation's objectives. This may take several forms, such as presentations at board meetings, reports detailing membership levels and performance against budgets, or consultation meetings at which both parties can address issues of mutual interest. It may also involve formal and informal presentations to staff and other stakeholders who play a day-to-day role in the long-term success or failure of the scheme.

Creating a brand

For communication to be effective, it must be clear from whom it is being sent. This is particularly important for a membership body, which as explained in Chapter 1, may be either an entirely independent entity or integrated with an affiliate organisation. It is important that the intrinsic status of the membership scheme is conveyed appropriately through its 'brand image', as the perceptions of potential members will to a large extent determine whether they will show any actual interest in joining. Elements that contribute significantly to a brand's image include the organisation's name, the tone of its communications and its visual identity.

Visual identity

Visual identity is the creation of a unique marks or graphic symbols that capture the essence of a business, organisation, product or service. As one of the key elements in a branding and marketing strategy, any logo or identity symbol should be used consistently.[1] In coming up with a coherent 'look' for a membership scheme, designers responsible for visual identity will consider the nature of the scheme, the identity of its affiliate (if any). They will also take into account the demographic and socio-economic profile of likely members, the nature of the benefits being offered to members, and the forms of communication through which the visual identity will be conveyed (for example, leaflets, t-shirts, newspaper and magazine advertisements, websites and stationery). This understanding will enable them to propose appropriate colours, fonts and imagery.

Use of language

As copywriters know only too well, the style of communications used by an organisation tells volumes about its culture. Levels of formality in written communications, for example, create expectations about the friendliness of an organisation; and the use of street language might suggest that an organisation serves a predominantly young market. Its 'verbal identity'[2] can help a membership organisation connect more emotionally with its target audiences. Names, expressive language, conversations, narrative and storytelling can all convey the true nature of the organisation in the same way as logos, symbols, colours and graphics.

The extent to which a membership organisation is linked to and involved with an affiliate organisation will influence the choice of names that identify it. There are several issues to consider.

How to refer to a scheme

Most membership organisations are faced with options on this very simple point. They may choose to call it a 'membership scheme', a 'friends association', a 'supporters club', a 'trust' or a 'society', for example. Although some legal restrictions may apply (for example, in the use of the word 'trust') the choice is a wide one. Related to this are decisions about how to refer to sub-sections of the scheme, such as a corporate section or a junior section. Consistency across the different sub-sections normally helps to reinforce the overall brand identity.

Football supporters' club names

Even if different membership schemes have broadly similar functions, they may be referred to in very different ways:

Arsenal Football Supporters Club exists to help further the interests of Arsenal Supporters everywhere

Clubffc is the name of a club for adults (16 and over) who want access to match tickets as well as the benefits of membership of Fulham Football Club

LOFT is the abbreviated name for The Leyton Orient Fans' Trust.

What to name a scheme

The actual name of the scheme itself can also cause dilemmas. Major decisions have to be made about how closely the scheme's name is linked with an affiliate organisation. For example, a fully integrated membership scheme may adopt a name that is unrelated to its parent organisation if it wishes to convey an impression of cosiness and separation from the corporate body to which it is attached; but it may adopt a closely related name if it believes there is goodwill to be gained through the association. Indeed, even a social club scheme with only an informal relationship with an affiliate organisation may choose to link its name with that affiliate. It may hope to benefit from the potential kudos that could arise from sharing its name (though from the affiliate organisation's perspective, this may not always be welcome, especially if the affiliate has no formal or informal structures for influencing the direction of such a scheme).

Brand names

The names of membership schemes may be descriptive (for example, The Art Club – an entry level membership at the New Art Gallery Walsall), acronyms (for example, YCUK – for the youth section of Coeliac UK), or contemporary (The Cool Cats Club – for junior members of the Cats Protection League), as well as the very straightforward 'friends of…' designation (for example, Friends of the Imperial War Museum).

How to refer to members

A related decision is how to refer to those who join. They may simply be known as members, but alternatively as friends, supporters, associates, or patrons. Further decisions may have to be made about how to refer to members at different tiers within a scheme. For example, those who join at the most basic level of a scheme are sometimes referred to as 'bronze members'; the next tier up is for 'silver members'; the one after for 'gold members'; and the top tier may be referred to as the 'diamond club'. Such a progressive naming convention should be used with care, however, as subsequently inserting additional tiers to the scheme may result in the need for a new naming convention, or alternatively, the creation of some very strange alloys!

Naming tiers

The naming of the different tiers within a membership scheme need not necessarily be a sober exercise, as the following examples demonstrate!

- **California Oak Foundation:** Acorn, Seedling, Sapling, Heritage Oak, Oak Grove, Oak Woodland

  Source: www.californiaoaks.org (14 January 2004)

- **San Diego Aerospace Museum:** First Flight, Aero Squadron, Kitty Hawk Club, Wings Club, Mercury Club, Apollo Club

  Source: www.aerospacemuseum.org (14 January 2004)

- **Victoria & Albert Museum:** Doric, Ionic or Corinthian Patron

  Source: www.vam.ac.uk (13 January 2004)

- **The Dreaming Theatre Production Company:** Nodding Acquaintance, First-name Terms, Drinking Buddy, Own Set of Keys, Our Beshtesht Mate in the Whole World

  Source: www.thedreaming.co.uk (12 December 2003)

- **Malvern Theatres:** Easy Street, The Best Years of Our Lives (senior), Happy Days, The Full Monty

  Source: Malvern Theatres membership leaflet: 'Clueless or Bananas?'

- **The Kennedy Center:** Sustainer, Contributor, Donor, Sponsor, Patron's Circle, Golden Circle, Producers' Circle, Chairman's Circle, Maestro's Circle, Directors' Circle, Trustees' Circle, Laureates' Circle

  Source: The Kennedy Center membership leaflets: 'Membership Month', 'The Circles 2003/2004'

- **One in Ten:** Executive Producer, Film Critic, Studio Director, Movie Mogul

  Source: www.oneinten.org (14 January 2004)

- **National Theatre:** Advance Member, Priority Member, Supporting Cast, Patron, Benefactor, Life Benefactor

  Source: www.nt-online.org (14 January 2004)

- **The Baltimore Zoo:** (Corporate Membership) Family of Otter, Pride of Lion, Herd of Elephant, Eagles' Aerie

  Source: www.baltimorezoo.org (14 January 2004)

- **Shared Experience:** Luvvie, Darling, Absolute Sweetheart

  Source: www.sharedexperience.org.uk (14 January 2004)

Membership marketing communications

As discussed earlier, different groups need to be addressed using different forms of marketing communications. Some of these are one-to-one methods, used to engage a person thought likely to have an interest in a membership scheme. Other methods attempt to generate interest and involvement among people who have, to date, not shown any signs that they might be good prospects for deeper involvement with an organisation.

Printed literature

This form of marketing communication is used by virtually all membership schemes. A promotional leaflet or brochure can perform a range of tasks for the scheme. It can, provide background information about the organisation; attract attention to the existence of the scheme and the benefits it offers; and give practical guidance on how to join, as well as providing a member-ship form to fill in.

Design and print quality

All the usual decisions have to be made about design and print quality, including:

- the leaflet size (will it fit, and be visible in, a leaflet rack? and will it fit in a standard size envelope?)
- paper stock (coated papers are good for glossy colour print; but uncoated is both cheaper and more suited to self-completion application forms)
- colour or mono print (the former for impact, but will it appear too ostentatious to the target market?)
- photographs or illustrations (photos tend to date more quickly, but can be more eye-catching)
- paper weight (an impact on postal costs as well as print production)
- special finishes (varnishes, gold-blocking and lamination can all create an impressive appearance, but their appropriateness depends upon the image and brand values which are being communicated).

The message

The messages contained in leaflets will vary depending on their purpose, but whatever the message, it should be conveyed with absolute clarity. Membership schemes, particularly tiered ones, can be quite complex and the design and wording of a leaflet will make a big difference to its impact among readers. Testing out design concepts and proofs on potential members, to assess their readability and clarity, is a valuable exercise.

Clear forms, making it easy to understand the costs of joining and the process of doing so, are of the utmost importance. These forms also provide a useful opportunity for the organisation to gather full details of the person joining, including postcode, e-mail addresses and both land line and mobile phone numbers. Postcode mapping will enable the organisation to view its catchment at a glance, and contact details enable the member to be reached with details of special events or special offers. It is vital to test application forms with existing and potential members prior to printing, as a simple omission or confusing term may render the entire run of print completely useless, resulting in the costs of reprinting and associated time delays. It is also important that the information gathered on the form is in line with the requirements of the Data Protection Act 1998[3] (see Chapter 5).

Membership leaflets can also be a useful vehicle for further fundraising. The leaflet can suggest that the new member might also like to make a donation to the organisation at the same time as joining. Those who perceive the membership package to be particularly good value for money might be minded to add a small amount to their membership fee as a gesture of goodwill.

Boston Symphony Orchestra

The Boston Symphony Orchestra uses its direct mail letter to potential members to solicit donations in several ways. It starts by asking for a cash pledge, but also asks whether the potential applicant actually wishes to receive any benefits in return for that pledge. Furthermore, it offers the applicant the chance to receive an information pack about including the Orchestra in their will, and asks them to indicate whether their employer might be willing to match the value of cash they have pledged. The form also asks the applicant to indicate in which month of the year they wish to be sent a renewal reminder. The incentive? Unless they do this, they are told that they will receive reminders in November, February, May and July!

Source: Boston Symphony Orchestra direct mail letter to Ms R. Priestman, Boston, MA (undated)

Distribution

The effectiveness of printed leaflets and brochures will depend very much on their distribution. There are various options. To reach an organisation's existing members and others known to it, they can be enclosed with a letter and sent in the post (see direct mail, below). If the organisation is based in a public building, they can usefully be made available in leaflet racks in a reception area or foyer. To reach those who currently have little, if any, contact with or awareness of the organisation, then print can be also be distributed to other organisations' leaflet racks in public places – hotels, doctors' surgeries, and libraries, for example – normally by commercial print distribution service providers. To reach further afield, leaflet inserts can also be distributed with relevant magazines or journals. The scope of each distribution mechanism should always be assessed, in order that its relevance to target membership prospects can be evaluated.

Advertising

Advertising a membership scheme is a good idea if suitable media can be found in which to do so. Often, such media are related to the affiliate organisation. For example, the membership schemes of theatres are often promoted through programmes and in their season brochures as well as local entertainment magazines such as 'What's On' guides. They may even be promoted through the membership scheme's own magazine, which may have a circulation and readership that is much wider than just the current membership base (see case study below).

Equity

The actors' union Equity's quarterly magazine represents the main point of contact with the union for the majority of its 36,000 members. Its winter 2003 issue was specially designed to spread the word about membership and to help its members to recruit other professionals who have either lapsed from the union or never joined. The magazine stated 'We want you to give them your copy of this magazine so they know what they are missing by staying outside of Equity'. As part of the union's commitment to recruitment and retention of members, the special issue contained features about the services offered by the union, including training opportunities, and an account of its successes in campaigning, negotiations and the information it provides on issues affecting its members. The editorial further encouraged members to be 'champions for Equity' and 'talk up the union whenever you have the opportunity'.

Source: Equity magazine, Winter 2003

Relevant independent media, particularly magazines which specialise in a related field to that of the membership organisation or affiliate organisation, may also be a cost-effective means of reaching potential members. For example, health support membership organisations might promote membership in publications that are widely read by doctors and other health professionals, on the basis that these people may recommend that their patients join.

British Riding Clubs

British Riding Clubs launched an advertising campaign in 2003 in a bid to raise still further their already successful levels of membership. In the previous year, membership of affiliated riding clubs recovered from the impact of foot and mouth disease to reach 36,000, exceeding all previous records. The 2003 campaign offered a prize of a new PC for the affiliated club that increased its 2003 membership by the highest percentage. The membership drive was supported by advertisements in the equestrian press, the distribution of posters to affiliated clubs to use in their areas, and the distribution of 'Join a Riding Club' leaflets around the UK. These initiatives were also supported by the further development of the British Riding Clubs website and the launch of merchandising initiatives.

Sources:
Press release: 'British Riding Clubs to Launch Membership Incentive Scheme' (25 April 2003)
www.bhs.org.uk (13 January 2004)

Direct mail

Assuming that a membership scheme has access to its own list of members and potential members (see above) then it is in a good position to send promotional literature by post.

Those that don't have their own lists can still use direct mail, though they are at the disadvantage of having to rely on renting lists of supposedly relevant names from third parties. If this method of direct mail is chosen, it is worthwhile testing the rental list by mailing a sample with the proposed offer, to ascertain response rates and value for money (see Evaluation, below). Many list owners will be happy to permit such tests especially if they are confident in their lists.

Mailing 'piggy-backs' provide another possible cost-effective alternative to using a scheme's own list, or indeed as an addition to other direct mail campaigns. Here, managers of a membership scheme negotiate with another non-competing organisation which has a similar market profile to the scheme, enabling a leaflet or letter to be included within a third-party mailing. Response rates are generally lower than for owned or rented lists, but nevertheless, this technique can be useful in locating potential members who might not be accessible through other means.

Copywriting

The most important element of a direct mail package is not the leaflet or brochure though, but the letter that accompanies it. It is the letter that personalises the communication, and has the potential to convert it from being just another piece of junk mail to a highly persuasive medium. Several fundamental principles apply to direct mail letters for membership schemes, just as for any other purpose. Clever copywriting can achieve very successful results, and can be the catalyst that encourages people to read the material and join the scheme. The component parts of a letter should be:[4]

- **The opening:** a headline or opening section that attracts the reader's attention and induces them to read on.
- **Description and explanation:** to hold the reader's interest and build an understanding as to the nature and purpose of the scheme.
- **Argument:** to create interest and desire for the benefits of the scheme.
- **Persuasion:** an exploration of the ways in which the scheme can deliver real benefits to the reader.
- **Inducement:** a special offer giving the reader an extra reason to sign up now, rather than just think about it.
- **The climax:** to cement any intentions to sign up and make it easy for the reader to respond immediately.

Special offers

An inducement can also encourage people to join a scheme, particularly if it is a time-limited offer. It can be made available through a direct mail campaign, but may also be used in other circumstances, such as at events and open days (see below), when the special offer can encourage people to join there and then.

The most appropriate form of inducement will vary between schemes, but may commonly take the following forms:

- **Reduced membership fee:** sign up now and it won't cost you as much as it will if you leave it until later.
- **Extended membership period:** sign up now and it will be 15 months, not 12, until your membership expires.
- **Invitation to a special event:** sign up now or you'll miss a very special never-to-be-repeated opportunity.
- **Discount voucher for merchandise or events:** sign up now and you'll get money off later.

Derngate Theatre

During the 1990s Derngate Theatre was attempting to build more enduring rela-tionships with people who had a genuine interest in the theatre and were likely to purchase tickets. As part of the process, the theatre asked those who had signed up for its free mailing list – a list of over 15,000 customers who had specifically requested to be sent information about forthcoming shows – to pay £3 if they wished to continue to receive this information. This was the first step in a wider relationship strategy. To incentivise people to join the paid list, and also to counter the argument that the new arrangement would cut off information from people who otherwise might have chosen to purchase tickets, everyone who joined was given five £1 ticket discount vouchers. These were redeemable against any purchase made in the subsequent 12 months.

In effect, joining the paid mailing list became a win-win option, in that the theatre refined and cleaned its mailing list whilst at the same time customers received a net payment of £2, albeit in vouchers. A further benefit was that the theatre sold additional tickets. In order not to lose the custom of the more sporadic customers who made less regular purchases, (i.e. those for whom the paid mailing list was not appropriate) the theatre continued to make use of its box office database to analyse and mail specific marketing materials to those customers whose past purchasing behaviour indicated that they may have a strong interest in specific types of show.

Evaluation

There is little point in going to the expense and time involved in undertaking direct mail without some sort of ongoing evaluation, especially given that direct marketing is one of the most measurable forms of marketing activity that there is. Without some form of testing and analysis as to who the most likely prospect members will be, the wastage in terms of print and postage may be significant, to say nothing of the annoyance of people who are simply not interested, and view the communication as 'junk mail'.

At the very least, quick and dirty research into likely 'hot prospects' for responses to membership recruitment campaigns can be undertaken by simply contacting a few people from a mailing list to hear their verbal response to the planned mailing campaign. Formal pre-testing usually takes the form of a much smaller mailing of a test sample from within the total mailing list. The impact of such a mailing is best measured by a simple comparison of the direct costs of sending the mailing versus the direct income achieved (whether in membership fees or donations) over a limited timescale. Having undertaken the tests the evidence can be used to inform the decision on a subsequent larger mailing.

A range of measures can be taken to evaluate the wider cost-benefit of direct mail, including:

- number of items mailed;
- number of responses received;
- timescale over which responses are received;
- cost of the mailing per item (include postage, print, mailing house or internal staff costs);
- cost of response handling;
- number of ancillary purchases (for example, merchandise, or theatre tickets);
- value of ancillary purchases;
- timescale over which ancillary purchases occur;
- impact of external factors (does the time of year, postal delays, first- or second-class postage, the way the letter is written or the time of arrival have an impact on the response?);
- the profile of the respondents (is there a difference in response rates between different types of people, especially within the test mailing? This might inform the final mailing in terms of who is selected or what message is used);
- qualitative factors (what changes have been made to the depth of relationship with the customer as a result of the mailing?);
- long-term implications (does the mailing have a long-term or cumulative impact on the purchase behaviour, trust or depth of relationship?).

Telemarketing

Direct mail can deliver carefully crafted messages to those who are thought to be good prospects for joining a membership scheme – but what it can't do is enable the organisation to respond to any questions or reservations that the recipient may have about the scheme. Telemarketing can provide a valuable opportunity to do this.

It is most valuable as a membership marketing technique when an organisation has a list of customers or donors who may be persuaded to form a longer-term relationship with it.

Telemarketing of a membership scheme can take several forms, but in essence, it is simply a structured telephone conversation between the organisation and a prospective or existing member. This might happen 'inbound', for example, in the course of normal contact between an organisation and its supporters or customers. Alternatively, such calls may take place 'outbound' where the organisation (or an agency on its behalf) takes the initiative and proactively calls existing or potential members.

Inbound

Telemarketing prospects should be clearly flagged on relevant databases. Staff who take inbound calls must be trained about the membership scheme, and briefed about any special offers and how to sell them when a prospect next calls in. A formal scripted dialogue is seldom helpful because of its tendency to make the telemarketer sound clipped, in most cases a general discussion guide or conversation plan can be useful to ensure that all relevant questions and other pieces of information are communicated. Mechanisms should be put in place to record the outcomes of such conversations so that managers can gauge the effectiveness of this approach. For example, it is helpful to note the volume of identified prospects making contact by telephone; the consistency and effectiveness of up-selling; and the nature of any feedback being given about the scheme.

For an organisation that employs significant numbers of staff who take calls, and who have access to some basic technical resources, this can be a very cost-effective way of selling a membership scheme and of gathering market intelligence. It can be established as part of the daily routine. Where staff numbers are too few or insufficient in-house resources exist, or where the expected response volume may be too high to handle in-house or may not fit in with working hours, inbound telemarketing of this kind can be outsourced through agencies.

Outbound

As its name suggests, outbound telemarketing takes place on the initiative of the organisation. Response rates for outbound telemarketing are dramatically higher than for both direct mail and inbound telemarketing – for fundraising, experience shows that definite pledge rates of around 15% are common[5] – but costs are also higher (mainly staff wages and management overheads). In the end, cost-income ratios tend to be the same as for direct mail, but outbound telemarketing will generate around 10 times as much gross income due to the higher response.

Telephone Preference Service

Outbound telemarketing is perhaps the most intrusive form of marketing, so strict adherence to both the spirit and the letter of the Data Protection Act 1998 will help to ensure that best practice is observed. Having first checked that a list of prospects has been legitimately obtained and processed, a key requirement is to check this list against the Telephone Preference Service (TPS) list. Telemarketers must exclude individuals registered with TPS from their marketing campaigns, as it is unlawful to make unsolicited direct marketing calls to individuals who have

---

indicated that they do not want to receive such calls. A number of agencies perform this service, many offering a more-or-less 'while-u-wait' service online. The Direct Marketing Association (DMA) has published a code of practice for direct marketers. For telemarketing, advice is given on subjects such as reasonable hours for calling, courtesy and procedures, and the use of power and predictive dialling, for those with access to such technology.

Further information is available from the Telephone Preference Service www.tpsonline.org.uk and the Direct Marketing Association www.dma.org.uk. The DMA Code of Practice is downloadable free of charge.

Organisations may find that the best first use of outbound telemarketing will be to raise purely philanthropic donations, which tend to be of higher value on average than membership subscriptions. Having secured a donation, outbound telemarketing is subsequently extended to membership development. In general, telemarketing is especially successful when used in relation to existing customers who are already known to feel positive towards the organisation or its membership scheme. Its use here might be not only to seek renewal of an existing membership or repeat a previous donation, but to convince the customer, through a personal conversation, to increase the level of their financial involvement.

In-house campaigns can succeed where there are enough staff to both make the calls and manage the campaign, or where prospect lists are relatively small, but capacity issues tend to lead most organisations to outsource their outbound telemarketing to external agencies eventually.

Given the high initial costs of outbound telemarketing (whether run in-house or outsourced), it rarely makes sense to measure the return purely in terms of year one income and the lifetime value of a member should be taken into account from the outset. To help reduce long-term costs and enhance lifetime value it is implicit that outbound telemarketing campaigns should aim to recruit members by direct debit, ideally using paperless direct debit (also known by the major banks as AUDDIS), which can be set up over the telephone (see Chapter 5).

Orchestra of the Age of Enlightenment

In March 2000 the Orchestra of the Age of Enlightenment (OAE) ran a telemarketing campaign to promote its Friends scheme to mailing list members and attenders at its concerts.

Just over 5,000 people were selected from the above groups and a pre-call letter was sent to around 2,800 people for whom a usable telephone number could be found. The letter outlined the details of the new scheme and let prospects know that a telephone call would follow, allowing them the opportunity to opt out by phone or mail if they did not wish to receive a call. Calling began after allowing prospects around 10 days to respond to the letter.

OAE made contact with 1,556 people in all: 268 people (17%) said they would definitely join the scheme and a further 306 (19.7%) said they would consider doing so. A further 43 people pledged a philanthropic gift to OAE. All of these people were sent a letter confirming the details of their pledge, a personalised donation form and a freepost reply envelope.

OAE's scheme was tiered, with levels as follows:

Basic Friend	£25 per year
Bronze Friend	£125 per year
Silver Friend	£250 per year
Gold Friend	£500 per year
Platinum Friend	£1,000 per year

Of prospects approached, 91% said they would join at the Basic level, but around 9% said they would join at the Bronze, Silver and Gold levels. In all, the campaign generated gross income of around £13,500 in the first year, against costs of around £10,000. Around 40% of the Friends' pledges were made on direct debit, meaning that measured over a four-year period, the campaign would deliver a 3:1 return on investment.

Source:

Case study prepared by Adrian Salmon, The Phone Room, Oxford. Telephone 01865 324000

Websites

In recent years websites have become the engine rooms of many non-profit organisations. As well as being places where customers go for information, they have increasingly become the shop window and retail outlets through which online visitors make purchases. They have also become a valuable resource for the marketing of membership schemes.

Benefits of a website

Websites offer some unique advantages over other forms of promotional activity for the marketing of membership schemes.

- **Reach:** being geographically unconstrained, the Internet enables web-based information to be easily distributed across the whole of the world. This creates access to potential members who live in other regions and countries.

- **Exclusivity:** by creating zones within a website that are password protected, membership organisations can keep members-only privileges exclusive to those who have joined.

Shakespeare's Globe

Shakespeare's Globe runs GlobeLink, an international membership scheme for schools, colleges and universities, as part of its education programme. In return for payment of an annual fee, all students and staff in an organisation, or department of a higher education institution, are entitled to password access to the resources and projects available on the interactive GlobeLink website. They are also eligible for discounts on lectures, workshops and teachers' courses, practitioner-led study resources, advance information, priority ticket booking ahead of the general public, and online publications. Tailored videoconferences can be developed for member organisations at additional charge, for example allowing discussions with actors, directors or designers. In addition the annual 'Adopt an Actor' scheme gives members an insight into the experiences of individual actors from the beginning of rehearsal to the final performance, through regular online bulletins and bespoke classroom activities.

Source: www.shakespeares-globe.org (10 December 2003)

- **Impact:** whereas leaflets are two-dimensional and static, websites can include better insights into the work of the organisation, for example, with video clips of its work.
- **Flexibility:** as websites can (and should) be updated regularly, they need never display irrelevant or inaccurate membership information. They can also include new information as it becomes available – such as details of forthcoming members' events.
- **Revenue generation:** a website can not only display information about a membership scheme and the benefits it offers; it can also facilitate a transaction, allowing people to join there and then.
- **Custom-targeted content:** the advances in web and database technology means that websites no longer need rely on purely 'static' web pages offering the same information to everyone, but can instead generate 'dynamic' pages which base their content on a combination of customer-selected preferences and options, together with stored information on past transactions and other membership data. Thus such pages can be created uniquely for each member.

Web domains

Membership schemes are presented online in one of two ways: as stand-alone sites dedicated to the membership organisation or scheme itself, or as pages on an affiliate organisation's website.

Stand-alone sites

Not all membership organisations have an affiliate, and even if they do, the relationship with that affiliate may be a relatively distant one. These organisations will have no choice but to acquire their own web domains at which they can set up their own websites and promote their schemes. However, some membership organisations that have very clear links with a specific affiliate choose to go down this route too. There are both advantages and disadvantages to doing this. A stand-alone site:

- need not conform to the design constraints imposed by an affiliate organisation's site;
- has total control over the content of the site;
- has a major presence in its own right rather than a minor presence on a much larger site;
- can employ techniques that will raise its own profile on search engines, rather than that of its affiliate;
- can create links with the affiliate's site, and be linked in to it, with the affiliate's consent;
- can be independently linked by other organisations' sites.

On the other hand, stand-alone sites:

- cannot normally adopt the corporate identity of the affiliate;
- must bear the costs of the site's design and maintenance;
- rely on the affiliate's goodwill in directing visitors away from their own site towards the membership site.

The potential for confusion is significant when there is little or nothing online to suggest that an affiliate organisation and a membership scheme are linked in any way. Indeed, if a membership site appears to be completely separate from its affiliate, this may arouse the suspicions of web visitors, particularly if they are considering joining the scheme (and therefore parting with their credit card details) online.

This confusion can be compounded if splinter groups emerge, all appearing to claim links with a particular affiliate. For example, the proliferation of fan club websites for artists, musicians, football clubs and the like, often leads to confusion as to which one is the 'official' or 'recognised' group.

England football supporters club

When the words 'England football supporters club' are placed into a search engine, seemingly relevant sites can be found at www.england-supporters.com, www.englandfc.com and www.england-supporters.co.uk. Trying to ascertain which is the 'official' fan club site is difficult. In fact, the last official supporters club was disbanded in 2001 by the Football Association, and a new one, 'englandfans' was subsequently launched, but membership is closed until August 2004, after the next World Cup campaign, and it is not easily accessible through a web search. Details are given on the Football Association's own website at www.thefa.com and englandfans' own official members website is at http://englandfans.thefa.com.

Affiliate organisation sites

By contrast, having a presence on an affiliate organisation's site is a relatively straightforward exercise. Even membership schemes which are constitutionally quite separate from the affiliate organisation can usefully be integrated with the affiliate's website for the purposes of promoting membership. The benefits for a scheme of being integral to an affiliate organisation's site usually seem to outweigh the disadvantages, though there will always be exceptions to this.

Hospital websites

Although they are an independent charitable voluntary organisation, the Friends of London's Royal Free Hospital display information about themselves on the website owned and managed by Royal Free Hampstead NHS Trust. To reach the Friends pages, visitors to the site have to click on the phrase 'how you can help' and will be offered a menu of four options, one of which takes the visitor to the 'Friends' section.

By contrast, the Friends of Addenbrooke's Hospital in Cambridge run a stand-alone site which is quite separate from the Hospital's own site. Furthermore, the Friends scheme has been incorporated into The Fund for Addenbrooke's, the professional fundraising arm of Addenbrooke's NHS Trust, which itself is located at another quite separate site. The two fundraising sites provide reciprocal links with each other, though the relationship between them is not discussed. Whereas the Fund for Addenbrooke's site is formally linked with the affiliate, the same is not true of the Friends' site – a search of the hospital's site for 'Friends of Addenbrookes' produces no results.

Sources:
The Friends of Addenbrooke's website: www.friends-of-addenbrookes.org (19 January 2004)
The Fund for Addenbrooke's website: www.theffa.org.uk (19 January 2004)
Addenbrooke's Hospital website: www.addenbrookes.org.uk (16 November 2003)
Royal Free Hampstead NHS Trust website: www.royalfree.org.uk/volunteers.htm (19 January 2004)

Website content

Precisely what material should be used to create a web presence for a membership scheme will depend partly on the extent to which the site is linked with that of any affiliate organisation. The closer the links are, then the less background explanation will need to be given. The following sections are common to many membership websites:

- **Explanation of the purpose of the membership organisation or scheme:** visitors to the site need to understand the reasons why the membership organisation exists, and how, if at all, it links with any affiliate organisation.

- **Background information about the affiliate organisation (if any):** this is particularly important for stand-alone sites which have few immediate links with their affiliate organisations.

- **Descriptions of benefits to members:** a full listing of benefits helps web visitors to understand the scope of the scheme.

- **Opportunities linked with the scheme:** this is particularly important if the membership scheme is used to identify potential volunteers.

- **Membership news:** the activities of members and any developments taking place through the scheme can be shared here.

- **Forthcoming events and special offers:** details of members-only events can be published here, away from the main publicity for events that are open to all. One-off discounts and other promotions can be promoted too.

- **Sale of merchandise:** some membership schemes make merchandise such as promotional t-shirts, lapel badges, car stickers and key rings available for their members to buy. Others go a lot further, and act as a merchant for items that may have relevance for scheme members, but not relate directly to the scheme itself. Both of these warrant exposure on a website.

- **How to make a donation:** anyone interested in extending financial support beyond that required to take advantage of the benefits of the scheme can be helped to do so here.

- **How to join:** a clear application form and very specific details to help web visitors choose the level of the scheme most appropriate to them is essential. A payment mechanism must be determined too (see below).

Online transactions

A key purpose for a website in marketing a membership scheme is to enable transactions to take place so that potential members can join. To enable this to happen, the online equivalent of the promotional leaflet has to be in place. The application procedures may be one of two types:

- a simple application form that can be printed out, completed by hand and returned in the mail or by fax, together with payment (and ID if required for proof of, say, student status);
- an online application form that can be submitted together with credit card details or instructions (ID has to be submitted separately under this system).

The main advantage of the former is its simplicity. Setting up a downloadable application form on a website is a straightforward task which does not involve any complex programming, and because any money sent by this route will arrive by mail, there are no grounds for fears over the security of Internet transactions. However, the main disadvantage is that the application process involves two stages – a web-based investigation followed by a manual application process. It's quite possible that some potential members will get as far as printing off their forms, but never quite get around to filling them in, signing their cheques and putting them in the post.

Online membership applications are undoubtedly more complex. In particular, secure arrangements have to be set up for accepting credit card details. Aside from countless web designers (ranging from one-man-bands and volunteers through to relatively large corporations), there are an increasing number of online banking and online credit card merchant service providers that are quite used to helping inexperienced would-be web designers prepare their sites for online transactions. Such service providers can offer a range of options, from designing and setting up the whole site through to offering the necessary credit card facilities as a 'bolt-on' to the existing website for the more experienced web designer. After setting up secure online transaction facilities, the next critical issue to resolve is the electronic connection – if any – with the membership scheme's database of members. Having encouraged a prospective member to pay money for membership via a website, it is a pity if the membership administrator then has to re-enter the data which has been sent over the web, because a link between the membership database and the website was not considered to be a priority at the outset.

Word of mouth advocacy

Word of mouth endorsement by a trusted individual of the value of joining an organisation is probably the most influential form of communication possible. Both anecdotal and more formal evidence[6] suggests that word of mouth is one of the most widely used techniques for promoting membership. In many cases, this happens without any intervention by the membership organisation, as members enthuse to their friends and colleagues about the benefits of joining the scheme. However, in some schemes, considerable efforts are made to formalise the process of encouraging word-of-mouth communications by setting up networks of advocates.

Organisations that manage social networks of volunteers (ideally members themselves) with close links into specific community groups have access to a valuable resource for promoting various forms of engagement, including membership. These people, often referred to as 'ambassadors', are motivated out of genuine personal enthusiasm for the aims of the organisation and can offer an immediate live and direct form of communication with potential members.[7] A skilled ambassador can address potential members' concerns on the spot, and is able to overcome the reservations people may have about getting more closely involved.

Dallas Symphony Orchestra

During the 1990s, Dallas Symphony Orchestra successfully deployed its volunteers not only for face-to-face advocacy, but also to undertake and manage telemarketing campaigns for both fundraising purposes and to generate new subscribers for its classical music seasons.

Source: Kinzey, D., (1998) 'Volunteers in Relationship Marketing: The Unlimited Resource', *ArtsBusiness*, issue 11, September 28

Other personal approaches

Sometimes it can be useful for membership organisations to take advantage of opportunities to recruit the general public face to face. For example, they may take stands at exhibitions, set up stalls at shopping centres, design shop window displays in collaboration with any retail sponsors, and use their own venues to establish booths where volunteers can talk through the benefits of membership with passing customers. As with advocates (see above), this approach to marketing a membership scheme can be a powerful one. The face-to-face opportunity to overcome any objections a person might have to joining, and to conduct a transaction there and then, can tip the balance and persuade people to join. It can also create a very public presence for the organisation, which can significantly raise its profile.

The Raptor Foundation at Scotsdales Garden Centre

The Raptor Foundation provides a rescue service and rehabilitation facilities for injured raptors. It provides a permanent home for birds of prey unable to return to the wild and is committed to increasing rare species and sharing knowledge and information on their medical treatment and rehabilitation. As part of its activities aimed at developing understanding of and support for its work, the Foundation maintains a permanent kiosk outside a garden centre located some 25 miles from its base in St Ives, Cambridgeshire. At the kiosk, visitors to the centre can see some birds of prey close up, and volunteer staff encourage them to visit the Foundation or to become a member. An annual family membership includes free entry for named members.

Sources:
www.raptorfoundation.org.uk (15 January 2004)
Publicity leaflet: 'Cambridgeshire Raptor Foundation'

Open days and seminars

Rather than going out to the public, the membership organisation can invite the public in. By arranging open days or seminars (in the case of organisations with nothing to 'show'), the work of the membership and any affiliate organisation can be explained in some detail to those who express an interest. Such events can be advertised in the press, and may even warrant editorial coverage; but also, the events provide an opportunity for current members to invite their friends and colleagues along.

Gift membership

Another opportunity for members to involve their friends and colleagues can be created through a 'gift membership' package. The benefits available through the scheme can be drawn together into a gift pack to be purchased by members and sent on their behalf to whoever they choose. Such packages have two roles – they encourage members to introduce their friends, but also they enable those friends to experience the organisation and the benefits of the scheme at no personal cost to themselves. There is a reasonable possibility that some of those who receive the gift pack will re-join in their own right when the time comes for renewal (though there is evidence to suggest that members who receive their membership as a gift are more likely to lapse than if they bought it themselves[8]). Sophisticated relationship marketing techniques can subsequently be used to renew the gift membership, either through the originating purchaser, or directly with the gift beneficiary.

The Ramblers' Association

The Ramblers' Association was founded in 1935 with around 1,200 members in its first year and over 300 affiliated rambling clubs. The Association now has a membership of around 139,000 and has over 800 local organisations affiliated to it.

In October 2003 the organisation launched a new gift membership initiative. Special gift membership packs contain additional benefits to those included in standard membership packages, including copies of Ramblers' publications, a pedometer, a personalised message (such as a Christmas card or birthday card) and a packet of Kendal Mintcake. Gift membership costs £10 more than the standard membership and is available in individual and joint categories.

The new package is intended to promote the sale of memberships as 'the perfect gift for birthdays and other special occasions like marriage or retirement'. Prior to October 2003 recipients of gift membership received the standard membership pack. Retention levels among these members are estimated to be between 40% and 50%, and these levels are expected to apply to the new-style gift members as well. However ongoing campaigns are in place to increase retention rates among members in general, for example by encouraging direct debit subscriptions.

Sources:
www.ramblers.org.uk (22 December 2003)
Information from The Ramblers' Association (22 December 2003)

Summary

In order for it to achieve its objectives, a membership scheme must reach out to potential members. Those who run the scheme must also establish good communications with those who work within any affiliate organisation, as these people are in a strong position to influence the success or otherwise of the scheme. A 'brand image' is important for a scheme, as this will determine how it is perceived both from outside the organisation and from within any affiliate organisation. Brand image is particularly influenced by verbal and visual identity, which should be addressed when a scheme is established. Marketing communications to convey the nature of a scheme and its benefits can take a range of forms, from leaflets to direct marketing, personal selling, websites, open days and exhibition stands. These techniques should be used as appropriate, depending on the communications objective and the nature of any target market.

1 www.mousewks.com – 16 November 2003

2 Simmons, J. (2003) *The Invisible Grail: in Search of the True Language of Brands*, Texere Publishing

3 www.informationcommissioner.gov.uk – 17 December 03 – for full information and guidance documents

4 Bird, D. (1989) *Commonsense Direct Marketing*, Kogan Page, p190

5 Unpublished figures from The Phone Room, Oxford, 2003

6 Slater, A. (2004) 'An audit of Friends schemes at UK heritage sites', *International Journal of Heritage Studies*, Vol. 9, No. 3, forthcoming

7 Jennings, M. (2003) 'A Short Introduction to Arts Ambassadors', Arts Marketing Association conference, July

8 Bhattacharya, C.B. (1998) 'When customers are members: customer retention in paid membership contexts', *Journal of the Academy of Marketing Science*, Vol. 26, No. 1, pp31–44

5 MANAGING A MEMBERSHIP SCHEME

Keeping a membership scheme running efficiently and effectively requires a range of processes and procedures to be set up and managed. Good communication between members and those running their scheme is essential, and a range of techniques can be used for keeping in touch. Good communication between those who manage the scheme and those who manage its affiliate organisation (or, indeed, staff in other departments, if the scheme is managed in-house by that organisation) is also vital. This is especially so if the scheme depends on the support of the organisation to deliver the benefits it promises to its members. Database management, financial management and a process for evaluating a scheme's success (or failure) are also covered here.

Managing communications

Members generally part with their money and offer their goodwill in joining a scheme, but as explained in Chapter 2, they do have expectations in return, even if these expectations are subconscious. In particular, they expect the scheme to provide them with some form of communication that will give link them with their chosen cause or affiliate organisation. These communications may take several forms.

Membership packs

The implicit enthusiasm that members show when they first join a membership organisation or scheme should be recognised appropriately. If members join by responding to a simple leaflet or advertisement, they may well only have cursory information available. Some form of membership pack should therefore be presented to new members. A pack provides the first opportunity to cement a long-term relationship. Normally, it can fulfil a range of functions, and the nature of these functions will determine its content. For example:

- to give more details about the work of the membership organisation and/or its affiliate;
- to provide contact details of those who manage the scheme;
- to provide information about forthcoming events;
- to draw attention to the scheme's website;
- to encourage a new members to participate in fundraising or other voluntary work;
- to publicise any reciprocal arrangements with other organisations (see Chapter 4);
- to explain how to take advantage of discounts and special offers available to members;
- to encourage new members to invite their friends and colleagues to join the scheme.

Such a pack might also include a copy of the latest newsletter or magazine, a car sticker or a lapel badge (to enable members to make public their membership) and if required, a membership card.

Membership cards

Whether or not to issue membership cards or other means of identifying members is another dimension to be considered. For any scheme which offers reciprocal benefits in collaboration with other organisations (see Chapter 3), or a scheme which offers benefits at a range of locations, such as a group of heritage venues, a card is a prerequisite and has a practical use. Similarly, if a corporate membership category permits an organisation's staff to access benefits, a card will normally be used to help the affiliate organisation identify those who are eligible. On the other hand, a scheme that offers open access to a set of facilities, such as a sports club, may use a more visible identifier such as a shoe tag; and membership schemes run entirely by mail, or those that offer no tangible financial benefits, may have no need for any formal mechanism for identifying members.

Aside from the practical reasons for supplying membership cards, in some circumstances, notably those schemes with a carefully branded image or those where membership is perceived to be exclusive, a membership card has a social cachet in the same way that a gold credit card may have done in years gone by. Consequently, if a membership card is to be issued, any decisions about its design, the materials to be used and any associated security devices such as magnetic strips, bar-coding or member photographs, should be taken in the light of its perceived value as well as more practical uses.

British Naturism

Membership of British Naturism is described as a means to help promote and protect naturism, and 'membership also gives you a sense of belonging to the naturist community, an important part of the naturist movement'.

Tangible benefits available to members include the quarterly magazine *British Naturism*, an information service and personal accident insurance. This cover, which is included in the membership package, applies to accidents incurred during the pursuit of naturist activities at any approved club or location including official naturist beaches in the UK.

British Naturism is a member of the International Naturist Federation, and its members automatically belong to the international body and are issued with an internationally recognised membership card on joining. These cards 'act as an assurance to naturist centres, such as a holiday resort, that the holder is known to his or her national body'. In order to ensure the safety of members many commercial holiday centres and naturist clubs require the possession of such a card as proof of identity and some also offer discounts to card holders.

Source: www.british-naturism.org.uk (29 September 2003)

Meetings

Face-to-face communications are an important part of the management of a membership scheme, as they permit two-way debate and can create opportunities for decisions affecting the scheme to be agreed.

Meetings with members

Although not all members will take an interest in the work of the scheme (a number will simply wish to access its benefits), some enjoy the opportunity to meet with others. Two main purposes may be established for such meetings:

- to permit members to contribute to the decision-making associated with the scheme
- to permit members to socialise.

Participation in decision-making

Whilst it will normally be an organising committee or management team that makes decisions relating to the running of the scheme, it can be helpful if a forum is created at which the views of the wider membership can be aired. The drawback of inviting everyone to have their say is that expectations can be raised, even for the most inappropriate courses of action. There is always a danger that any individual whose suggestion is considered at a public meeting will expect this to be implemented if the rest of the meeting was supportive. In management terms, the suggestion may be impractical or too costly, and it may have to be dismissed on these grounds. An element of expectation management may be required in advance of any meeting in order to avoid such a scenario arising.

The legal structure of a membership organisation (see Chapter 3) will to some extent determine the nature of formal business meetings that must take place. For example, in the case of incorporated organisations, company law requires that an annual general meeting (AGM) takes place and that certain basic rules are adhered to in relation to members' meetings and directors' meetings. Similar arrangements for formal meetings should also be in place for unincorporated organisations. Appendix E provides a useful outline for planning and running an AGM. For both types of structure, these will form part of the governing document (see also Chapter 3), which should make clear the role and powers of such meetings.

YHA

The Youth Hostels Association operates a network of 225 hostels across England and Wales. Over 310,000 members 'receive a warm welcome, comfortable accommodation, good food and affordable prices'. The YHA's charitable objective is 'To help all, especially young people of limited means, to a greater knowledge, love and care of the countryside, particularly by providing hostels or other simple accommodation for them in their travels and thus promote their health, rest and education'.

The YHA is a registered charity, run by its members. A national executive committee and national officers of the Association; a chairman, vice chair, treasurer and assistant treasurer are elected by its voting members, which is a right of membership. YHA also exists as a charitable company limited by guarantee – YHA (England and Wales) Ltd. The board of trustees of the company mirrors the national executive in composition, and is responsible for the effective management of staff and acquisition, operations and sale of properties. The chief executive of YHA reports to the board of trustees.

The organisation employs 1,200 staff, including 600 seasonal staff, and is supported by 2,000 voluntary workers. A primary aim of the YHA's five-year plan is to increase the number of people as volunteers in delivering the YHA objective.

Source: www.yha.org.uk (19 January 2004)

For an integrated membership scheme there will be no constitutional requirement to meet with the members *en masse*. In this case, it may be more productive to set up a range of specialist forums to which members with particular interests – fundraising, managing events or volunteering, for example – are invited to attend and share their views. In addition, 'meet-the-management' meetings may be popular occasions at which members can question those who run both the scheme and the affiliate organisation. Expectation management is key to ensuring that the purposes for and subsequent outcomes of such meetings are not misunderstood.

Social opportunities

As discussed in Chapter 3, members are often interested in the social benefits offered by a scheme, and may join in the hope of building social relationships with like-minded individuals. Meetings, usually hosted by guest speakers, can be seen as a very important element of the membership benefits.

Meetings of the organising team

Committee meetings, board meetings and/or management team meetings are necessary to enable decisions to be taken about the membership scheme. Such meetings are different from those involving the entire membership, but are essential to ensure the smooth day-to-day operation of the organisation. Minutes of the meetings are often circulated to members or are made available on request.

In the case of a social club scheme or public members scheme, such meetings will generally involve those with the titles 'chair', 'secretary', 'treasurer' and other officers identified in the governing document, often with a paid manager of the scheme, if any, in attendance. In the case of the smallest organisations, these people may be self-appointed individuals who have taken upon themselves the work of running the scheme. But in other cases, these people will have been democratically elected at an AGM or by postal ballot.

In the case of integrated membership schemes, management meetings may take place from time to time, and may involve volunteers as well as paid staff.

Meetings between a membership organisation and its affiliate

Other than in integrated membership schemes, the relationship between a membership body and any affiliate organisation generally exists at arm's length. In other words, each party is an independent organisation in its own right, and the relationship between the two is generally driven by the interaction between individuals working for each party, rather than any formal structural links. There are usually no formal reporting lines between the two, and no one individual in each organisation has any line management responsibility over anyone working for the other party. Consequently, good communication between the two is vital to keep the relationship positive. Each party needs to know what the other is doing, to minimise the potential for one undermining the activities of the other, and to help each meet their respective objectives. This may not be as straightforward as it sounds, as conflict between the two can arise in several areas (see Chapter 6). Informal meetings between the managers of two parties can be a valuable mechanism for minimising such conflict, as they permit an exchange of views and provide a forum at which any problems can be resolved. Some membership organisations have more formal arrangements to enable ex-officio representation by the affiliate organisation on their governing bodies (for example, the marketing manager or chief executive), either as observers or fully fledged voting committee members. Whilst there are benefits of such close formal ties, there is also the potential for a conflict of interest to arise between the two organisations, which can lead to tensions.

E-mails and text messages

New media, such as e-mail and text messaging, can play a role in keeping members involved with and updated about a membership scheme. Both are relatively inexpensive means of reaching large numbers of people, though they have their limitations. There still remain many households and individuals without access to e-mail or a mobile phone, particularly among older age groups. These are therefore unreliable methods for disseminating important information to all members. However, they can be useful for promotional activity, for example, to draw attention to forthcoming events or to encourage lapsed members to renew their memberships.

Arts Marketing Association

The AMA is the UK's professional development body for anyone involved in the arts and cultural industries in the UK. It has 1,400 members, and benefits of membership include:

- opportunities for professional development, including a mentoring scheme
- a quarterly journal (JAM) and other publications commissioned by the AMA
- events, conferences and networking opportunities
- access to a website which includes an online think-tank, resources, information and contacts.

In 1999 the AMA ceased sending printed newsletters to all of its members, and instead started sending monthly e-mail bulletins with links to its website. This change arose following a membership survey which revealed that members wanted to be provided with more up-to-date information on marketing and audience development issues. The survey was part of the organisation's annual research to evaluate member benefits, and revealed that 95% of members had access to e-mail. E-mail bulletins contain summarised information with links to the website so that members can easily scan through and decide which articles they would like to read in more depth. Hard copies of the bulletin are sent out to members if e-mails are 'bounced back'.

The use of e-mail has significantly increased the effectiveness of communication with AMA members. There have been several benefits:

- lower printing and postage costs, which brought the added advantage of freeing up funds to develop and improve the journal and website;
- less staff time taken to produce a newsletter;
- increased use of the website through links from the e-mail bulletin;
- establishment of a two-way dialogue, allowing an immediate response from members and avoiding delays in sending information by post;
- the potential for the individualisation of mass communication, using mail merge fields to insert personal details, for example individual passwords for the website;
- better support for the AMA brand.

The only drawback of using e-mail bulletins has been that e-mail is not appropriate for all members, and there are still some who choose to receive printed bulletins by post instead.

Sources:
www.a-m-a.co.uk (19 January 2004)
Interview with Julie Aldridge, Arts Marketing Association (January 2004)

Websites

Although access to the Internet is by no means universal either, a website can be another means through which members can be kept involved with the organisation. However, the task of keeping a website up to date with useful information is seldom simple, and tends to be beyond the capability of membership organisations that rely solely on volunteers. Consequently, the websites of membership schemes which link into affiliate organisations are often used purely to publicise the existence of a scheme and its benefits (see Chapter 4) rather than as an information source or resource. Larger membership organisations, however, particularly where there is no external affiliate involved, may use their websites to provide actual services to members, and the resource provided on the web may be an important benefit of membership, and must be continually maintained (see Delivering benefits, below).

The Association of MBAs

The Association of MBAs comprises around 12,000 members from 80 countries, of whom around two-thirds are senior managers, board directors or chief executive officers. The Association offers a regular programme of networking meetings, events and lifelong learning activities in order to further the professional development of its members. In addition to these events, membership includes subscription to the Association's magazine *MBA Business*, preferential rates on health clubs, health care schemes, leisure pursuits, financial services and fast-track hotel and car reservation services. It also offers a range of benefits through its website, including the Members' Address Book which can be updated online by members; links to sources of business information; and online registration with MBA Career Horizons, a group of organisations offering job search, interim management, career planning, skills training, and personal development services.

Source: www.mbaworld.com (22 December 2003)

Newsletters

Newsletters are the life-blood of many smaller membership schemes, though larger professionally run schemes often publish magazines instead. Some national organisations produce both – a magazine for all members and regional newsletters containing information about meetings of local groups, the activities of local members or forthcoming regional events, for example (see also Chapter 3). These forms of communication are very valuable as they keep members in touch, even if they have very little other contact with the scheme. However, the costs of design, printing, packing and postage can be prohibitive, especially where the membership fees charged are minimal.

Managing the database

At the heart of every membership scheme there will be a list of people who belong to the scheme. Self-evidently, this list is of critical importance, as it determines who is eligible to take advantage of the benefits offered by the scheme, and who is not.

Selecting a data management system

These days, all but the smallest of schemes will store details of their membership on a computer database, and gone are the days of the card index and photocopied labels. The best solution may be a simple spreadsheet, off-the-shelf membership database software or a comprehensive bespoke system. The choice of software will depend upon factors such as the information needs of the membership scheme, the budget available, staff or volunteer skills and the nature of existing technology.

Alternatively, if an affiliate organisation keeps a database itself – as in the case of theatres which issue tickets using a database-driven box office ticketing system, or charities which hold a central fundraising database – it is almost always desirable for the membership database to be fully integrated within the main database. This will mean that details of all transactions that have taken place between an individual and the affiliate organisation can be recorded alongside their membership records, which may be useful for any future targeted marketing campaign. It also means that eligibility for limited membership categories related, for example, to a person's home address or recent purchase history, can be checked. Such joined-up record-keeping has other benefits. For example, if a member moves house, acquires a spouse, or even dies, the updating of that person's record by any department in the organisation will ensure that the membership record is automatically updated too.

For schemes which are not integrated with an affiliate, a separate database may be inevitable. In these circumstances, good communication between the membership organisation and affiliate is of paramount practical importance. If membership benefits are provided by the affiliate, but the membership database is held and managed by an independent membership organisation, it is crucial that key information on members is shared if both organisations are to manage their affairs effectively. For this to work successfully (and legally), sound management systems and strict adherence to the principles of the Data Protection Act 1998 (see Chapter 4 and below) are imperative.

Data fields

In most 'off-the-shelf' software database packages, the data fields (i.e. the categories of data you can store about people) are pre-determined; but in the case of bespoke systems or those for which user options are available, choices can be made as to the information that should be stored about each person who joins a membership scheme. The types of data that should be collected and entered into the computer, and the ways in which it will be processed, should be considered at the outset. This is not only for obvious practical reasons, but also to ensure compliance with Data Protection legislation (see below). As a starting point, the following database fields should be considered:

- title (Mr/Mrs/Ms/Miss/Dr/Professor/Sir – and a space available for non-standard titles)
- first name or initial

- surname
- suffixes (such as honours – in some membership schemes, a significant minority of members may have designations which are important to them)
- preferred name (how does a member prefer to be addressed – first name, title and surname, awarded title and first name etc.)
- details of spouse and other family members
- address (house number and street, village or district, town or city, post-code and country)
- alternative address (e.g. vacation home, if relevant)
- telephone and fax numbers (home, work and mobile)
- e-mail address
- source of application (leaflet, or word-of-mouth recommendation, for example)
- starting date of membership
- period of membership
- type of membership (tier and/or category)
- membership fee paid
- additional voluntary donations
- other relevant information (such as volunteer or donor status)
- general correspondence flags (such as letters and welcome packs sent, or responses received to direct mail campaigns)
- transaction details (such as renewals, non-renewals, reason for non-renewal etc. where known)
- opt-out from further direct marketing approaches (see Data Protection, below)
- notes.

Databases should be kept as 'clean' as possible, and to help this, software can be designed to accept only certain formats of data. For example, postcodes and telephone numbers should always be entered in an agreed format and dates should be recorded in a consistent style. This consistency is important to enable the data to be used for marketing purposes. For example, analysis of postcodes can enable scheme managers to identify the geographic catch-ment of their scheme, and thereby understand the districts and regions in which new prospects are most likely to live. If some postcodes are entered without numbers, letters and spaces in the appropriate places, then the aggre-gation of data becomes unreliable.

Spellings are also important. Should a lapsed member submit a new appli-cation to re-join a scheme, then it is important to be able to recognise that this person has been a member before, and to revive the original record, rather than set up a brand new record for them. If the spelling of that person's name or address has been made incorrectly, then it will be difficult to match the two. Failure to match the renewal with the original record can lead to subsequent problems, for example sending a direct mail letter targeted at lapsed members (see Chapter 4) to a person who has already re-joined.

Data Protection legislation

In the UK a raft of legislation, such as the Data Protection Act 1998 (see Chapter 4), Freedom of Information Act, and the Privacy and Electronic Communications Regulations, has been established with a view to protecting the rights of individuals about whom data is obtained, stored, processed or supplied.[1] As a result of this, almost any person, company or organisation within the commercial, public or private sector who records personal data about living individuals (even information as simple as names and addresses) is required, under the 1998 Act, to register with the Information Commissioner about the information they hold and how it will be used (see Appendix F).[2]

The process of notification applies whether the records are held manually or on a computer. It requires data controllers (the term used in the 1998 legislation to refer to those who make use of the data) to declare the ways in which they may use the information they collect. For example, a membership scheme may hold details for the purposes of delivering benefits to people who have paid to access them. However, the scheme's managers may also wish to use the names and phone numbers on their list for telephone fundraising campaigns, or to exchange their list with another organisation which is not a direct competitor but has complementary aims. These uses of the data must be made explicit in the notification.

There are some exemptions from notification for not-for-profit organisations.[3] The rules are complex, but some small clubs, voluntary organisations and charities that keep records of existing, lapsed or prospective members in order to establish and maintain membership or support for a not-for-profit affiliate organisation may be exempt.

Retaining members

By placing the focus of marketing activity on generating new members, schemes can experience the 'leaking bucket' effect, where customers are being lost because insufficient marketing activity generally, and customer service specifically, is being directed to them.[4] This has historically been a major problem for many membership schemes, but is not always widely recognised because it is quite possible that total membership continues to grow at the same time as sizeable proportions of the membership base fail to renew.[5]

Increasing the rate of member retention can have a significant impact on the cost effectiveness of the scheme. For example, an 80% retention rate means that 20% of customers will be lost each year. In other words, the entire membership database will have to be replaced every five years. This is a costly exercise and will require significant marketing effort. On the other hand, if the retention rate can be increased to 90%, it will take 10 years for the whole membership database to turn over, as only 10% are lost each year.[6] The annual marketing expenditure needed to attract new members is therefore halved. The measure of 'churn' – the rate of turnover of the membership – is one of the key evaluation statistics that can be used to assess the health of a membership scheme and diagnose its problems (see Evaluating performance, below).

When handled well, the process of renewing membership can be used to great advantage. As well as encouraging people to re-join the scheme, the renewal point can be an opportunity to persuade members to upgrade to a higher tier of membership (known as 'up-selling') and/or make a donation to the organisation. It may also be an opportunity to sell related products (known as 'cross-selling'). For example, a heritage organisation may use a renewal letter as an opportunity to promote its own-branded merchandise, or an arts centre to sell tickets for a forthcoming event.

There are two fundamental areas where effective management can contribute to the greater retention of members: the processes for managing renewals and the service levels achieved in delivering the benefits of the scheme.

Delivering benefits

Key to sustaining and growing the loyalty of existing members is the delivery of the benefits they are promised when they join. All of the basic principles of customer service apply to the delivery of membership benefits, just as they do to the delivery of any other product or service. The fact that members' motivations for joining a scheme may embrace an element of altruism (see Chapter 2) does not mean that any corners should be cut in delivering the promised benefits. It simply means that some (but by no means all) members may be quite forgiving on the occasions where service levels fall short of what is promised. Mechanisms for generating feedback – including meetings (see above) but also complaints – are important means of evaluating the extent to which the promised benefits are being delivered to members' satisfaction (see Evaluating performance, below).

Integrated membership schemes and membership organisations tend to be in a position to take responsibility for delivering benefits themselves. For example, if a museum runs a scheme that offers free entry to special exhibitions, a quarterly magazine and discounts in its restaurants and cafés, then the management of the museum is responsible for ensuring that the different departments within the organisation provide these benefits to members. However, social club schemes and public members' schemes, which are independent bodies with some form of link to an affiliate organisation, may be dependent upon their affiliate to deliver many of the benefits that they offer to their members. In this case, the relationship between the affiliate and the scheme is a key determinant of the quality of service that can be offered to members. Any breakdown in communication between the two can lead to disappointment for members, who will often attribute blame to those who run the scheme, regardless of whether it is they or the affiliate organisation who are really at fault for problems with the service delivery.

Public of European Theatres

In 2000, to celebrate its twelfth anniversary, the European Theatre Convention in conjunction with the 36 theatres which comprised its membership, launched a new network scheme, the Public of European Theatres. The scheme offers 'a standing invitation to any season-ticket holder of any theatre member in all the other European theatres of the network'. To access the benefits, attenders need to obtain a Public of European Theatres card from their own theatre and (also through their own theatre), arrange a reservation for a free ticket which can be collected at the destination theatre on a selected date. The benefit is limited to one free ticket per season ticket holder. According to the scheme's managers, '36 theatres are thus creating a bridge… giving birth to the first European network of attenders'.

Sources:
European Theatre Convention website: www.etc-centre.org (14 January 2004)

Problems can arise with staff training. Those working in front-line customer service roles for the affiliate organisation must be fully aware of the benefits being offered to members (and members of any other schemes where reciprocal arrangements apply). Breakdowns in communication can lead to tensions at the point of redeeming benefits. Other problems can arise with database management. If the affiliate organisation manages an integrated database which includes data relating to members, then those who run the scheme will depend on the affiliate to extract appropriate names for targeted benefits such as, special member-only offers and newsletters. Should they fail to do this, then lapsed members may continue to receive benefits reserved for current members, and current members may fail to receive the benefits they are due.

Managing renewals

Another factor that exerts a significant influence over the retention of members is the efficiency and persuasiveness with which the renewals process is conducted. One survey at a theatre in England found that almost a third of respondents to a membership survey stated that one of the reasons they had failed to renew was because they had simply never been asked.

Geological Society of London

The Geological Society of London sends renewal notices to all its Fellows annually in November, saying 'Payment is due on 1 November. You should pay by the end of the year to ensure that all services (e.g. access to the library) continue. We strongly advise you to renew before the end of March, as non-payers will not be sent their journals after 31 March. The final deadline for renewals is 30 June, which means that everyone has just over 8 months in which to pay. The records of those who have not paid by then are lapsed'.

Until 2000 this work was carried out internally by the accounts department of the Society, but as the membership grew the task became too large to be managed in this way. As a result the process has been streamlined in association with Kendata Print Services. A two-page A4 form has now been created, consisting of a letter and brief questionnaire on one side, and a barcode and financial information on the other. These forms can be personalised with information from the Society's records. On return the barcode is scanned by the Society's accounts staff to speed processing, and the replies to the questionnaire can be scanned by a bureau service and returned in a compatible format.

Sources:
www.geolsoc.org.uk/template.cfm?name=renewals (18 January 2004)
www.kenda.co.uk (7 January 2004)

The renewal point

There are two alternative scenarios for renewal points, each of which has advantages and disadvantages.

Rolling renewals

For some organisations, it is appropriate to sign all members up for a specified period of time (often a year) at a set price. In that case, their renewals become due precisely 12 months from the day, or more usually from the month, they were set up. This gives members the opportunity to enjoy a full year's worth of benefits before being asked to re-subscribe. It also spreads the administrative burden of managing the renewals process across the full year. However, such a system does rely upon efficient data management systems to identify when each individual's renewal falls due, and requires a constant level of reasonably sophisticated administration year-round.

Fixed point renewals

For other organisations, it is more appropriate to renew the entire membership at a fixed point in time. Those who wish to join after that point may be offered a reduced rate if their application is made late in the membership cycle, but their renewals will fall due at the same time as all other members. This may be a useful approach for a sports club which is only very active for certain months of the year, and where benefits may be of limited value at other times, and for those where the complexity of administration cannot be constantly managed throughout the year. In the case of seasonally sensitive sports clubs, full-price membership may be charged until this standard membership cycle ends and reduced rates apply after the season right through until the next renewal point. The advantage of this system is that it can be designed to recognise the time-related value of membership benefits, but its disadvantage is the sudden pressure it puts upon scheme managers – particularly those who manage a large membership base – when all the renewals fall due at the same time.

Studland United Nudists

Studland United Nudists was formed by users of Studland Bay in 1995, in order to represent their interests to the National Trust which inherited the land in 1982. The group required a simple method of managing renewals and opted for a standard membership renewal date of 1 November, which allowed reminders to be sent in the same mailing as AGM material. Members joining between 1 November and 31 March are asked to renew on the following 31 October, and members joining on or after 1 April are not asked to renew until 31 October the following year. As relatively small numbers of new members join between January and April, this system produces only a few members who receive either 18 months or 10 months in their first year of membership. A database is used to identify those due to renew their membership and an asterisk on the mailing label generated is used to ensure that a renewal pro-forma is inserted in the appropriate envelopes when the AGM material is sent out to all members.

Source: www.studland-nudists.co.uk/membership_renewal.htm (19 January 2004)

Renewals communication

Although membership schemes vary and a certain amount of testing is required, a month or two prior to a membership expiring it will normally be appropriate to invite the member to re-join. It is often assumed that such an invitation should automatically be sent to members in the post. Indeed, the mail is generally a cost-effective medium for sending out high volumes of standardised documentation, and may be appropriate for schemes that attract a lot of people who pay a relatively small amount of money to join. However, as shown in Chapter 4, many schemes include tiers that will appeal to relatively few people because of the relatively high cost of joining them. These highly valuable members may be better served by more personal forms of communication. Telephone contact may help to cement the relationship between these members and the organisation, as well as providing a channel through which more persuasive two-way interpersonal communication can be conducted. The phone is also an effective vehicle for up-selling or cross-selling (see above), as the caller can explain the nature of the up-graded benefits that the member may never before have considered, and can complete a credit/debit card or direct debit (see below) transaction there and then.

In addition to the chosen method for contacting members, the message must be considered too. For example, the term 'renewal notice', often used in a letter asking members to re-join, is strangely reminiscent of a telephone account or electricity bill. It can sound like a demand for money, which must be grudgingly paid. Much more enticing is use of language that conveys the chance to re-join as being an unmissable offer. An 'invitation' to continue an involvement with an organisation, or an 'opportunity' to receive even more benefits, is therefore likely to be more appealing than a straight request for money. All the rules of good copywriting (see Chapter 4) apply to renewal letters and forms, just as they do to communications with prospective and first-time members.

The Lincoln Center

From July 2002 to July 2003 The Lincoln Center in New York joined forces with its official automotive sponsor, Lexus, to offer the Lexus Enhanced Membership Program to its members. This one-year programme aimed both to promote the scheme to new members, with Lexus contributing a portion of the membership charge, and to encourage existing members to renew their membership at higher levels, again with Lexus contributing to the increased cost. 'Renewing members – don't forget you must move up at least one level to participate in the Lexus Enhanced Membership Program!'. Members were also advised that they would receive a promotional mailing from Lexus and details of special offers.

Source: Membership leaflet: 'The Lexus Enhanced Membership Program'

Reminders

Not everyone who receives such an invitation to renew will act on it straight away. Some will put it to one side, intending to complete the form or reply to the letter when time permits. Others will be in doubt as to whether they wish to re-join, and intend to think about it for a while before responding. Inevitably some forget, and don't re-subscribe. Of these, a proportion could undoubtedly be persuaded to re-join if they are reminded to do so. Consequently, it is important for those who don't renew to be sent reminder communications. These can take the form of follow-up letters, but also e-mails, text messages or even telephone calls. E-mails and texts are relatively inexpensive, and phone calls create a good opportunity for persuasion as well as enabling the caller to gather feedback about the membership scheme, which can be used to evaluate it. The timing, nature and frequency of reminder communications will depend both upon the value of the prospective membership to the organisation and the budget for renewals. Again, a certain amount of testing is required over time, to ascertain the optimum methods of communication and the timing of these.

The Metcalfe Society

The Metcalfe Society, founded in 1980 to support anyone interested in Metcalfe family history, has accumulated around 1,500 members both in the UK and overseas. The Society offers its members the opportunity to buy a subscription for multiple years (priced in multiples of the current annual rate) and thereby avoid future increases in subscription rates. The Society operates as a registered charity and is also a member of the Federation of Family History Societies, the Guild of One Name Studies and the Council of Family Societies. Benefits of membership include a journal published three times a year, a lending library, an annual 'Mecca Muster' and AGM, a Metcalfe badge and coat of arms, and access to a 'members only' area of the Society's website which contains its records and existing research and resources.

Source: www.metcalfe.org.uk (7 December 2004)

Reviving lapsed members

As explained in Chapter 4, one of the important targets for marketing activity is lapsed members of a scheme. Keeping in touch with them, even if they ceased to be members a while ago, can be valuable, particularly if their reason for not having renewed their membership is known and relates to an aspect of the scheme's benefits that has since been improved. Needless to say, it's important to keep records that will make it clear when a person has died, or give any other reason why no further contact is appropriate (see Data fields, above).

Managing the money

Virtually all membership schemes and organisations have to deal with money in the form of cash, cheques, credit or debit card payments, or direct debits and standing orders (see above). For integrated membership schemes, the management of these incoming revenues is seldom a problem. The affiliate organisation's financial systems will embrace the activities of its membership scheme, which will be treated in exactly the same way as all other financial flows into the organisation, whether from trading activity, donations, legacies or grant funding. However, it is important to be able to identify and separate membership scheme monies from the organisation's other funds. For membership schemes that are independent legal entities, arrangements have to be created for handling incoming revenues and accounting for them.

Cash and cheques

For membership schemes that control their own bank accounts, secure mechanisms need to be in place for the banking of and accounting for cash and cheques (see Accounting for the money, below). Cheque payments are generally still the most favoured method of payment through the post, and if large volumes of cheques are anticipated, this should be borne in mind when negotiating service charges with the scheme's bankers.

Credit and debit cards

An increasingly popular means of payment for services these days is the use of credit or debit cards. Membership organisations wishing to accept these as a means of payment can do so by setting up card merchant accounts, and subject to appropriate undertakings being made when negotiating this facility, credit or debit card payments can then be taken by phone, by post or in person. The processing of such transactions is invariably via an electronic unit using a telephone line to the credit card processing company, which means that the administration and security issues that arise in banking cheques or cash are avoided.

Subject to additional undertakings, card payments can also now be taken by secure methods over the Internet, and there are a number of major online agencies able to process credit and debit card transactions on behalf of organisations. This means that the sophisticated knowledge and investment that might previously have been required for a membership organisation to process its own online transactions is no longer required, and such transactions can now be conducted at low cost and with minimum hassle.

Automated payment mechanisms

The whole renewals process can be made much simpler if a scheme makes it possible for members to take advantage of regular payment mechanisms through which they can renew without having to resubmit further forms or documentation. Automated mechanisms can enhance renewal rates since the onus is on the customer to cancel his or her membership in order to leave the scheme. (Other forms of payment such as cash, cheque or credit/debit card require a positive action by the customer at every renewal point, to continue membership.) For the member, they ensure that membership is continuous, and that the relevant fee is taken automatically, without having to write cheques or remember to post them.

Direct debit[7]

This is one of the simplest ways for organisations to collect regular or occasional payments from members and is used increasingly for the benefit of both businesses and their customers. It saves time for both parties, reduces the costs of collecting money and ensures that payments are made direct into the accounts of the membership organisation. Some customers, especially older customers for whom the advances in banking services may seem somewhat mysterious, may distrust any form of automated payment and be reluctant to use this method of payment. Also, direct debit payments can only be collected from UK or Irish bank accounts, so for membership schemes that attract primarily overseas members, this may not be an appropriate payment mechanism. However, in reality there are few other drawbacks to the system for either the organisation or the customer.

Organisations that accept payments by direct debit have to operate reasonably advanced administrative systems. They must inform customers of the dates on which money will be taken from their bank accounts, and the amounts that will be taken. They must also inform them whenever membership prices change. They are obliged to offer a guarantee to refund immediately any monies taken in error. They must also have an excellent banking and credit history, since legally binding undertakings have to be made if they are to be accepted by the clearing banks as direct debit originators in the first place. In order to execute the required administrative systems, sophisticated computer databases are generally needed to set up, track and process membership transactions, and to operate banking industry-approved protocols for electronic payment communication between the membership organisation and BACS, the organisation which administers the national direct debit programme.

Direct debit has recently been revolutionised with the advent of the paper-less direct debit. Hitherto, all direct debit instructions had to be personally signed by the bank account holder, but subject to further additional under-takings by organisations, they may now process direct debits by telephone, over the Internet, face to face or via a telephone touch-tone key pad. To find out more about the direct debit system, organisations should contact their own banks, since the process of becoming accepted as an originator involves the bank 'sponsoring' the client organisation into the system.

Using direct debit

Direct debit payment for membership fees is encouraged in various ways:

- **The National Trust** offers an extra three months' membership free as an intro-ductory offer to new members who pay their annual subscription by direct debit. Encouragement is also available for existing members, who are told '…if all our members paid by direct debit we could make a saving of over £100,000 a year on administration costs'.

  Source: www.nationaltrust.org.uk (14 January 2004)

- **The Friends of Great Ormond Street Hospital** operate an annual direct debit as a means of paying membership fees. The application form allows applicants to choose both the month in which the payment will be taken, annually, and the amount paid.

  Source: www.gosh.org (13 January 2004)

- **The Ramblers' Association** encourages payment by explaining the benefits of direct debit to its members. 'Paying by Direct Debit … will reduce our administrative and bank charges, and save you having to write cheques each time you renew your membership. Half our members already pay this way …'

  Source: www.ramblers.org.uk (14 January 2004)

- **Plantlife – The Wild-Plant Conservation Charity** allows prospective members to choose their preferred subscription level by direct debit according to their own personal circumstances, though each subscription provides the same membership benefits.

  Sources: www.plantlife.org.uk (14 January 2004)

- **Diabetes UK** is one of many organisations that offer members a discount for paying by direct debit – in their case £1 a year.

  Source: www.diabetes.org.uk (17 January 2004)

Continuous credit card authority

Similar to the banks' direct debit scheme, a continuous credit card authority enables a membership organisation to take regular or occasional payments automatically from a customer's credit card. It works in a similar way to direct debit in that the customer signs an open agreement permitting the organisation to collect variable amounts from the credit card account until such time as the customer cancels the instruction by notifying the organisation. The organisation undertakes to notify the customer the dates and amounts to be deducted, in advance. The advantages to both parties are similar to those for direct debit, but for the customer there is less formal protection, in that credit card issuing agencies and banks are currently under no obligation to follow up fraudulent or incorrect payment collections from organisations. Whilst one might hope that membership organisations would strive to ensure fairness and accuracy, the lack of formal obligations upon credit card issuers to act on behalf of credit card holders in pursuing the less than scrupulous, tends to deter many customers from choosing this payment method. The entire UK credit card industry is currently under the government spotlight, and such undertakings may ultimately be forced upon it in the future.

Standing order

Here the customer remains entirely in the driving seat by authorising his or her bank to make specific payments to the membership organisation on specific dates, and to stop those payments at any time. The organisation is simply the recipient of the payments and cannot directly control the payment values or the dates on which payments are made. To set up a standing order, a customer has to contact their bank with details of the amounts and dates of payments, as well as the membership organisation's bank details. In order to keep track of those customers from whom it is expecting payments, it is helpful if the membership organisation issues its own pre-printed standing order mandate form and requests its return to them, prior to forwarding it to the customer's bank.

Whilst a standing order gives the customer optimum power in the financial transaction and requires less formal administration by the organisation, it is more cumbersome to the customer who has to notify the bank of any changes to the amount or dates of payments. The painful experience of many membership managers suggests that, for the organisation, additional work is generated by the significant minority of people who forget or simply do not get around to notifying their banks of increased membership payments or changed dates. Under these circumstances the organisation either has to accept out-of-date payment rates from some customers, or become entangled in long communication exchanges with customers in order to pursue the correct amounts. Furthermore, any decision to increase membership fees tends to depress renewal rates for standing order customers, in comparison with customers who pay by direct debit or continuous credit card authority customers.

Automated payment mechanisms in any form can offer a number of positive benefits to a membership scheme, if only because withdrawing from a scheme requires a decision followed by a positive action from the customer. In any membership scheme there will be a broad spectrum of members, including those who would renew at almost any cost, but also those who, if they thought about it long enough, might permit their memberships to lapse. The automated nature of payments has a tendency to retain these people for longer than might otherwise be the case.

Accounting for the money

The bank account

A bank account is at the heart of the money management process for any membership organisation. Independent membership bodies must set up appropriate bank accounts – current accounts for paying out and paying in cash, and interest-bearing deposit accounts for holding any reserves. There are stringent legal and administrative procedures that cover the setting up of bank accounts, which aim to prevent fraud and money laundering, and also to ensure that an organisation is acting within the terms of its governing document. Banks and building societies require copies of such documents together with any formally adopted resolutions by the organisation. They must also be able to verify the identity of at least two members of the governing body. If the organisation is registered as a charity, the bank or building society will check the information provided with the Charity Commission when the account is set up. Named individuals will be identified as signatories for cheques, and it is usual for a single signatory to be permitted to sign cheques for small amounts, while cheques for larger amounts will need to be signed by two people. The level at which two signatures are required will normally depend upon the scale of the activities of the organisation.

When an account is operational, every effort should be made to ensure that the money held in it is managed honestly and accounted for accurately. An organisation should reconcile its bank statements regularly, to ensure that the amount of money recorded by the bank as being held in that account reflects the transactions that have been conducted since the previous reconciliation.

Financial records

The transactions conducted through integrated membership schemes will be recorded along with all the other financial activities of the organisation, and separate accounting systems are not required to support the scheme. Normally, a scheme will be given a numeric departmental code, which is simply an identifier code relating to all the transactions conducted in relation to the scheme. This enables the transactions of the membership scheme to be separated out and analysed – for instance, to ensure cost-effectiveness or to check against any budgeted figures for the activity.

The same is not true of independent membership organisations, which must not only bank the money they generate and pay out, but also record these transactions in full (see Book-keeping, below). They must also account for all their financial activities, and present such accounts formally to their members (see Financial management, below).

Book-keeping

Book-keeping is the process for recording an organisation's transactions on a day-to-day basis. The principles of book-keeping remain the same, whether they are implemented through computer software such as a spreadsheet or an accounts package, or by quill pen and parchment. Some form of accounts computerisation is the norm these days, and with easy-to-use accounts software costing less than £100, this is often a worthwhile investment for even the smallest of membership organisations. Push-button technology makes light of the otherwise laborious ongoing chores of entering financial data and generating financial reports. Detailed guidance on book-keeping is beyond the scope of this book, but in the not-for-profit sector, specialist advice is available[8] for charities, and in particular, for people with limited accounts experience.

Book-keeping should be well controlled and monitored, as the acronym 'GIGO' (Garbage In, Garbage Out) certainly applies here. The figures recorded will subsequently be used to generate a wide range of information, including management accounts (see below). Furthermore, the quality, accuracy and level of detail of the information recorded will have a direct bearing on the year-end workload when final accounts are prepared (see below), and this in itself will affect the fees charged by an accountant in preparing these accounts. It is a good idea to keep the accountant informed of any material changes throughout the year, and to seek advice from time to time as to the preferred format for the financial records.

Financial management

Budgets

Few membership schemes are ever managed without some form of financial plan (also known as a budget), and fewer still are likely to thrive in the long term without one. A budget should be the organisation's best assessment of its likely costs and income over a period of time – usually a year at a time (see also Chapter 3). It should be neither an overly optimistic wish list, nor a pessimistically hopeless under-assessment which will be easily over-achieved and thus of no practical use other than as a false comfort to the budget-setters! Creating a budget is a logical step to take after the strategic objectives of a membership scheme have been agreed. The process of creating a realistic financial plan becomes easier after a scheme has been run successfully for a period of time, as there will be a history of financial achievements and a better understanding of the financial impact of different courses of action. At the outset, scheme managers have to rely on a combination of their past experiences in related fields and any information they can glean from similar membership schemes.[9]

As each financial year progresses, an organisation's financial information gradually moves from being a budgeted plan into a historic record of what actually happened. With a combination of knowledge of the financial impact of events in the year to date, together with what is known or anticipated for the remainder of the year, it is possible to make more accurate forecasts through to the end of the financial period. Whilst the original budget should not be changed, the scheme or organisation would not be acting in its own best interests if it failed to take account of new information as it becomes available. Such information gives managers the opportunity to address any issues by taking remedial action to return to budget, or indeed to improve on an already successful year.

Management accounts

The purpose of management accounts is to present information to help managers run their organisations effectively, and indicate how successful they have been in performing their activities[10] to date (see also Evaluating performance, below). For any membership scheme, regular financial reports should be prepared, but the management accounts for an entire membership organisation are likely to be different in structure and detail from any financial reports produced by a department that operates a membership scheme as one of a number of functions. Furthermore, the frequency with which these reports should be produced will depend on factors such as the scale of the scheme, any other management reporting arrangements in place (for an integrated scheme), and the dates of financial period ends and board meetings.

As a minimum, membership organisations (as opposed to integrated schemes) will normally produce regular profit and loss accounts, and possibly cash flow statements, to help them get a firm grip on the ongoing financial situation of the organisation.

- **The profit and loss account** shows the direct costs of running the organisation against its income to date, together with the organisation's overheads, such as salaries, building costs such as heating, lighting and cleaning, as well as marketing etc. Rather than simply listing a series of anonymous-looking figures, it is helpful if financial reports relate 'actual' figures to budgeted figures so that a comparison (or 'variance') against the plan or forecast can be assessed, both during the period of the report and cumulative to date. These should be accompanied by a set of notes explaining the reasons for any variances. The content of such reports is reasonably standard in format, although the precise layout and level of detail required can be varied to suit the situation.

- **The cash flow statement** provides a timeline showing money coming into and going out of the organisation. In other words, the value and timing of actual cash being generated from the membership, and the value and timing of payments being made to suppliers. In large organisations, or where a membership scheme generates and spends large sums of money, a cash flow statement will be a useful document to produce from time to time, as no organisation, no matter how successful on paper, can survive without a ready supply of cash.

A department within an organisation that manages an integrated membership scheme is likely to rely on the wider organisation's management accounts (which are often broken down to department level such as 'marketing', 'development', 'production' etc.). However, to ensure that the scheme is achieving its financial objectives, its managers will be especially interested in any items listed within those accounts that reveal the direct costs and income that arise exclusively as a result of the activity of the membership scheme.

Financial accounts

Annual financial accounts follow a standard structure, and their purpose is to summarise an organisation's resources and its activities at the end of each financial year. They should comprise a year-end profit and loss statement (see above), which records the financial outcome of the organisation's activity over the previous financial year; and a balance sheet, which records the assets and liabilities of the organisation at the year end (including buildings, furniture, office equipment, stocks, cash and deposits, monies owed by and to the organisation, advance income held on behalf of members and so on). The whole subject of preparing annual accounts, and the raft of legislation which governs their structure, is the subject of numerous publications, and specialist guidance is available for those responsible for charity accounting.[11]

There is no need for the managers of integrated schemes that are part of wider organisations to prepare their own financial accounts. The financial data relating to their schemes will be automatically incorporated in the accounts of their organisations. However, a set of annual accounts must be prepared by most other membership organisations. In the case of an incorporated organisation, annual accounts must be filed annually with Companies House, and registered charities in England and Wales must also file them with the Charity Commission. For non-incorporated associations and trusts (excluding those that also happen to be charities) there is generally no legal requirement to produce accounts, although it is likely to be a requirement of an organisation's governing document or its funders.

In general, whether or not annual accounts have to be filed with official bodies, there is invariably an important role for a professional adviser such as an accountant who will need to prepare and/or examine the accounts. Whether or not such a person undertakes this work on a *pro bono* basis as a member of the organisation, he or she will require the organisation to pass across its records of the transactions that have taken place during the previous 12 months (see Book-keeping, above) at the first available opportunity after the year end, generally after income and expenditure for the year has been banked or paid, and after bank accounts for the period have been reconciled. As ever, an on-going dialogue with the professional adviser is the best course of action to ensure a smooth procedure and compliance with both the law and the organisation's governing document.

Protection against fraud

The consequences of financial irregularities for any membership scheme can be catastrophic, and not just in terms of cash and any potential legal action against the organisation.[12] Confidence will also be eroded in the eyes of members, affiliate organisations, donors and other stakeholders. One of the most common reasons that fraud occurs is a weakness of internal controls. People do not usually start off with the intention of committing fraud, but too much reliance and trust placed on certain individuals, coupled with poor internal systems create the environment in which fraud can occur.

Internal financial control systems need to be based on clear responsibilities for managing the money. An important principle of internal control is segregation or division of duties. This prevents any one individual from being able to authorise, record and process a complete transaction. For example, when the same person receives cash from members, records it in the cash book or accounts system, pays it into the bank and prepares the bank reconciliation, it is very difficult to detect dishonesty or error. Cash can easily be misappropriated and hidden by false record-keeping.

The Arachnoiditis Trust

The Arachnoiditis Trust was set up originally as a self-help group for people suffering from the condition known as Arachnoiditis, a pain disorder caused by the inflammation of one of the membranes that surround and protect the nerves of the spinal cord. It was registered as a charity in 1994 in order to relieve sickness amongst sufferers; to provide information and advice; promote research into the condition; and publish and disseminate the results of the research.

Following complaints from a former trustee, the Charity Commission undertook an investigation into the accounts, record-keeping and general management proce-dures within the organisation. The original complaint to the Commission stated that accounts had not been presented to either the membership at an AGM, nor to the Commission. Additionally, there were doubts about the validity of the appointment of trustees, and there appeared to have been a reduction in the income from membership fees, despite claims that membership appeared to be increasing. Although not all the original complaints could be substantiated by the Commission, which had already experienced its own difficulties in obtaining information from the trustees, it had some concerns about the day-to-day administration of the charity. After liaison with the trustees, the Commission satisfied itself with regard to up-to-date accounts, minutes of meetings and the fact that trustees had been validly appointed. It provided guidance to the charity as to how it might be more effectively managed in future, gave advice as to how membership records should be kept, and suggested that the charity might benefit from the involvement of other people with relevant skills.

With continued concerns about the reasons for the fall in membership fee income, the Commission undertook further investigation. The investigation found that four membership lists were held by different people, resulting in discrepancies in the numbers of members recorded and the identities of these people. It concluded that over a number of years, 'the quality of record keeping relating to maintenance of the charity's membership list and associated matters had declined to the extent that, by early 2003, there were serious inadequacies'. It stated that 'poor admin-istrative procedures generally, and in particular its inadequate membership records' had led to a number of problems, and found that the record-keeping with regard to the subscriptions, donations and other income was also deficient (though, it found no evidence to support allegations of misappropriation of funds in relation to the apparent decline in membership income).

Members who failed to renew their memberships were not deleted from the membership or mailing lists; standing orders were not updated by members to reflect membership fee increases; unpaid subscriptions were overlooked; and incorrect membership fees were being paid by some members. Other discoveries included a number of unbanked cheques made payable to the charity, dating back several years.

Immediately prior to the investigation, a new board of trustees was formed which cooperated fully with the Commission. It identified and began to rectify a range of administration problems. The Commission acknowledged the positive changes within its formal report, and offered further support in the future. One of the consequences of the new approach has been the compilation of a central up-to-date membership database, ensuring that subscriptions are handled correctly in future. Improved administrative procedures have also been reported to the Commission, and these will enable the charity to evaluate better its ongoing membership management.

Source:
Compiled from the results of an inquiry by the Charity Commission, under section 8 of the Charities Act 1993
www.charity-commission.gov.uk/investigations/inquiryreports/arachnoid.asp (13 January 2004)

Evaluating performance

Although financial statements give a good indication of the financial health of a membership scheme, they are limited in the information they provide. Other mechanisms are required to give an organisation a clear understanding of how well the scheme is performing.

Why evaluate?

The purpose of evaluating a membership scheme is to establish the extent to which it is achieving its objectives, and to identify the factors that have led to its successes and failures. Assuming that SMART objectives have been established at the outset (see Chapter 3), those who manage a scheme will have clear expectations as to what it should achieve and it is these expectations against which success should be judged.

Measurement dimensions

The objectives of a membership scheme create the framework within which evaluation must take place, and within this framework, four specific dimensions should be measured.

Member experience

An important part of the evaluation process relates to members' experience of the scheme. The figures might suggest that a membership scheme is performing satisfactorily because it is not losing any members, but the figures may conceal an underlying dissatisfaction with key issues. Feedback from members therefore forms a vital part of the evaluation process, and a regular and rigorous process for gathering qualitative and quantitative research should be established. Questionnaires, focus groups and telephone interviews can all be valuable processes for gathering the views of members, which should inform the development of the membership scheme, and in particular the benefits it offers and the price levels of the different tiers (see also Chapter 3).

Financial outcomes

Given that many membership schemes are created with a view to generating revenues for an organisation, the measurement of the financial outcomes is vital. In the absence of such measurement there is no way of knowing how much money a scheme is contributing to the organisation's operations, if any. Sadly it is not unknown for schemes to be regularly making a loss without anyone being aware of this – either because proper account is not taken of the true costs of providing the benefits, or because the income derived is insufficient to pay for the benefits, even if they have been correctly valued. Four key financial measures that indicate the health, or otherwise of a scheme include:

1 Revenues from membership fees, broken down by tiers of the scheme
2 Revenues from the trading activities of members of the scheme
3 Donations by members of the scheme
4 Direct costs of running the scheme (staff, marketing, events etc.).

Such financial measures are valuable in aggregate on an annual basis, as they can be used to assess the scheme's performance against its budgets (see Financial management, above). However, financial measures can also be used to assess the average contribution made by individual members over the lifetime of their membership. This is often an argument put forward for using telemarketing to recruit new members (see Chapter 4). Whilst the cost of recruiting each new member may not be covered by the membership fee in any given year, the lifetime value of that member is likely to more than pay back the investment in their recruitment. A range of individual financial measures, broken down by tier, might include:

- average annual revenue per member
- average lifetime value per member
- average cost of servicing each member
- average hours volunteered per member (where applicable).

Whilst a scheme will also incur overheads, these may not always be relevant in measuring the financial health of a scheme. For example, the overheads of integrated membership schemes will be subsumed into the general overhead of the organisation, and it can be difficult to allocate overheads accurately to the scheme. Usually an arbitrary view is taken by over-worked financial managers, purely to help give an idea of its real-world cost. Only when a scheme is a totally independent and all overheads are attributable to it will such indirect costs be an essential part of the financial evaluation process.

External impact

This can be the most difficult to evaluate, but will be the most relevant for pressure groups and other schemes which exist with the objective of influencing the policies of others, especially governments and governmental bodies. Aside from using measurement techniques such as qualitative and quantitative research, the impact of advocacy work can be measured in a number of ways. For example, the number of 'column inches' and the breadth of media in which an organisation is able to secure editorial coverage are helpful measures, if media coverage is an objective. Equally, for a campaigning organisation, concrete results such as changes in legislation can also be evident.

Marketing effectiveness

The effectiveness of a scheme's marketing can be measured along a range of dimensions, but these should almost always include:

- number of existing members
- number of new members
- size of total membership relative to the size of the total customer base (for schemes which are affiliated to organisations which also serve non-member customers)
- retention rates of members
- proportion of members who move up or down between tiers
- advance subscriptions paid
- average length of membership in years and months
- average lifetime value

- response rates to renewal communications
- speed of response to renewal communications
- response rates to promotional materials.

All of these can be further explored by categories such as membership tier, market segment, time period or geographic area.

The process of evaluation can lead to a range of conclusions, both positive and negative, and should contribute to a regular review of the scheme (see Chapter 6). For example, it may be found that a scheme is financially unsound, that the benefits offered to members do not match their expectations or that the marketing is failing to reach its target audience. Alternatively, the evaluation may conclude that a scheme encourages loyal behaviour and its marketing is persuasive and effective. Conclusions such as these should lead to a series of recommendations, and subsequently actions. For example, the structure of the scheme may need to be fundamentally re-thought (see Chapter 6), the benefits offered to members may need to be re-packaged within different tiers (see Chapter 3) or the administrative support dedicated to the scheme may need to be increased.

Ambassadors Theatre Group

An integrated Friends scheme at the New Victoria Theatre, Woking, was established not only as a fundraising mechanism, but also to foster loyalty, audience development, ticket sales and customer feedback. The scheme offers benefits such as discounts on tickets, drinks and merchandise, priority booking, invitations to special events, ticket exchange facilities and a copy of Ambassador magazine, produced by its parent company Ambassador Theatre Group (ATG). The scheme has a tiered structure that includes single, joint and family categories, a discounted category for student or senior Friends, and opportunities for higher levels of involvement. For example Gold Patrons are acknowledged in programmes and on a supporters board, have a brass name plate on a chosen seat in the auditorium, and are invited to VIP corporate events.

Members are recruited at the point of sale, through the box office. Recent recruitment drives have focused on the promotion of the higher levels of the scheme, which have succeeded in making the 'Silver Friend' category more popular than the basic level of membership. This entitles members to enhanced discounts, ticket exchange facilities, invitations to first night cast parties and social events, preferential rates at other ATG venues and access to backstage tours. The scheme also enjoys a high level of continuity with 84% currently opting to renew their membership. This rate is highest amongst those using direct debit as their payment method, a facility which has been introduced within the last five years.

The present scheme, now three years old, (which itself replaced a scheme launched 11 years ago when the venue opened) is currently being relaunched with new print following extensive research. Regular evaluation of the scheme is implemented by the organisation, monitoring membership levels and income on a monthly basis against budget targets and records from the previous year and considering the associated expenditure required by the scheme. In addition questionnaires are regularly distributed to assess levels of customer satisfaction, and ticketing patterns are tracked to identify levels of frequency, artform crossover, ticketing spend and the comparative value of the Friends scheme in this respect. Recent research indicated satisfaction with existing benefits, notably the ticket discounts, and suggested that membership rates could be increased without meeting pricing resistance. As a result the organisation plans to encourage members to increase their commitment by joining the higher level tiers of the scheme.

Source: Information from Pat Westwell, Group Head of Marketing, Ambassador Theatre Group (December 2003)

Summary

Keeping a membership scheme running smoothly requires attention to a range of day-to-day issues. Communication is key to this. Information must be disseminated to members, and feedback gathered from them; and people must be invited to join the scheme and to renew their memberships. Systems must be in place to manage the membership database, to manage the revenue streams that are generated through the scheme, and to account for its finances. In order to keep track of ongoing achievements, procedures for evaluating the scheme should also be in place.

1 Tomlinson, R. (2000) *Data Protection: A Guide to the Data Protection Acts and their Implications for Managers in the Arts and Entertainment Industry*, Arts Marketing Association

2 The registration process is known as 'notification' and full details can be found at www.informationcommissioner.gov.uk.

3 *Notifications Exemptions – A Self Assessment Guide* (2001) Information Commissioner's Office, April

4 Christopher, M., Payne, A. and Ballantyne, D. (1991) *Relationship Marketing*, Butterworth Heinemann, p21

5 Jordan, G., Maloney, W. A. and McLaughlin, A.M. (1994) 'Interest Groups: a marketing perspective on membership', conference proceedings, Political Studies Association, pp545–559

6 Christopher, M. (2002) 'Building Customer Loyalty – You Know it Makes Sense!', *Journal of Arts Marketing*, Issue 04, January

7 www.directdebit.co.uk – 5 January 2004 – for full details of direct debit

8 Morgan, G.G. (2002) *The Charity Treasurer's Handbook An introduction to voluntary sector finance and accounting*, The Directory of Social Change

9 A number of excellent free advice packs, including one on developing budgets, are available to download at www.funderfinder.org.uk/advice_pack.php

10 Reza, M. (2003) 'Financial Statements: What, Why and How', *ArtsProfessional*, issue 64, December 15

11 Sayer, K. (2003) *Practical Guide to Charity Accounting*, The Directory of Social Change

12 Reza, M. (2002) 'Preventing Fraud – A Question of Control', *ArtsProfessional*, issue 34, September 23

6 WHEN A SCHEME NEEDS TO CHANGE

Membership schemes operate in a dynamic environment influenced by internal change within affiliated organisations as well as wider changes in the external environment. Furthermore, members themselves exert considerable influence over the nature and character of a scheme. Consequently, even the best schemes should be reviewed from time to time, to ensure that they are continuing to fulfil their purpose as effectively and efficiently as possible. A range of problems may emerge if an organisation needs to change as a result of a review. Strategies for managing such change are also discussed in this chapter.

Changes in the internal organisational environment relating to a scheme, coupled with changes in the external environment relating to a wider constituency, mean that however well a membership scheme has been set up, it will need to adapt to new demands and situations. Rather than waiting for problems to arise, it is preferable to conduct periodic reviews of the scheme. These will flag up any major issues before they turn into problems.

Reviewing a scheme

A straightforward review can be based around what is commonly known as a 'SWOT analysis'. This is an approach to problem solving which starts with an assessment of the **O**pportunities and **T**hreats posed by an organisation's internal and external environment, and then considers the organisation's **S**trengths or **W**eaknesses that will influence its ability to benefit from that changing environment.

SWOT analysis

Opportunities: what is happening within the organisation or in the wider environment that has the potential to enhance the role of the membership scheme?

Threats: what is happening within the organisation or in the wider environment that has the potential to undermine the membership scheme?

And…

Strengths: what are the strengths of the scheme that will enable it to take advantage of any opportunities and deal with any threats?

Weaknesses: what are the weaknesses of the scheme that will hinder any attempts to take advantage of opportunities and deal with any threats?

Identifying opportunities and threats

The external environment

Changes in the external environment are defined as those over which an organisation has very little, if any, control. Certain types of change have the potential to create major opportunities and threats for membership schemes, and others will simply mean that those who run these schemes will have to change the way they do things in response to those external forces.

Legislative change

New laws may mean that the structure, administration and activities of a membership scheme have to be changed to meet new constraints or to take advantage of new opportunities. For example, the tightening of Data Protection legislation in recent years may require those who run independent membership schemes to work more closely with their affiliated organisations if they are to benefit from the data held by those organisations about potential members. Changes in child protection legislation may mean that police checks have to be conducted even for volunteers who have worked with children for many years. Changes in constitutional law can mean that the legal framework under which a membership scheme operates becomes less effective and a new legal status, and its consequential form of governance, is required for the organisation.

Community Amateur Sports Clubs

In April 2002 the Inland Revenue introduced tax concessions for community amateur sports clubs. The major benefits are that all interest income and capital gains are exempt from corporation tax; property and fundraising income is exempt from corporation tax; individuals can claim gift aid and inheritance tax relief in respect of donations to a club; and clubs can reclaim income tax on contributions received under gift aid. However, nearly 12 months after the tax concessions were introduced, research suggested that few eligible clubs were exploiting this opportunity. Of those that were, nearly 20% were cricket clubs.

Sources:
'Sport Clubs Missing Out' (25 March 2003) at www.footballfinance.co.uk/press/casc.asp (15 January 2004)

Changes in taxation

As explained in earlier chapters, the tax treatment of membership schemes is very complex, and depends on the activities pursued under the auspices of the scheme and the extent to which the scheme is integrated with an affiliated organisation. Even minor changes in the tax rules can influence the advisability of, for example, being registered for VAT or being registered as a charity. The relatively recent changes in tax rules for personal donations (see Gift aid, Chapter 3) has incentivised charitable organisations to pursue this form of individual fundraising far more vigorously than in the past.

VAT and London Zoo

Little did The Zoological Society of London (London Zoo) realise, when it went to the European Court of Justice for a ruling on why it was having to charge VAT on its admissions, that it was about to gain a landmark judgment that could change the entire VAT regime for charities in the cultural sector across the UK. Having lost its case, HMCE issued new guidance to cultural organisations, explaining how in many cases, admission charges would in future be treated as exempt from VAT, potentially saving millions of pounds a year for customers of those organisations. This has important implications for VAT-registered organisations running membership schemes that incorporate admission to cultural facilities as part of their membership fee. The admission element of the fee may well become exempt in future, resulting in a lower charge (or higher net membership income to the organisation).

Sources:
Various news reports and documents from leading accountancy practices
HMCE Notice 701/47 Culture: www.hmce.gov.uk/forms/notices/701-47.htm (19 January 2004)
HMCE Business Brief number 28/2003: www.hmce.gov.uk/news/bb2803.pdf (19 January 2004)

Changes in the funding environment

Many membership bodies are affiliated to organisations that receive public funding, whether directly from the government, from a non-governmental public body, from a local authority or another charity or trust. Changes in funding policy can have major repercussions for membership schemes. For example, should such funding suddenly cease, then a membership scheme may be placed under a lot of pressure from any affiliated organisation to generate substantial revenues in order to help make good any shortfall. This may conflict with the objectives of a scheme, which may exist primarily for other purposes. Similarly, a government grant may be offered on condition that an organisation generates matching funding. The organisation may wish to use the revenues generated through the membership scheme as part of this matching funding, though the members themselves may prefer the cash to be used for other purposes.

National Maritime Museum

A typical 'public members scheme' (see Chapter 1), the Friends of the National Maritime Museum (NMM) is administered from an office in the Museum and operates as a charitable organisation quite separate from the formal Museum structure. Since the scheme's launch 21 years ago, the Friends have raised £1.4 million. In Spring 2000 there were approximately 4,500 friends, and a new paid Director was recruited to expand and rejuvenate the Friends. She joined a part-time paid Membership Secretary, a part-time Treasurer working on a contract basis and a team of volunteers. A full-time Events Officer joined in 2002.

Since 2000, there has been a significant decline in membership, resulting from two problems – the implementation of a government initiative from 1999–2001 to permit free admission at national museums, and an ageing membership base. As in other similar organisations, the NMM membership package had been built around free admission and a bundle of other benefits such as private views, a Friends room, an annual publication, Friends events, discounts in shops and cafés, free parking and reciprocal free admission at other maritime museums worldwide. The scheme had to be repackaged, as its major financial benefit was rendered instantly redundant.

The Director had anticipated that free admission may have an effect on the organisation, following research conducted in 2000 to evaluate members' motivations, behaviour and attitudes to giving. Members were asked whether a free admission to the public would stop them renewing their membership; 7% said it would – a group which included people who were more likely to be from Greater London and to visit frequently. The problem of an ageing membership base was also highlighted through the research, which reported that 41% of members were 65 years or over.

In response to the challenges that faced the Friends, a new leaflet was launched, enhancing the offering and carefully promoting privileges to major paying special exhibitions, events and access to curators and conservators behind the scenes. Images on the leaflet were chosen to appeal to a diverse audience and to promote the Friends as an inclusive organisation. Gift membership was also promoted. At the same time membership fees were raised in an attempt to sustain income levels: joint membership increased from £28 to £40, single from £22 to £28, concessionary from £18 to £22 and life membership doubled in price too.

Despite a drop in membership having been anticipated, the actual decline in membership was greater than feared. It gathered momentum during 2003, resulting cumulatively in a loss of about 1,400 members, an erosion of about a third of the original membership base. Several features characterised this loss of members:

- There was a time-lag between the start of free admission and non-renewals or membership, as people became aware of the new free entry policy.
- An estimated 5% of the decline was attributed to death of Friends due to the ageing membership base.
- A more subtle change was the down-grading by senior citizens from joint or family to single membership In the past grandparents had held family memberships to enable them to bring their grandchildren. They still wished to receive publications, but due to free admission now only needed single membership to receive this benefit.

However, families and joint members seemed to renew their membership, and anecdotal evidence suggested that they were high-earning local people who saw their membership as a method of supporting the Museum.

What does the future hold for the Friends? Integration into the Museum has become a possibility due to changes in tax structures, and the potential strategic value of Friends has been recognised; however the financial benefits of alignment are still to be calculated. If this were to occur, a fundamental shift in the way the Friends and staff involved in fundraising, corporate development and events operate will be required in order to recognise each other's strengths and resources and to maximise the potential of these. Free admission for members to future exhibitions could be a lever for reversing the decline in members, and a move towards the implementation of new methods of payment, for example direct debit, should help to retain existing members.

Case study prepared by Alix Slater, Senior Lecturer, University of Greenwich, and Polly Larner, Director, Friends, National Maritime Museum.

A growing or declining market

Some membership organisations are subject to steadily growing (or declining) demand as external factors make the benefits they offer attractive to a wider (or narrower) group of people. For example, some medical membership charities experience considerable growth in the size of their markets as the incidence of the disease they are attempting to combat rises.

Gingerbread

Since Gingerbread's formation in 1970, the divorce rate in Britain has trebled, and now one in four UK families is headed by a lone parent. In line with these changes, Gingerbread, the leading support organisation for lone parent families, has quadrupled its staff team, set up 10 regional offices, and now hosts 190 local support groups.

Source: www.ncvo-vol.org.uk (15 January 2004)

The growth of a potential membership base can create enviable opportunities for schemes to extend their reach, but it can also generate significant pressures. When the market grows, a scheme may be under-resourced to deal with higher levels of demand, and it may have to re-think the benefits it offers if those being delivered would be unsustainable on a much larger scale. A complete re-assessment of the structure and functions of a scheme may be called for under these circumstances. Similarly, if issues arising in the wider environment are the root cause of a decline in membership, then the long-term role of the scheme must be brought into question.

The Barmy Army

The Barmy Army is a group of dedicated cricket fans that follow the England team around the world giving highly vocal and visual support. The group aims to 'make watching cricket more fun and much more popular'. Dubbed 'The Barmy Army' by the Australian media during the Ashes series in 1994–95, the group began a merchandising business and became a registered company in 1995. Until now, a different 'Barmy Army' is created at each game, comprising those able to attend each match; but the organisation is now working to establish a more formal membership scheme, including a loyalty card system.

Source: www.cricket.org (12 December 2003)

New competitors

Some membership organisations are fortunate to have few competitors, as no other organisation is able to deliver the type of benefits that they do or the market is so small as to deter others from attempting to compete. Many, however, do face competition in the form of other membership schemes offering broadly similar benefits. From time to time new competitors may emerge, with the effect of de-stabilising an existing scheme. In very unfortunate cases, this may occur with an organisation purporting to support the same cause or organisation as an existing scheme (see Wimbledon Football Club, below). Under such circumstances, the challenge facing a scheme is to distinguish itself sufficiently from its competitors, so that potential members do not join the wrong one through confusion, or do not view themselves as having to choose between two similar offerings, but believe that a particular scheme offers them uniquely special benefits that simply can't be matched elsewhere.

The internal environment

Changes in the internal environment are defined as those which arise specifically in relation to an organisation and over which it has an element of control. Such changes tend to arise with less prior warning that those in the external environment, and can have a de-stabilising effect on a scheme.

Changing needs of the affiliated organisation

As organisations grow, their membership schemes should grow with them, and grow in the same direction as them. For example, an organisation may change some of its underlying policies because of significant changes in its external environment, or in response to the perceived needs of its major stakeholders (for example, if the criteria under which public funding will be granted changes; or if customers or donors are deserting the organisation). A powerful and influential membership body should undoubtedly be consulted before any radical decisions are taken, and it is always to be hoped that good communication between the organisation and its members (see Chapter 5) will dissipate any problems associated with such change.

Gordon Craig Theatre

Some years ago, the Gordon Craig Theatre was both owned and managed by Stevenage Borough Council (the Council still owns the building, but it is now run by a non-profit distributing company, Stevenage Leisure Limited). Its Arts and Entertainments Manager was concerned about the need for a larger, more loyal audience for drama and formed a steering group to set up a friends scheme in order to achieve this aim. When it came to structuring the scheme there was a problem. The local authority was both owner and operator of the venue and there-fore any membership fees and donations raised through the scheme would have to be paid directly to the authority, with no firm guarantees as to whether any of this money would find its way back to the Theatre. That was an internal headache, but there was also a very real issue externally. How many individuals and businesses would be happy to use their spare cash to make discretionary payments to the Council, as well as having to pay their business rates and council tax bills?

The obvious solution at the time was to set up an external friends group as an unin-corporated association which could be both self-governing and beneficial to both parties. Thus the Theatre Club was born, appealing to keen theatre-goers who were attracted not only by a desire to support the Theatre, but also to make use of promised ticket discounts and attend frequent social events.

In the early years, the arrangement worked well for both the Theatre and the Friends. Managers from the Theatre would attend the Friends' meetings to report on the latest activities of the Theatre, and in particular, the forthcoming artistic programme. The association members were offered a range of ticket discounts and invitations to the 'first night' post-show parties with the Theatre performers. The Theatre and the Friends split the income derived from membership fees. The Theatre managed the administration of the Club through its box office and marketing database system, and the club banked the cheques and accounted for the money.

However, in the late 1990s, Stevenage Leisure took over the running of the Theatre, and the few minor aggravations between Theatre and association started to esca-late. In the view of the Theatre, the Club, which by now had grown to around 1,700 members, had become more limited in its appeal. It had turned into a more general theatregoers' club that organised trips and events at multiple venues – including one of the Gordon Craig's primary competitors, the Milton Keynes Theatre. Membership enquiries were directed to the Friends secretary, rather than to the Theatre itself, but the Theatre still provided costly benefits such as ticket discounts and parties for a seemingly well-heeled minority of its customers. The lack of formal representation by the Theatre on the Club's committee, whilst not a hindrance in the early days of mutual cooperation, had, in the eyes of the Theatre undermined the relationship between them. The Friends, however, perceived the Club to be committed to supporting the Gordon Craig Theatre and did not see itself as profiting from the arrangements. Half their membership income was donated to the Theatre, for example the Friends helped to fund the decorating of the green room.

The management finally admitted that the Club might have run its course following an incident relating to the artistic programme. One manager reported:

'I went to a meeting to announce the forthcoming season to the committee. When I announced that *The Vagina Monologues* would be performed in October, the committee went quiet. They refused to organise a first night party or even speak the play's title! Finally, one of the members said: "Despite the fact I've had one for the past 53 years, I have never felt it necessary to discuss it in public!"'

Sources:
Information from a senior manager and the membership secretary for the Gordon Craig Theatre (December 2003 and January 2004)

However, if members are not considered by the organisation to be important stakeholders, or if the policies in question are so fundamental to the well-being of the organisation that not to change would seriously undermine its work, then managers may choose to change direction regardless of the views of members. This effectively casts members adrift. Some will remain as members, some will inevitably leave, but others will attempt to apply pressure to the organisation to reverse its decisions. Major donors may threaten to withdraw their financial support; splinter membership groups may set up in competition to the main membership scheme; members may lobby the governing body to vote against the proposals if they disapprove; and if they have voting rights over the activities of the organisation members may call a special general meeting to overturn the decision, or to bring a vote of no confidence in those running the organisation. Such conflict can be hugely detrimental to both the organisation and the membership scheme. Time, effort and money spent in negotiation with disenfranchised members is invariably worthwhile, though it is by no means certain that a peaceful, mutually beneficial solution is achievable in the short term.

Wimbledon Football Club

In 1995 the Wimbledon Independent Supporters Association (WISA) was formed by a small group of enthusiastic Wimbledon Football Club supporters, who viewed the Wimbledon FC Official Supporters Club as being too tied in with the Club to campaign for the interests of the majority of its supporters. Over the years, member-ship of the group grew and as more pressure was placed on the founding members to run the Association, they realised that there were simply too few of them to carry the workload. At that point, five years after setting up, the group decided to adopt official status by creating a constitution and set up a formal committee.

When Wimbledon Football Club subsequently announced that it was planning to move from its South London base and relocate to Milton Keynes, some 70 miles away, WISA members were united in their opposition to the move and mounted an ener-getic campaign to resist it. By lobbying the Club, the relevant local authorities, the media, and the government, WISA quickly earned respect throughout the footballing community, but nonetheless its views went unheeded. So when the Football Association Commission finally gave permission for the proposed relocation to go ahead, WISA immediately set about creating a replacement football club to enable the history and identity of the Club to live on in Wimbledon itself. AFC Wimbledon was born.

Despite playing in an amateur league six divisions below former FA Cup winners Wimbledon FC, AFC Wimbledon sold more season tickets in its first season, and more than 1,000 fans had to be turned away from the Club's first home game as the gates were closed on a capacity crowd of over 4,000. Barely 12 months later administrators were appointed to work with Wimbledon FC's management to produce a viable solution for the survival of their Club, which was facing a deep financial crisis.

Sources:
Cozens, C. (2002) Wonderbra man gives Wimbledon extra support, the *Guardian*, August 22, www.guardian.co.uk (2 November 2003)
www.wisa.org.uk (2 November 2003)
www.wimbledon-fc.co.uk (2 November 2003)

Changing needs of members

Sometimes it is the needs of members that change rather than the needs of the organisation. The benefits provided by a scheme may become less relevant over time, as society changes and individuals find different ways of meeting their needs. A key indicator that this is occurring will be the dwindling of support for a membership scheme. For example, the number of people who belong to a trades union[1] in the UK peaked in 1979, but has declined consistently ever since. The decline coincides with a period during which continual changes in employment law have required employers to adopt more employee-friendly policies, rendering a traditional role of the trades union – defending workers' rights in the face of powerful organisations – less relevant for many. Under such circumstances, serious questions have to be asked as to whether the objectives of a membership scheme are still relevant; whether the provision of new and different benefits will revive the role of the scheme; or whether the scheme has outlived its useful purpose and should be closed altogether. The latter is likely to be extremely controversial, as members who remain in a scheme long after others have deserted it are probably those who value it the most and are most reluctant to let it go.

Independent schemes that close under such circumstances may find that other schemes spring up in their wake, possibly with a less formal organisation structure than existed previously. When integrated schemes close, there may be backlash from the die-hard members who may, as explained above, attempt to apply considerable pressure to the organisation to retain the scheme and continue to offer benefits to members. However, given that there will be little support for such a move beyond the remaining members themselves, the influence of this group is likely to be limited.

The Royal British Legion

The Royal British Legion provides financial, social and emotional support to those who have served and are currently serving in the armed forces, and their dependants. The Legion was founded in 1921 as a voice for the ex-service community, and is now one of the country's largest membership organisations, with over 550,000 members in the UK and around 13,000 members overseas. The organisation operates a network of clubs and branches across the country and provides opportunities to become involved in its welfare and fundraising work. The Women's Section of the Royal British Legion has around 72,000 members and a network of 1,400 branches.

In 1999–2000 membership levels fell by 3% and the charity reported that 'branches and counties are having difficulty in finding [voluntary] officers to manage their activities'. Facing an ageing and gradually declining membership in 2000, the Legion began a process of change including a strategic review and a working party to consider a more appropriate corporate governance structure. It also started work on a new plain English Royal Charter, in order to facilitate the interpretation of the organisation's rules and speed its decision-making processes. A membership review was carried out from February to August 2002. Over 519,000 questionnaires were sent to members, and attracted a 32.1% response rate. A further 435 members sent letters and suggestions, and over 1,423 took part in 69 focus groups held around the UK.

The findings were used to inform an action plan, 'Taking the Legion Forward' (TLF), to reinvigorate the Legion. A special newsletter was produced and incorporated in *Legion* magazine, informing members of the reasons for change, the findings of the review and the progress of its implementation. It stated: 'The action plan is not a "top down" exercise. The goals and actions that will enable us to become a thriving model charity are based on the responses and ideas that you and other interested parties have given us. Over the next 18 months or so, you will be hearing much more about it. And, you'll have the opportunity to comment and contribute'.

Twelve core recommendations were derived from the review process:

- Redefine the purpose of Royal British Legion membership.
- Make membership more inclusive to all sections of the community by combining the 'Ordinary' and 'Associate' categories of membership into a new category of Member.
- Create a new focus for membership (and its support to the charity) at county level, encouraging greater flexibility in how the structure and activities are coordinated within each county.
- Create a new positive image for Legion membership, with maximum publicity at national and local levels.

- Make membership more attractive by introducing new activities and creating new 'membership value'.
- Transform Legion clubs into attractive social centres, creating an integral role for them in the new membership organisation.
- Give members closer involvement in the policies and development of their own organisation.
- Transform *Legion* magazine into a high quality, informative and enjoyable journal that is attractive to a broad spectrum of ages.
- Ensure that the membership is self-supporting financially and that members have full, regular, transparent information on all aspects of membership finances.
- Introduce simpler and more cost-effective recruitment, records and membership administrative procedures – with a high priority on quality and efficiency in handling first-time applications.
- Attract more members from the service and ex-service communities.
- Develop stronger links with all other ex-service membership organisations – reinforcing the Legion as the leading ex-service charity.

2003 was described as the organisation's 'Year of Transition', enabling the Legion both to conform to best practice models for large charities and to revitalise its membership.

The amalgamation of the Ordinary and Associate membership categories into a single level, removing the distinction between those who have served in the armed forces and those who have not; aims to send out a powerful new signal to younger potential members and to enable the Legion to create a new image of being an attractive and relevant organisation – and one which is open to everyone to join. However this move has proved highly controversial. The recommendation was proposed as a Charter Motion at the 2003 Conference of the Legion and arguments for and against the motion were reported in the fourth TLF newsletter. One member, said: 'As far as I know, none of the Trustees of the RSPB have got feathers and lay eggs! These are successful charities being run by people who believe in the aims of the charity, the majority of them not being in a position to benefit from the charity'. And another observed 'The new class of member has the potential to turn the Legion from a membership organisation for the support of the ex-service community into an organisation for the membership'. Although the vote revealed majority support for the change, a two-thirds majority was required to carry the motion and this was not achieved. The topic will continue to be debated within the Legion and formally reconsidered at Conference in 2004.

Sources:
www.britishlegion.org.uk (15 December 2003)
The Major Charities, An Independent Guide
TLF Newsletter 1, *Legion*, March/April 2003 p1 and p8
TLF Newsletter 4, *Legion*, September/October 2003 p2

Dwindling organisational support

This is most likely to arise when a scheme fails to achieve its objectives, or is viewed by an affiliated organisation as being ineffective at doing so. Sometimes it may arise due to a breakdown of communications between those who run a scheme and those who run the organisation with which it is associated. A change of management (within the scheme or the affiliated organisation) can also lead to a reduction in the support given by an organisation to a scheme, if someone who is less committed to the scheme is given responsibility for its management or coordination. Historically, membership schemes have tended to be founded by passionate pioneers and when these 'champions' move on, lose interest, or in some cases 'die in the saddle', the scheme may start to go into decline. Whilst the immediate catalyst for change might appear to be the 'change at the top', it is more likely that the scheme is no longer focused on the current needs of either members or the affiliate organisation, hence the dwindling membership.

There are a number of ways in which an affiliated organisation may withdraw its support. It may reduce the staff time and money it invests in running the scheme; it may limit the facilities, including premises and databases, that are made available for the running of a scheme; or more damaging still, it may reduce the range or withdraw the privileges it provides as benefits to members of the scheme. Without such benefits the scheme may have little to offer its members and its very existence can be threatened.

Derby Playhouse

The friends scheme at Derby Playhouse was disbanded following consultation with the group in 2002. Derby Playhouse itself originally developed as a professional producing theatre from an amateur group. The friends of the theatre emerged as part of this process, undergoing a series of incremental changes as the original amateur base of the organisation shifted towards increasing professionalism. At various times members of the friends had participated in the work of the organisation, not only as volunteer stewards but also as actors, board members and advocates.

In recent times, although fully integrated with the Playhouse, the friends scheme lacked a coherent structure and appeared to operate more in the manner of a social club group. Members enjoyed ticket discounts, social events, trips to other theatres and a newsletter, produced by Derby Playhouse itself, in return for an annual fee of £12 (at the time of closure). Although ostensibly part of the theatre and keen to support its work, the small friends group was highly vocal and largely autonomous, required labour-intensive support from the theatre which nevertheless was unable to realise the fundraising potential of maintaining such a group. It was ultimately decided to discontinue the scheme.

Source: Interview with Geoff Sweeney, Derby Playhouse (15 December 2003)

Emergence of an elite or clique

As a membership organisation or scheme develops, those who are most passionate about its work tend to come to the fore and move into more prominent roles. In the case of independent schemes, these people are the ones who are most likely to put themselves forward for the positions on the organisation's governing body. In both independent and integrated schemes, they are likely to be the most visible at social occasions and the keenest to participate in the marketing of the scheme. If these people are broadly representative of the wider membership and potential membership, this is normally no bad thing. A corps of committed individuals upon whose long-term loyalty the organisation can depend is often a very valuable asset. However, if this group of highly-motivated people starts to be viewed as a clique, or is considered to be taking decisions that are not in the wider interest of the whole membership, then the scheme can start to crumble. A dominant group of people at the centre of a scheme can create an air of exclusivity around it and deter others who may feel alienated by this. The scheme may be characterised by high levels of 'churn' as renewal rates fall (see Chapter 5).

Friends of Yorkshire Museums

A report on friends organisations for museums and galleries in Yorkshire revealed an ageing (75% retired) and two-thirds female membership. Only 1% of members reported themselves as having an ethnic minority background.

While 88% of respondents reported a cordial relationship with the affiliate organisation, at least 10% of the friends surveyed seemed less friendly. One museum officer said 'Friends groups can be helpful, but they can also be the tail wagging the dog ... you can end up with the friends groups dictating the priorities of service'.

Source: Edwards, C. (2002) 'Friends like these: a study of the contribution of friends and support organisations to Yorkshire's museums, archives and libraries', Resource, Yorkshire Museums Council and British Association of Friends of Museums, in Hill, L. *et al.* (2003) *Creative Arts Marketing*, 2nd Edition, Butterworth Heinemann

---

Identifying strengths and weaknesses

An evaluation of the strengths and weaknesses of a membership scheme is normally based on its achievements, especially its financial impact, the effectiveness of its marketing activities, the experiences of its members and/or its external impact (for a full discussion of evaluation, see Chapter 5). However, a scheme's strengths and weaknesses should always be evaluated in the context of the opportunities and threats that face it. To do otherwise would paint a false picture of the elements that are capable of leading it to (or preventing it from) achieving its objectives. For example, a scheme may deliver a wide range of benefits, and superficially this may be viewed as one of its key strengths. However, if an affiliate organisation is threatening to cut back its support for the scheme, or if the membership benefits are ceasing to be relevant to a sizeable proportion of the membership base, then that range of benefits may be a major weakness of the scheme.

Another dimension in which strengths and weaknesses can arise is through the managerial and administrative resource base of the scheme.

Administrative resources

If the size of a scheme's potential membership is growing rapidly, if existing members are becoming more demanding, if new benefits are offered to members, or if new tiers of membership are created, then a scheme's administrative resources may become inadequate to meet the demands placed upon them. For example, more staff may be required to manage the processing of membership applications and renewals; more sophisticated software may be required to manage the increasing complexity of a scheme; and larger or more permanent premises may be required to accommodate the increased levels of activity. Such demands may create potential weaknesses that can seriously undermine a scheme, and may require urgent attention.

Ludlow Assembly Rooms

The Friends and Supporters scheme at Ludlow Assembly Rooms was changed in November 2003 in order to take advantage of a new box office database, add new and higher levels of subscription, allow gift aid on subscriptions and to bring Friends' activity into VAT registration. The previous scheme, which had been in operation for 10 years, had over 500 members and brought in an annual income of around £2,000. Some doubts about the changes were expressed by existing Friends but this was overcome by effective consultation.

Information from Paul Whitehouse, Ludlow and District Community Association, (December 2003 and January 2004)

Managerial resources

As schemes grow, and the range of human and other resources under their control grows with them, then there is a much greater need for strong leadership. As well as being responsible for the strategic direction of an organisation, leaders play a vital role in unifying the membership and liaising with any affiliate organisation. Weaknesses in management can be catastrophic for both independent and integrated membership schemes. When leaders fail to represent the needs of members effectively, then informal cliques may spring up within the membership body and splinter membership groups may form, either as formally constituted or informal groups. Failure of leaders to recognise and respond to changes in the environment, and to guide the organisation strategically in an appropriate direction, can lead to a range of problems. Independent schemes may experience serious conflict with affiliate organisations, whose managers may become frustrated at the failure of scheme leaders to take advantage of clear opportunities that arise (potentially withdrawing their support if the problem is deemed sufficiently serious).

The Derngate Society

Derngate Theatre was a prestigious £10 million state-of-the-art theatre when it opened in 1983. Controversially in its day, the capital costs were underwritten by the local authority, and from the outset, an increasingly vociferous minority within the local community began to complain about the levels of public funding to support the Theatre's artistic programme – and in particular its international classical music series.

In response, the then management assembled a group of influential like-minded individuals from the local residential and business community to establish a group of supporters who shared the desire to ensure the concerts were adequately funded and attended. Known as The Derngate Society, and ultimately registered as a charity, the new friends association was entirely independent from the Theatre, with its own board of trustees, and a constitution which defined its legal and operating status. The Society continued to exist for more than a decade in this form. Whilst permitted to attend meetings as ex-officio committee members, Theatre managers had no other constitutional role and thus no formal right to influence the policy and activities of the Society. They were, nevertheless, expected to provide office and administrative facilities as well as ticket discounts and other benefits to the Society's membership.

Whilst the Derngate Society was originally set up for the specific purpose of advocacy, over time, the needs of the Theatre changed as did the needs of the members, many of whom had joined in subsequent years, often in search of benefits which had not been conceived at the Society's outset. Although the activities of the Society broadened over time in an attempt to meet the increasing demands of the membership, activities tended towards social gatherings such as 'meet-the-artist' suppers, raffles and lucky prize draws and visits to other theatres. A combination of factors including the lack of volunteers with either the technical skills or available time to develop and market those activities, meant that by the mid-1990s membership numbers had stagnated at between 400 and 500, representing less than 0.2% of the Theatre's annual audience.

Source: Former staff and members of The Derngate Society

Managers of integrated schemes may also lose the support of their own top management, which can be reflected in budget cuts for the operation of the scheme.

Choosing a way forward

Having assessed the influence of a changing environment on a scheme, and evaluated the scheme's strengths and weaknesses in that context, it is possible to determine an appropriate strategic direction for the scheme. When that direction has been agreed, then the role of the management becomes much clearer – to muster the appropriate resources to implement that strategy.

Strategies for change

There are five generic strategic directions that an organisation can pursue. Four of these directions will take schemes forward, though the fifth is an option for schemes that have come to the end of their useful purpose:

1 **Service provision:** sustain or enhance the value of the services and benefits provided to *existing members*, with a view to securing member loyalty and improving renewal rates.

2 **Service development:** deliver new services and benefits that will appeal to *existing members*, with a view to securing member loyalty and improving renewal rates.

3 **Membership development:** sustain or enhance the value of current services and benefits, and communicate these to potential *new members* with a view to expanding the size of the membership base.

4 **Diversification:** deliver new services and benefits that will appeal to potential *new members*, with a view to re-positioning the scheme in the eyes of these potential members.

5 **Dissolution:** disband the scheme as it no longer serves a useful purpose.

The choice of strategic direction will be informed by the outcome of a SWOT analysis. This analysis highlights the most pressing issues facing the organisation, and the strategic option chosen should address these issues. Clearly, the dissolution of a scheme is incompatible with the other directions, but there may be significant advantages to developing other strategies simultaneously if resources permit. For example, if the evaluation of a scheme reveals that members are unhappy with the benefits provided through certain tiers of that scheme, then a restructuring of those tiers may be required to retain their loyalty (a service provision strategy). However, this restructuring may also present an opportunity to attract new members, who previously felt that the scheme failed to offer value for money (a membership development strategy).

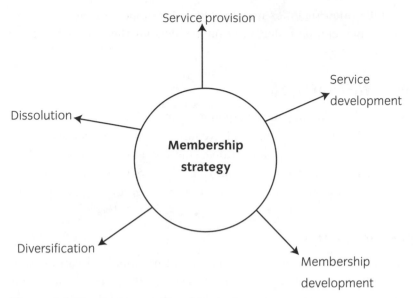

Figure 6.1 Developing membership strategy

Diversification and dissolution are both potential strategies when a scheme's circumstances change dramatically. They are the most radical of all the potential strategies, and are the most likely to be controversial amongst members and affiliate organisations alike. Both should be considered in the light of the aims and objectives of the whole scheme. If the scheme's objectives have become irrelevant (for example, if a particular cause for which an organisation is campaigning is resolved), then tough decisions have to be made as to whether there is any reason for the organisation to continue to function – and if there is, for what purpose and for whose benefit. Alternatively, if it becomes clear that the organisation is unable to sustain its services and benefits – for example, if an affiliate organisation ceases to exist or withdraws it support, then the future of the organisation looks equally bleak and will have to be re-considered.

Managing change

The process of changing a scheme can be a traumatic one. This can be true both for those involved in managing an organisation, whose role is to implement the change, and for members of an organisation, who will be affected by the change.

Types of change

Some types of change that arise in membership schemes are relatively unlikely to meet any serious resistance, and the process of change can be straightforward and uncontroversial. Small, incremental changes that are made either in reaction to circumstances as they arise, or as part of the ongoing management of a scheme can usually be implemented without either consultation or controversy. Members tend to recognise that those in charge have to take decisions, and that it would be unrealistic to expect the entire membership to be involved in minor issues. However, when any proposed change is strategic in nature, perhaps emerging from a review of the scheme or from an unexpected event that has major consequence for the scheme, then the process of change management should be handled much more deliberately and carefully.

For example, as a scheme grows it may become uneconomic to deliver certain benefits; yet proposals to withdraw benefits or make them more costly to acquire are often highly controversial. Such issues should be the subject of discussion with members before action is taken, so that the reasons for any change in benefits are clearly communicated and objections to the proposals can be taken into account.

Edinburgh International Book Festival

The Book Festival Friends at Edinburgh International Book Festival was relaunched in June 2003 in order to increase the financial viability and fundraising potential of this integrated scheme. In its previous incarnation the single-level structure offered discounts on tickets, in addition to advance information, events, a newsletter and priority booking in return for a £15 fee. The need for change emerged as the Festival expanded, essentially outgrowing the scheme. Furthermore, the financial implications of the benefits offered had not been adequately costed at the outset and the inclusion of ticket discounts made the membership fees ineligible for gift aid.

A survey of existing Friends, prior to the relaunch, found that the key motivations for joining were to obtain the benefits of advance information and priority booking, combined with the wish to support the Festival. As a result, the design of the new scheme focused on these factors and removed the element of discounted tickets. A new three-tier structure was established using a low entry level of £10 (£15 Joint), in order to offset any criticism over price rises in the scheme in general. This level primarily offers advance information without the facility for priority booking. A mid-level membership costs £25 (£40 Joint) and offers five additional days of priority booking and an invitation to the Festival reception. The highest level, priced at £75 (£115 Joint) provides an opportunity for more philanthropically motivated members and offers reserved seating for events and an invitation to the Director's Programme Preview reception, in addition to the benefits offered at the lower levels of the scheme. Although there was some resistance to the changes, particularly amongst longstanding members of the previous scheme who feared that the identity of the Festival and the Friends might be altered as the organisation increased in size, these reservations do not appear to have affected commitment to the organisation. Levels of renewal into the new structure have remained high.

Further evaluation of the new scheme is intended following a full year of operation and an increase in staffing. The scheme is currently managed by the organisation's Sponsorship and Development Manager, who also has other substantial responsibilities, and the appointment of a dedicated part-time coordinator is proposed in order to facilitate further development and research.

Sources:
Interview with Sophie Moxon, Sponsorship and Development Manager, Edinburgh International Book Festival (15 January 2004)
www.edbookfest.co.uk (15 January 2004)

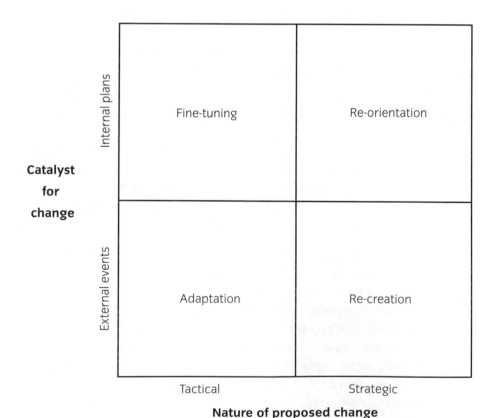

Figure 6.2 The process of change

Another situation in which change may well be resisted arises when an affiliate organisation decides to develop an integrated scheme 'in-house', and wishes to distance itself from the activities of an independent scheme. Members of the existing scheme may feel under-valued and resist the idea of joining the new scheme unless they can be convinced as to the advantages of pursuing this route.

A regional museum

A regional museum runs three concurrent schemes with different governing structures, each focused upon meeting different objectives.

The Friends of the museum is a society founded in the late 1960s. It is a registered charity with the aim of fostering a public interest in the museum and helping, through members' subscriptions, to acquire works of art and antiquity to enrich the collections. The self-contained charity is separate from the organisation and has control of its own funds and spending decisions. It is managed by a committee of volunteers and has a representative member of the staff at committee meetings. Benefits offered include a twice-yearly magazine, a programme of activities, invitations to private views and to go behind the scenes, and discounts at the museum café and shop. The greatest privilege of membership is described as 'to know that your subscription is helping to support a museum whose collection of art and antiquities are of international importance'. The scheme has a single-benefit package with a set fee structure for individuals, joint and lifetime membership, and some concessionary rates for over 60s, young people under 26, students and families. It has around 2,000 members.

The Young Friends of the museum was set up as an arm of the Friends society, but is managed by volunteers who are also staff of the museum. The Young Friends scheme was set up in recognition of the limited appeal of the main scheme, which, although it does offer educational activities and activities for young people in their teens and early twenties, attracts mainly an older group aged 50 years plus. In addition to the Friends' benefits, events are organised specifically for the Young Friends, and discounts are offered on events organised by the museum's education service. This scheme is focused on meeting audience development needs rather than fundraising objectives.

The museum also has a Patrons scheme, which is managed by paid staff with professional fundraising expertise. It offers an opportunity for philanthropy, rather than being benefit-led. There are two tiers, a top tier with a £500 membership fee and a lower tier at £150.

The Friends scheme was founded in an era when the organisation was well funded and any money it raised provided the 'icing on the cake' for the museum. However there is now a much greater need for the museum to generate more income to fund the wider core business of the museum. The current Friends scheme is benefit-driven and although the Friends are afforded great respect in return for their goodwill, their support does not contribute to the primary financial needs of the organisation, as funds are exclusively spent on supporting acquisitions.

There are plans to develop all fundraising activities in the next two years, as the current structures are not as efficient at meeting organisational objectives as the museum would like, not least because membership of each scheme is managed through separate databases and each scheme has a different structure of governance.

Source: This case study is based on an organisation that prefers to remain anonymous.

The problems of change

Whenever change is proposed, there are three potential problems that may have to be addressed: resistance to change, loss of control and a shift in the power base.

Resistance to change

Resistance to change is common among membership groups, not least because those who join membership schemes may do so because they have a particular interest in and affection for the work of the organisation. This commitment may lead them to hold strong views as to how the scheme should be best managed, and they may attempt to resist change if it does not fit in with their own perceptions as to the most appropriate route to take.

Resistance to change may emerge for a number of reasons:[2]

- **Personal views:** people may think that the current scheme is fine, or that proposals to change it will not work; and some may resist change simply because it was not their idea.
- **Habit and fear of the unknown:** it may be easier to keep things as they are, as change can mean upsetting a well-established routine. A sense of security may disappear.
- **Misunderstanding of the benefits:** the gains to be made by change may not be clear. Only the problems relating to the change itself may be apparent.
- **Disturbing existing relationships:** people may feel threatened and experience a sense of loss if current structures, benefits and relationships are changed. Some may fear a loss of status under a proposed new scenario.
- **No trust in change makers:** there may be no trust in the people who are making the change, perhaps because mistakes have been made in the past. Members may feel that there are hidden motives for the change.

- **Lack of involvement:** people may feel that they are not influencing the direction or outcomes of the change and that no one is listening to their views.
- **Too much work:** the amount of effort involved in the change may be daunting.

If the potential for resistance goes unrecognised, then conflict will almost inevitably arise. This may manifest itself as conflict between members of a scheme who may hold different views as to whether or how an organisation should change; it may be between the members and those responsible for the running the scheme; it may be between members of a scheme's governing body; or in the case of independent schemes, it may be between the management of the scheme and the management of the affiliate organisation. Consequently, the importance of anticipating and deflecting resistance should not be underestimated, as its repercussions can be significant.

Victoria & Albert Museum

The Friends of the V&A is a registered charity and a company limited by guarantee. It is an autonomous organisation governed by a self-appointed executive committee, which includes several key staff members. Membership is run by the Friends of the V&A and subscription payments are dealt with by the membership office. There are currently over 19,000 members.

The organisation's charitable objectives are to foster, assist and promote the charitable work and activities of the V&A, or of any other art gallery or museum (which is not conducted for private profit and to which the public have access as of right) selected by the Committee of Association.

In November 2000 the Museum launched a new Patrons Scheme (subsequently updated and refined in October 2003) for higher value individual supporters, providing tailored benefits to enable members to play an active part in the cultural and artistic life of the Museum. The Patrons Scheme aims to provide an alternative source of income to help fund major projects, as well as some of the core activities of the Museum such as acquisitions, research, education, conservation and exhibitions. Membership of the Patrons Scheme is managed by the Development Office and attracted 100 members in its first two years.

In May 2001 an Extraordinary General Meeting of the Friends was called to put forward a special resolution to amalgamate the Friends into the Museum. The meeting was inquorate but after considering the strong feeling of a group of Friends against the resolution the proposal was dropped. Although the Friends have since become more closely aligned with the Museum, they have maintained their autonomous status. The Friends now support the V&A branding and membership has been repositioned to membership of the 'Museum' rather than of the 'Friends'. There is now an agreement that the Friends are answerable to both the Museum management and the Friends Executive Committee. These changes have helped to reach a balance between the Friends' wishes as an autonomous organisation and the evolving aims and needs of the Museum.

The two concurrent membership schemes are structured and designed in such a way that they do not compete for members. The Friends support new acquisitions as well as some of the Museum's audience development and marketing needs, such as the Student Membership package. The scheme is loyalty-driven through the provision of benefits. The Patrons Scheme offers a higher level of involvement in return for a much higher contribution, and provides unrestricted income, serving the fundraising objectives of the Museum. A newly introduced 'ladder of affinity' has been developed to help upgrade and retain members at all levels.

Sources:
Information from Sarah Carthew, Flora Smith and Judy Ridley, Victoria and Albert Museum (January 2004)

Loss of control

Sometimes members, scheme managers or other stakeholders believe that as soon as the process of change begins, the promised benefits of that change will be realised. In reality, things may get worse before they get better.[3] Any change upsets an established system, the status quo is disturbed and control is often temporarily loosened. Instability may be introduced into a membership scheme, which might have been operating, albeit sub-optimally, on comfortable and well-established habits for many years. The process of managing the transition is a delicate one. It begins with the management of stakeholder expectations – ensuring that all parties to be affected are aware that the promised benefits of the change may take some while to be realised. In addition, adequate resources should be allocated to ensure that the depth and length of the dip in performance is not so great as to de-stabilise the entire scheme. If the disruption to the scheme is too great, or the benefits take too long to come through, then there is a risk that members will withdraw their support and the change process will fail to achieve its objectives.

Shift in the power base

It is important to understand the power base on which a membership scheme sits, as any major change can upset the political dynamics of a situation. Stakeholders who formerly held very little influence can become key to the change process, and those who were previously in positions of responsibility may lose their power base. It is important to identify those whose power base will shift, anticipate their likely reaction to the change, evaluate the extent to which their reaction could undermine the change and prepare contingency arrangements to deal with any adverse reactions.

Such reactions can take a range of forms. In the case of an independent membership scheme, opponents to change may seek to enhance their power base by garnering support from members to resist the change formally, even to the extent of persuading others to sign up to a call for a formal meeting through which they may attempt to prevent the change taking place. In extreme circumstances they may call for a vote of no confidence in those who are running the membership scheme, and attempt to replace them on the organisation's governing body. Disgruntled members of either an independent or integrated scheme may vote with their feet by setting up a new membership organisation with broadly similar aims to the original one, but which differs with respect to the change issue (see page 165 Wimbledon Football Club). They may withdraw their volunteer labour; they may lobby an affiliate organisation for support in resisting the change; and, if all else fails, they may resign from the scheme and persuade others to do the same.

To offset some of the negative reactions it is important to draw in the support of those who are in a position of power to support the change, and to use their support to influence others who may be more resistant. For example, if those who run independent membership schemes wish to introduce change that will clearly benefit an affiliate organisation, then it is important that the affiliate organisation communicates its support for the proposals to members. Similarly, if those who run integrated schemes wish to make changes to their scheme, then it is important that they discuss their proposals at an early stage with the most active representatives from amongst the membership. It is possible to deflect a lot of criticism by ensuring that these people are 'on side' and willing to be actively supportive before the wider membership is addressed, though this is often easier said than done. Supporters of change may be reluctant to come forward, particularly if the change being proposed is in any way controversial, and those supporters may themselves lose their own friends or supporters if they nail their colours to the mast.

Planning for change

Even when the strategic direction of a scheme has been agreed, the change process associated with this is likely to create problems; but as suggested above these can, to some extent, be avoided through careful planning. The purpose of a change management plan is not only to ensure that the organisation ultimately achieves its new goals, but also to build defences for the organisation whilst simultaneously helping all involved to pass through the four typical stages of 'grieving' for the old ways of doing things,[4] namely:

- **Denial:** avoidance of the new system
- **Resistance:** refusal to participate in the new system
- **Exploration:** assessing the impact of the change on self
- **Commitment:** viewing the new system as a challenge.

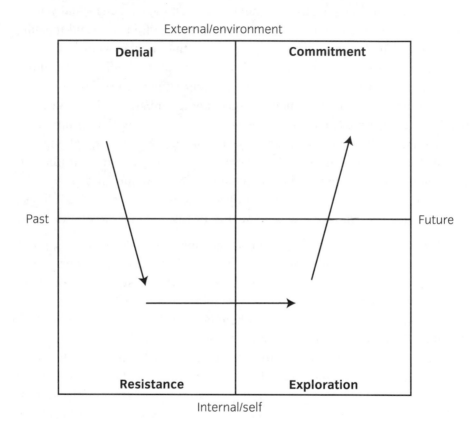

Figure 6.3 The change model

Adapted from Scott, C. D. and Jaffe, D. T.

There are three critical phases in the change process: preparing for change, communicating change and implementing change.

Preparing for change

- Assess the culture and history of the organisation and the general acceptability of the proposals to the membership, including a rough calculation as to the proportion of members that will ultimately find change acceptable. This could be vital if ever a vote of confidence is called in the scheme's leadership or if the long-term viability of the scheme is under threat because more existing members are likely to leave, following the change, than new members join.

- Establish a realistic timescale and budget for the change, and ensure that management, staff and volunteer levels are sufficient to achieve the change. Issues such as legal processes (for example, registering or de-registering a charity) and financial activities (for example VAT registration or de-registration, company incorporation, setting up new bank accounts) have a tendency to work to their own timescales, and often hinder the development of other necessary management activity (for example marketing and publicity about the new scheme, or the purchase of equipment or services).

- Consider who will be affected by the change, and how they may feel about it – particularly those who will lose their position, influence, authority or group of friends. Identify the nature and extent of resistance and the like-lihood of this being mobilised in ways that could undermine the proposed change. Prepare for the likely scenario, including taking legal advice, if appropriate, to ensure that the proposed change cannot be expensively contested in court. There may be opportunities to re-deploy the skills and interests of those likely to be most affected (and most resistant) to the change, into other areas such as fundraising, organising social events, promotional activities and other voluntary activities.

- Establish sources of support for change, and the ways in which this support can be employed in overcoming resistance to change and in managing the transition.

Communicating change

- Communicate the proposed changes to key stakeholders and leading opinion formers first, since their leadership will help to 'sell' the process to the membership at large.

- Communicate the timescale for the change.

- Encourage key people to be involved and 'own' the change process from the start.

- Try to create the sense of a change process which is doing something *with* the membership, not something which is being done *to* them.

- Keep people fully informed and where practical, involve them in decision-making that directly affects them, especially through meetings to talk about the change process. If those responsible for planning and managing the change are considered too 'partisan' for the process of consultation and communication, find people who will be perceived as more independent to engage in the dialogue. If meetings are to be held, consider places mutually regarded as 'neutral territory'.

- Sustain a positive attitude to the changes in everything that is said and done, and avoid the tempting prospect of 'dishing dirt' specifically to undermine the opponents' case.

- Identify those individuals at the root of any resistance, meet with them individually and attempt to negotiate around their concerns.

- Publicly acknowledge the past support and time given by both committee members and the membership at large, especially where the benefit has been to both the membership organisation and its affiliate organisation.

Implementing change

- Establish a network of 'change agents' comprising those related to the membership scheme who are willing to support the implementation of change in various ways. This may include members of the scheme itself, those who manage the scheme, those on the scheme's governing body and those who run any affiliate organisation. Diversity of support can help to head off pockets of resistance that may arise from various quarters.

- Ensure that the change strategy has been fully established prior to its implementation. Among other things, this will mean ensuring that the change agents are fully briefed on their roles in delivering the change, the timescale and how to handle ongoing concerns and queries posed by the membership. The plan will need to address 'what if?' scenarios so that the most obvious setbacks do not arrive as a complete surprise. Change processes that have not been clearly thought through have a habit of unravelling, and if there is remaining dissent amongst the existing membership, it will naturally become focused upon the weakest point in the plan.

- Develop visible rewards, so that those who give their commitment to the new system soon start to see and enjoy the benefits of the new over the old, and understand why the change was important. Such rewards may include a 'free transfer' from an existing scheme to a new one, a discounted fee for a limited period of time or an introductory free period. Unless an automatic transfer of membership is offered, the process of persuading existing members to join a new scheme may take a long time and result in apathy and drop-out by less active members.

- Ensure that new and amended benefits are delivered in a timely and efficient manner. Proposing a change process on the back of improved benefits, and subsequently failing to deliver these, will have more serious repercussions than simply effecting change without any future guarantees of benefits.

- Where possible, operate a feedback and evaluation process so that members are engaged throughout the process. This will in many cases help to 'bring over' less vociferous opponents.

Of course, no matter how well change is planned or how hard people work at the change process, it is inevitable that some people will be lost along the way. But if this has been predicted at an early stage, the damaging consequences can at least be anticipated and actions taken to minimise their impact.

Summary

Periodic reviews of membership schemes are important, as they create an opportunity for scheme managers to consider any ways in which changes in the external and internal environment may affect the scheme's effectiveness. They also provide a formal opportunity for the scheme's strengths and weaknesses to be considered in relation to that environment. As a consequence of such a review, future strategies and tactics can be developed. If it becomes clear that significant changes will be required for the scheme to continue to fulfil its objectives efficiently and effectively, then a careful process of change management should be put in place. Failure to do so can leave a scheme vulnerable to the activities of those who resist change, and who potentially have the power to undermine the scheme.

---

1 www.dti.gov.uk/er/emar/trade_data02.pdf – 15 December 2003

2 www.scoutbase.org.uk/library/hqdocs/facts/pdfs/fs310602.pdf – 18 December 2003

3 http://viney.com/DFV/During/18/18.html – 18 December 2003

4 Scott, C. D. and Jaffe, D. T., (1995) *Managing Change at Work: Leading People Through Organizational Transitions*, Crisp Publications Inc

APPENDIX A

Checklist for setting up a scheme

- What are you trying to achieve?
- Is there evidence of a need?
- Are your aims narrow or wide; and will you know when you have achieved your aims, or will your aims be ongoing and long term? For example, are you trying to achieve something for the greater good of society; the support of particular groups of disadvantaged of afflicted people; advance, defend or protest at something; or form a social group of like-minded people?
- Is there any other way of achieving your aims?
- Are there others out there who are already undertaking the same work, and if so, should you join in with them? Could you volunteer your services?
- If not, what will be different or unique about your aims, or the way in which you will achieve them?
- What support and resources do you have around you (people, money, professional expertise)?
- Do you believe that by formalising together in a group, you may attract more people, money and professional expertise?

If you get to this point and you want to continue...

- Is there a need to formalise into a group. If yes, what form of structure do you need/desire? Legal and financial advice should generally be taken before a final decision is made, but consider for example, issues such as the likely scale of the 'organisation'; the potential levels of income and expenditure; whether there is a need to fundraise from the public. Are there opportunities for grant funding from public bodies and if so, do those bodies have a view on what type of structure they will consider funding? (It is often the case that groups start off as unincorporated associations before progressing organically towards a more formalised structure such as incorporation and/or charitable status).

- Having decided upon the structure of the organisation, together with your 'provisional committee' members you will need to develop a governing document that will lay out the legal identity of the organisation and a framework for its future operation. This may be a constitution (for an unincorporated association) a deed of trust (for a charitable trust) or a memorandum and articles of association (for a limited company). In most instances you will require legal assistance for this stage, but you can do a lot of the ground work first by considering the earlier questions: what are you trying to achieve and how; what resources will you require; what people are you setting up to serve; what sorts of people you need to assist you; whether you will need to apply for funding; are you likely to need to employ staff eventually, buy or rent premises, and so on. Until this work is completed, you will not be able to set up bank accounts, apply for funding or undertake contracts.

- You have assembled the provisional committee and are now armed with a constitution, so you can proceed to organise banking facilities, apply for funding and start the process of delivering your aims. Do you have all the people you need to start? Do you have a plan for the first one, two and three years? Where will you be based? How will you tell people about your new organisation? How can people join? How can people access your services? Answers to these and many more questions should form the basis of a written development plan. Careful refinement of this plan will ensure that the tasks are located in the right order of priority and chronology, and will help to identify any gaps that still remain before you begin work. This plan, or an abbreviated version of it, may well be required by any potential funder, and a less detailed version of it may help you to attract both volunteers and beneficiaries to your new organisation.

- Use the plan to allocate responsibilities between you and your colleagues, according to the technical skills and interests you each have. It is important at this stage to ensure that no one person is left with the lion's share of the work, and also that communication between you is good enough so that if someone moves on, or becomes unavailable for periods of time, that others can take over the extra workload without the organisation failing in its infancy. If the workload is still too great, or if gaps in skills and knowledge have been identified, work with your colleagues to find, coerce and enthuse additional individuals to your cause.

- Make sure your committee regularly meets – at least as often as your governing document requires – and continually review progress throughout the year.

- Your first annual general meeting should be a cause for celebration of your achievements – after all, you have survived the first 12 months, and will by now hopefully be looking at how to develop your fledgling organisation into a long-term success.

This checklist is an extremely brief synopsis of what may be a typical route from an idea through to creation of an organisation to deliver that idea. There are numerous excellent publications which look at this process in considerable detail, including:

The Voluntary Legal Sector Handbook, 2nd edition, Adirondack, S. and Sinclair Taylor, J., (2001) Directory of Social Change.

APPENDIX B

Sample questions for assessing members' experiences of cultural organisations

For members

How often do you attend this theatre/museum/gallery?

- three or more times a year
- once or twice a year
- less than once a year
- never.

For how many years have you been a member of this scheme?

- less than a year
- one or two years
- three to five years
- six to ten years
- more than ten years.

How important were the following in your decision to join our membership scheme?

- the opportunity to receive a package of discounts and benefits
- the opportunity to become involved in the work of the theatre in a voluntary capacity
- the opportunity to share a social experience with like-minded people
- the opportunity to give financial support to the theatre.

How much do you value the following benefits of your membership?

- the advance/priority booking period
- the opportunity to work as a volunteer
- the private room/private bar facility
- discounted tickets
- the newsletter
- advance information on shows
- standby tickets (when available)

- social events organised by the membership social club
- meet the artists/curator receptions
- free open day invitations
- competitions and prize draws.

What do you think about the annual fee you pay for membership?

- good value for money
- a little expensive
- very expensive.

Would any of the following benefits be of interest to you as part of the membership scheme in future?

- more regular and professionally produced magazine with exclusive articles and offers
- flexible ticket exchange scheme
- more opportunities to meet artists at receptions
- invitations to private views
- the chance to attend open rehearsals and 'get-ins' for shows
- regular special functions hosted by the theatre/museum for the benefit of the membership
- discounts on the hire of private catering and entertainment facilities
- discounts and benefits at other arts or heritage organisations
- more opportunities to volunteer or get more deeply involved with the theatre/museum/gallery
- personal recognition of your involvement within theatre programmes/ exhibition guides
- credit facilities for tickets, food and drinks at the theatre/museum/gallery
- organised visits to other cultural organisations and events
- a chance to help secure future funds and other support for the theatre/ museum/gallery
- annual hosted social event to recognise the work of the members
- opportunities to meet the theatre/museum/gallery board and management to exchange ideas and news.

For lapsed members

Are any of the following reasons why you did not remain a member of the membership scheme?

- I didn't have time to take advantage of the benefits
- I didn't really enjoy the social events
- I didn't think the membership scheme was especially well run
- the membership fee is too expensive for me now

- the scheme doesn't feel the same as it used to
- there were not enough activities and other benefits
- no one has asked me to renew my membership
- I didn't feel it provided value for money
- my personal circumstances have changed
- my friend/partner/spouse is not longer able/prepared to accompany me to the theatre/museum/gallery
- other (please state).

Would any of the following encourage you to join or re-join the membership scheme?

- an invitation to join/re-join
- better ticket discounts
- a longer advance booking period
- cheaper membership fee
- more regular and professionally produced magazine with exclusive articles and offers
- flexible ticket exchange scheme
- more opportunities to meet artists at receptions
- invitations to private views
- the chance to attend open rehearsals and 'get-ins' for shows
- regular special functions hosted by the theatre/museum/gallery for the benefit of the members
- discounts on the hire of private catering and entertainment facilities
- discounts and benefits at other cultural or heritage organisations
- more opportunities to volunteer or get involved with the theatre/museum/gallery
- personal recognition of my involvement within theatre programmes
- credit facilities for tickets, food and drinks throughout theatre/museum/gallery
- organised visits to other cultural organisations and events
- a chance to help secure future funds and other support for theatre/museum/gallery
- annual hosted social event to recognise the work of the members
- opportunities to meet the theatre/museum/gallery board and management to exchange ideas and news.

About the respondent

Which of the following age groups are you in?

- Under 16
- 16–19
- 20–24
- 25–34
- 35–44
- 45–54
- 55–64
- 65+

Please indicate your sex:

- male
- female

If you bought a national newspaper today, from which group of titles would you be most likely to buy?

- Telegraph/Times/Independent/Guardian
- Mail/Express
- Sun/Star/Mirror

Which of the following best describes your employment status at present?

- full-time employment
- retired
- part-time employment
- unemployed
- student
- other (please state).

What is your postcode?

APPENDIX C

Setting a budget

Whether or not a membership scheme is independent or integrated with an affiliate organisation, there are many common direct costs and revenues which need to be taken into account within the budgeting process. The following list gives an indication of those items which may be included in a 'revenue' budget – that is, no account is taken of capital expenditure (computers, office furniture, buildings etc.).

Income/revenue

Sales
Revenues to be derived directly from the activities of the scheme. These may include membership fee income, funding grants, sponsorship and donations plus any other incidental membership-related sales

Cost of sales/expenditure

Staff
Those exclusively employed to administer the scheme (including staff, part of whose time can be specifically allocated to membership administration)

Marketing
The costs of promoting the scheme to potential new members (for example, production and distribution of printed literature, direct mail, website[1] design and maintenance, advertisements etc.)

Administration
Specific costs of servicing the membership, including joining and renewal (for example, application forms, membership cards, postage etc.)

Benefit provision
Nearly all member benefits will have a cost associated with them (for example, ticket/admission discounts, newsletters, 'free' items such as reports)

Overheads
For integrated schemes, overheads – or the more general running costs of the organisation – may be attributed to the department which manages the scheme – marketing,

development etc. – and not to the scheme itself, which is likely to be one of several functions of that department. For an independent membership organisation, the overheads will comprise all those indirect costs for the organisation as a whole which do not specifically relate to the management of the membership. Thus for a small independent organisation, the overheads will comprise all those indirect costs which cannot be specifically attributed to the management of the membership records (including heat, light, rent, rates, insurance, stationery, telephone etc.). For larger independent organisations where there may be a membership department, these overheads may be allocated proportionately by department, but correspondingly, direct costs such as benefit provision may in fact become those of another department – for example, customer services, volunteering, campaigns etc.

---

1 Consider where costs fall carefully. In this example, the website would serve as an aid to recruitment, but it could as easily be regarded as an administrative cost if the site permits people to renew membership, or as a benefit provision department, but correspondingly, direct costs such as benefit provision may in fact become those of another department – for example, customer services, volunteering, campaigns etc.

APPENDIX D

Benefits planning grid

Example of benefit planning and allocation for a theatre

	Base level	Bronze	Silver	Gold	Subscriber	Sponsor	Funder
'Free' mailings of events brochures	■	■	■	■	■	■	■
Meet-the-artist events		■	■	■	■	■	■
Priority booking periods		■	■	■	■	■	
Ticket discounts		■	■	■	■	■	
Invites to meet-the-management occasions		■	■	■	■	■	
Invitation to exclusive open day events		■	■	■	■	■	
'Free' newsletters	■	■	■	■		■	
Discounts on purchases from local retailers		■	■	■		■	
'Free' programmes				■	■	■	■
Free tours of the organisation				■	■	■	■
Invitations to guest lectures			■	■	■	■	
Opportunities to volunteer			■	■		■	
Exclusive invites to premium ticketed events				■		■	■
Invite to the Chairman's annual dinner				■		■	■
Recognition in theatre programmes				■		■	■
Personal telephone booking service				■	■	■	
Opportunity to join the organisation's board				■		■	■
Seat naming				■		■	
Personal guide for events				■		■	
Discounted use of private function room			■	■			
Discounted purchases from gift shop			■	■			
Reciprocal membership of other organisations			■	■			
Invitations to open rehearsals				■	■		
'Free' use of private function room				■	■		
Advertising in theatre programmes						■	■
Name plaque on function room wall						■	■
Building naming						■	■
Sponsor an artist opportunities						■	
Discounts on series/subscription bookings					■		

The above is an example of how a theatre might begin to structure its benefits packages across the entire spectrum of stakeholder and membership groups. Obviously there may be many more tiers to the scheme than shown here, and a sponsor who invests £500 would not anticipate receiving the same level of benefits as one investing £500,000. However, this grid shows it is important to map out the entire spectrum in order to prevent benefit 'clashes' where one market segment is unnecessarily disadvantaged by another being offered the same or better benefits for a lower cost. This document may be used purely to inform internal management, and careful targeting of different market segments would in most cases not reveal one series of benefits to another segment. Planning benefit allocation in this way also enables the organisation to ensure that each target market is offered benefits appropriate to its needs or known demands, and for instance, helps ensure that there are sufficient differentiated benefits between each offering.

APPENDIX E

Organising an AGM

This section offers guidance on arrangements for a meeting that might suit a small organisation. For guidance on incorporated company annual general meetings, see *The Voluntary Sector Legal Handbook* 2nd edition, Adirondack. S. and Sinclair Taylor. J., DSC (2001).

Introduction

The main purpose of an annual general meeting (AGM) is for the committee to report back to all members about the activities of your organisation over the past year.

It is an opportunity for discussion about the issues and projects the membership wants to tackle during the coming year.

The AGM is also the time for electing new committee members into office and asking for new members to join the committee.

All organisations that receive funding must ensure their accounts are independently checked and that a statement of the accounts is available for viewing at the meeting.

Pre-planning

You will probably need to start planning your AGM at least eight weeks ahead. Get together with your committee to plan this.

Independent check of the accounts

You should have your books checked by a qualified accountant. Depending upon the role your organisation performs, you may be able to attract a generous discount or possible *pro bono* work from an accountant with an interest in your work. If chargeable, the cost of this will vary depending on how much money passes through the organisation's account and how well the books are kept.

To audit or examine the accounts, an accountant will need to see everything relating to your organisation's finances:

- bank or building society book
- all receipts/invoices
- income and expenditure sheets
- cheque books and paying in books
- all petty cash sheets for the year
- the previous year's audited/examined accounts, if available
- the auditor will give you a balance sheet with a statement of your accounts, which should be copied and made available at the AGM.

Setting the date of the meeting

Bear in mind all the usual considerations: time, day of the week, popular television programmes or sporting events. You will need to check that any invited guests and other key committee members are available on your chosen date. If a number of them are not available, you should choose another date. Often, there is a stipulation about the period of notice required, prior to an AGM, within your governing document (constitution), so check that you have left enough time between notifying your members and the date of the meeting.

Venue

Choose a suitable venue and check it will be available. Make sure that the venue is convenient for people in your area to get to. Is there a large enough room for the meeting? Do you require any special equipment to enable disabled members to attend (for example, access ramps or an induction loop for the hard of hearing)?

Larger rooms such as a local school hall are ideal but sometimes they can be pricey. Ensure that you have sufficient funds in order to meet the cost.

Guest speakers

Although the AGM itself is a formal business meeting, you may wish to invite a guest speaker to present a discussion on a topic of interest to the membership. This can help to attract more people to attend and give a focus to the meeting.

Notice of meeting

Having checked the rules for the notice period within your governing document, you will need to issue formal notice of the AGM to all voting members of the organisation. Again your governing document may stipulate the process of notification, but if not, this can be done by:

- sending a letter or leaflet to all the voting members on your database
- placing posters and leaflets in prominent places (if there are obvious places where large numbers of your members will see them)
- telephone or in person
- e-mail and website.

You may wish to send a reminder notice closer to the meeting, particularly if there are confirmed speakers and other social activities due to take place at/after the meeting. An agenda should be included within this information, if it has not already been sent within the earlier notice.

Preparing the agenda

The agenda for the AGM should generally be drawn up by the chair and secretary of the organisation after consultation with the rest of the committee.

Send the agenda to all committee members and any invited guests at least two weeks prior to the meeting to enable them to prepare for the meeting.

Include the agenda on the leaflets and posters to advertise the meeting so that those attending will know what is to be discussed.

Allocate a set time for each agenda item so that all the business of the meeting can be completed within the advertised time.

Changes to the governing document or constitution

Occasionally there may be a need to make changes to the governing document. Such changes have to be voted on at the AGM. Proposed amendments should be clearly stated in the notice of the meeting, and copies of the constitution should be made available to enable those attending to vote on the proposed changes; whether to accept or to reject them. The governing document itself should stipulate precisely how changes to it may be made. In general, such proposed changes will need to be circulated to the membership in advance of the meeting, and a specific minimum number or percentage of votes will normally be required for the changes to be carried at the meeting.

On the day

There are a number of arrangements and considerations that will need your attention. These are set out below. The total time for an AGM should be no more than one and a half hours.

Setting up the room

Arrange access to the meeting room at least half an hour before the meeting is due to start. Make sure that the top table is set out. Make sure that there are plenty of chairs available. Put a copy of the previous year's AGM minutes and a copy of the balance sheet and any other information you are supplying on each chair or at the door that leads into the room. If you are providing refreshments, make sure that this is arranged in plenty of time so that the start of the meeting is not held up while you wait for the kettle to boil! Provide water or soft drinks for the top table. Have an attendance sheet for people to sign as they enter the meeting room so that you can contact people with any further information.

Quorum

Make sure that you have the quorum for the meeting to proceed. The quorum is the minimum number of people who need to be present in order for the meeting to be valid. If the quorum is not reached then the meeting should be cancelled and a new date set for the meeting. The quorum will be stated in your organisation's governing document.

The meeting

Welcome and introductions

The chair should welcome everyone to the meeting and introduce invited guests and committee members, so that the members know who is present. Committee members could consider wearing name badges if the meeting is likely to be attended by large numbers of people who may not be familiar with the different personalities. Let people know that there will be a chance to ask questions later on in the meeting.

Minutes of last annual general meeting

Copies of your organisation's previous AGM minutes should be made available to everyone at the meeting (unless this is your first AGM when this does not apply).

You do not need to read out the minutes of the previous AGM, but the chair should ask if they are a true and accurate record and someone, usually a committee member, will agree that they are. If the minutes are queried and there are corrections made, these should be minuted by the secretary for inclusion in the current year's AGM minutes.

Chair's report

The purpose of the chair's report is to update the members on the activities of the organisation during the previous year. It is important to let people know of your success! Tell people briefly how these successes have been achieved. For example, include the highlights of the year – whether campaigning successes, artistic triumphs, great social occasions, personal achievements of members and so on.

Treasurer's report

Copies of the balance sheet should be available at the AGM. The treasurer should give a brief verbal report on how much money the organisation has, how money has been spent and where it came from (for example grants from specific bodies, fundraising, donations and membership fees).

Election of committee

This is usually a formality and more often than not members are re-elected into the same positions. However, it does present an opportunity to recruit new members onto your committee and get some fresh faces involved with the organisation. It may be that some committee members want to resign from their positions and do not wish to stand for re-election. You can enlist some help with the election process. Some governing documents require that election nominations should be received prior to the AGM, whilst for others, elections must be held by secret postal ballot.

Assuming all key committee posts are to be elected (some may be returned unopposed if no one chooses to run against them) an independent person such as a professional person or senior manager should be invited to preside over the election in order to ensure fairness. This should be arranged with that person beforehand if possible.

The presiding officer (the person dealing with the election) will:

- Thank the committee members that are stepping down for their work on behalf of the organisation over the past year.
- Ask for nominations in turn for each of the committee roles which have become vacant.
- Ask for any nominations to be seconded.
- Ask for any other nominations.
- If there are no other nominations, ask for a show of hands as a vote for the nominee to be elected into position. As long as there is a majority vote, individual votes need not be counted.
- If more than one nomination, ask for a show of hands for each of the nominations and if the outcome is not obvious, votes need to be counted.
- State which nominee has been voted into post.
- When voting in 'ordinary' committee members (those who don't hold a named position) they are voted in by a majority show of hands.
- Ask the new committee members to join the top table.

Variations

Alternative arrangement for election of a new committee

An alternative is to elect (or re-elect) the committee at the AGM, and at the next committee meeting, the committee itself decides which individual is best suited to carry out each role on the committee, the chairperson, secretary or treasurer.

Nomination forms

You may wish (or be required by the governing document) to have nomination forms for people to fill in prior to the public meeting. These don't count as votes but are a useful way of recording who has been nominated and seconded. It is the people who are present at the meeting who vote the committee into position.

Paper ballot

If you prefer, you can carry out the vote by giving out voting slips and counting up votes for each nominee.

One nominee

If there is only one nominee for a position then you can ask if there are any objections to that nominee being elected into post and as long as there are no objections then this counts as a positive vote.

Speaker

If inviting a speaker, it is a good idea to have them talk about a particular issue of concern. AGMs are generally regarded as being rather dull therefore having an interesting speaker could improve the turnout! Allow some time for people to ask questions. If possible let the speaker know the sorts of questions they are likely to be asked. This will help them to prepare for the meeting, which will mean they are more likely to have the answers to the questions put to them.

Let the speaker know how long you would like them to talk for. Send a copy of the agenda to the speaker at least two weeks prior to the meeting, although in some instances you may not wish your speaker to attend the 'business' part if the meeting. Conversely, allow your speaker the option of not attending the AGM itself, but schedule their arrival in plenty of time for their talk, if using this option.

Open forum

Allow time at the end of the meeting for people to ask questions, of the committee or other key staff or volunteers. This may require some astute chairing, to ensure it does not become a platform for moans and gripes – or more likely, to ensure that the blank faces amongst the membership are encouraged to participate. The committee can take this opportunity to ask the audience what priorities they want the organisation to tackle during the next year.

After the meeting

Close of meeting – the chair should thank everyone for coming, thank the invited guests and pronounce the meeting closed.

Follow up

If people don't attend meetings, this doesn't necessarily mean that they're not interested. It can be useful to send out a letter or news sheet to all members following the AGM with details of what went on at the meeting, introducing the new committee and outlining any issues that were raised.

If any decisions were made at the AGM make sure that they are acted upon. The chair and the secretary should get together to agree that the minutes are correct before having them copied. Send them out to all the committee members.

And that's it ... until next year!

Source: Adapted from guidance notes to people setting up residents groups within Eastserve, the East Manchester New Deal for Communities project. www.eastserve.com – 16 January 2004

APPENDIX F

The following is reproduced from the Information Commissioner's website at www.informationcommissioner.gov.uk. The fees quoted were correct as at the time of going to press.

Notification

What is notification?

The Information Commissioner maintains a public register of data controllers. Each register entry includes the name and address of the data controller and a general description of the processing of personal data by a data controller. Individuals can consult the register to find out what processing of personal data is being carried out by a particular data controller. Notification is the process by which a data controller's details are added to the register. The Data Protection Act 1998 requires every data controller who is processing personal data to notify unless they are exempt.

Why do I need to notify?

The Data Protection Act 1998 requires every data controller who is processing personal data to notify unless they are exempt.

Failure to notify is a criminal offence.

Do I need to notify?

- Every data controller who is processing personal information must notify unless they are exempt.
- A data controller is a person who determines the purposes for which and the manner in which any personal information is, or is to be processed.
- Personal information means data which relates to a living individual who can be identified from those data or from those data and other information which is in the possession of the data controller. To check if you are exempt, answer the questions in our guide.

Exemptions are possible for:

- Some not for profit organisations.
- Processing of personal data for personal, family or household affairs (including recreational purposes).
- Data controllers who only process personal data for the maintenance of a public register.
- Data controllers who only process personal data for any one or all of the following purposes for their own business:
  - staff administration
  - advertising, marketing and public relations
  - accounts and records.

If you think you may be exempt please see Do I need to notify?, above.

Do I need to renew my notification?

Yes. The notification period is one year. The renewal fee is £35. Any change to this fee will be advised to you when you start the process of renewal. We will write to you before the expiry date of your register entry.

How do I renew my register entry?

The notification period is one year from the day we receive your correctly completed notification form. Your entry will then expire unless it is renewed. Prior to the expiry date we will write to you and explain the procedure for continuing your register entry.

The fee for renewing an entry is £35. Any change to this fee will be advised to you when you start the process of renewal. If you pay by direct debit you will not need to take any action to renew your entry in subsequent years. If you have previously paid the fee by some other method a direct debit form will be enclosed with the renewal reminder letter.

At renewal time you will be asked whether there have been any changes to the data controller name and address details of the contact details.

A letter will be sent to you to confirm that your entry has been renewed together with information about your new expiry date.

What do I do if my notification has expired?

It is very important that we receive payment of the renewal fee prior to the expiry of the entry. It is not possible to renew an entry which has expired. In these circumstances the data controller must make a new application for notification.

Completing the notification form on the Internet

It is possible to complete the notification form using the Internet. However, after completing the form online it must be printed and sent to us by post with the notification fee or direct debit instruction. Currently it is not possible to send the form to us electronically. You will be deemed notified on the day we receive your correctly completed forms and fee.

Completing the notification form online is a step-by-step process. You are asked to answer certain questions and provide information before continuing onto the next question. At the end of the form you can print it off and send it to us.

The first questions on the form are about the data controller who is notifying, for example their name, address and contact details.

The next stage of the online process involves choosing an appropriate nature of business template. Each notification must include a general description of the processing of personal data being carried out. On the register this description is structured by reference to purposes. You will find a selection of templates which describe the processing which is likely to be being carried out by a range of different businesses. After selecting the template appropriate to your business you need to check that it accurately describes the processing which is being carried out. You may amend the template or add additional purposes to it. If you cannot find a relevant template, either call the notification help line or select the nearest template suitable to your needs and amend it accordingly.

The following stage of the online process involves providing additional information for example, the security statement and statement of exempt processing. Some of this information is mandatory, so failure to return this part of the form renders your notification invalid and it will be returned to you.

The final stage is to print the form, sign the declaration and return it to us with the notification fee or completed direct debit instruction. If after printing the form you find that you have forgotten to include something, then you can write in ink directly onto the form and we will include it in your notification.

Manual records and notification

There is no requirement to notify manual records which come within the scope of the Data Protection Act 1998.

However, you can choose to notify them voluntarily. Further information about manual records can be found in our publication The Data Protection Act 1998 An Introduction.

How to notify

There are 3 easy ways to notify:

- **By Internet**

  You can complete the online notification form online, print it and send the form to us.

- **By telephone**

  You can telephone the notification help line (01625 545 740) and a draft notification form will be sent to you based on the information you will be asked to provide on the telephone.

- **By completing the Request for a Notification Form**

The changes introduced by notification

Notification replaces the registration system established by the 1984 Data Protection Act.

Below is a summary of the main differences:

- Broadly speaking data users become data controllers.
- Broadly speaking computer bureaux become data processors and do not need to notify.
- Register entries will still contain a description of the processing of personal data. However, this description is in very general terms. The detailed coding system no longer exists.
- You do not need to describe sources of personal data in your entry.
- Registration of disclosures are replaced by notification of recipients.
- You need to describe transfers of personal data outside the EEA only.
- You have to provide a statement about your security measures.
- You do not have to provide an address for the receipt of subject access requests.
- The 1998 Act provides some exemptions from notification but you can choose to notify voluntarily.
- The notification period is one year.
- A data controller can only have one register entry.
- Headteachers and governing bodies of schools may notify in the name of the school.

Source: http://www.informationcommissioner.gov.uk/eventual.aspx?id=316 – 16 January 2004

OTHER PUBLICATIONS FROM DSC

The following is a selection of titles available by mail order from DSC Books. Telephone 08450 77 77 07 with your credit card details or order online at www.dsc.org.uk/charitybooks, where you can find a complete catalogue.

Editions and prices were correct at the time of going to press but may be subject to change.

Directories

A Guide to the Major Trusts, Vol. 1: the top 300 trusts (making grants annually of over £1,600 million a year), DSC, 2003, £20.95

A Guide to the Major Trusts, Vol. 2: the next 700 trusts (making grants annually of over £127 million a year), DSC, 2003, £20.95

A Guide to the Major Trusts, Vol. 3: the next 500 trusts (making grants annually of over £20 million a year), DSC, 2002, £17.95

A Guide to Scottish Trusts: details of around 350 trusts which concentrate their grantmaking in Scotland, DSC, 2004, £17.95

The Welsh Funding Guide: details charitable giving for Welsh causes, DSC, 2003, £16.95

A Guide to Local Trusts: four volumes covering local trusts in the North of England, the Midlands, the South of England and Greater London, DSC, 2004, £18.95

The Grant-making trusts CD-ROM 2004: all the trusts from the CAF and DSC databases on one CD-ROM, developed by FundFinder for DSC, £120+VAT

Funding guides and handbooks

The Arts Funding Guide: Susan Forrester and David Lloyd, DSC, 2002, £18.95

Marketing Strategy: Peter Maple, DSC, 2003, £19.95

The Complete Fundraising Handbook: Nina Botting and Michael Norton, DSC, 2001, £16.95

Relationship Fundraising: Ken Burnett, Jossey Bass, 2002, £25.50

The law for the voluntary sector

The Voluntary Sector Legal Handbook: Sandy Adirondack and James Sinclair Taylor, DSC, £42 for voluntary organisations, £60 for others

Data Protection: Paul Ticher, DSC, 2002, £14.95

INDEX